Kitchen Suppers

Kitchen Suppers

Good Food to Share with Good Friends

Alison Becker Hurt

Doubleday

New York London Toronto Sydney Auckland

PUBLISHED BY DOUBLEDAY
a division of Random House, Inc.
1540 Broadway, New York, New York 10036

DOUBLEDAY and the portrayal of an anchor with a dolphin are
trademarks of Doubleday, a division of Random House, Inc.

Book design by Dana Leigh Treglia

Library of Congress Cataloging-in-Publication Data
Hurt, Alison Becker.
Kitchen suppers / [Alison Becker Hurt]. —1st ed.
    p.   cm.
Includes index.
1. Suppers.   I. Title.
TX738.H87   1999
641.5'3—dc21   99-10275
                                CIP

ISBN 0-385-48831-9
Copyright © 1999 by Alison Becker Hurt

For Harry and Harrison

with all my love

Acknowledgments

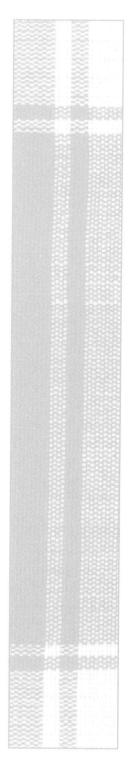

Kitchen Suppers could not have been finished without the enormous support and help of many people. I must thank them:

My husband, who painstakingly and patiently edited each word, dotted my *i*'s and crossed my *t*'s, and lovingly gave me kisses in between bites of experiments, while I was moaning through pregnancy, experiencing sleep deprivation while nursing our son, and trying to keep my thoughts in line.

My mother, for being the best mom a daughter could ask for. My father, for his love and support. My brothers, Jonathan, for looking after me, and Peter, for many backrubs. Ivy, for following me around the kitchen without a complaint. And my entire extended family, for the many meals they have eaten (and some they may not have wanted to).

My agent, Jane Dystel, whose encouragement and guidance throughout the process of creating and writing I could not have done without.

My editor, Judy Kern, who patiently waited for the manuscript and led me through the editing process with a brilliant hand.

My partner, Michael Chamberlain, and the staffs of Alison On Dominick Street and Alison By the Beach, for taking great care of the restaurants while I couldn't be in them.

Meg and Kim, for their unwavering support through thick and thin.

My friend Mimi Leiber, for countless cross-country phone calls and faxes, and her friendship. Rick Rodgers, who helped to straighten out the recipes so that real people could read them.

And all the friends who have graced our table, shared our food, and celebrated good times.

Contents

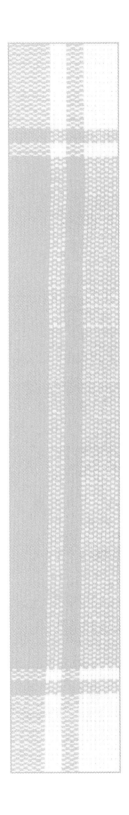

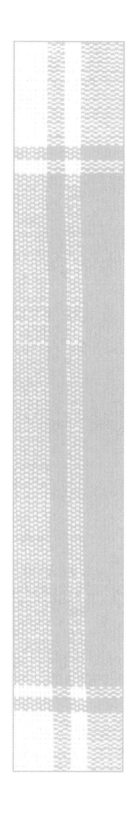

1. What Are Kitchen Suppers?

1. What Are Kitchen Suppers?

When I married my husband, we inherited the kind of large, formal dining-room table I had always dreamed of, complete with repoussé Kirk silver and miles of lace napkins, tablecloths, and runners. I love to cook, and I loved the idea of cooking grand and graceful dinners, and I did—twice. At the first dinner, my juicy roast pork landed on the lace tablecloth as I tried to serve it across the vastness of the table. So much for grace. And there was nothing grand about attempting to wash my soiled lace tablecloth in the bathtub. Needless to say, the tablecloth never got ironed because I was too exhausted.

Not to be discouraged, I summoned my courage, and at Thanksgiving, I tried the grand and graceful dinner routine again. Thanksgiving is my favorite holiday, for two reasons. I believe in giving thanks, and I believe in celebrating food. We invited twenty guests, which necessitated moving the furniture out of the living room and putting all the leaves in the table. I was giddy with excitement. The turkey was golden, the settings of beautiful china and crystal glistened. There was a profusion of flowers, eighteen-inch tapers twinkled majestically in the candelabra, and the kitchen was almost presentable. This was going to be *graceful* and *grand* if it killed me.

And it nearly did. Our dining room table almost collapsed, saved only by a kitchen sponge stuck under a leg. We ran out of spoons and had to eat dessert with a funny-looking fish fork. Three days later, I was still hand-washing the crystal and china, which, I was beginning to realize, was meant to live on an almost-permanent basis in a sideboard we did not have.

That Thanksgiving taught me a lesson I have been giving thanks for ever since. The food had been splendid and a good time was had by all, but I learned that this exercise in grandeur and gracefulness was only that. It seemed to take the heart out of creating the meal by causing too many worries and complications. And it was not about cooking, which is what I really love to do. Realizing this, I ran back to the comfort and safety of my checkered tablecloths and what I like to call "kitchen suppers."

If I could make up a definition for kitchen suppers, it would read something like this:

1. Meals that usually take place in the kitchen—but don't have to.
2. Meals that are what they are, and don't try to be anything else.
3. Meals that are cooked with ease and love.

My husband's cousin, Ala, once told me that cooking is about making people happy, and I think kitchen suppers make people happy. They are easy and uncomplicated in spirit if not always in creation. The only requirements are good food, good drink, good bread to break with good friends, and plenty of good humor.

The recipes and menus for the kitchen suppers described in this book are motivated by taste and by smell and by what I like to eat. They teach you not only to be an inspired shopper, but also to cook with the ingredients you have available—how to look into the refrigerator and create a meal out of so-called leftovers. I am an avid supporter of Share Our Strength, a program sponsored by American Express and my fellow restaurateurs that provides food resources to the hungry, and I do not believe in dumping good food in the garbage.

The recipes for my kitchen suppers do not require you to go back out to the store to buy more food items, because you can usually find something to substitute for whatever the recipe calls for that you don't happen to have on hand. The recipes do not require the sauce to be silky, though if it is, all the better. Kitchen suppers are never perfect—and yet they are perfect in their imperfection.

Most of the kitchen suppers you will read about here were cooked in our Sag Harbor kitchen, but the meals could take place anywhere—in your kitchen, in an old friend's home, or in the home of a new acquaintance. The stories that accompany the recipes and menus are not only about food. They touch on the lives and hearts of the guests at our table, and our hearts as well. My husband always reminds me of the time when he was sleeping off a cold on a particularly drafty winter night during a particularly difficult winter, and awoke sniffing the rich aroma of Lamb Shepherd's Pie wafting its way up the stairs and bringing the warmth of the kitchen along with it. He says that is love. And love is the aim and purpose of my kitchen suppers.

Kitchen, by definition, means not only a place but also the people who work there. Kitchen suppers are about the heart and soul of the kitchen, as well as the meals that come out of it. It does not matter if you are two people or twenty people. The kitchen table is a nice place to be. And kitchen suppers are one of the nicest things you can bring to the kitchen table and to each other.

And kitchen suppers do not have to include anyone else. A kitchen supper can be yours alone. Sometimes you may reach the point when the whole world seems to be pitted against you, and all your friends and family can't seem to understand what's happening to you, and, like some fang-toothed vampire from Transylvania, you growl under your breath, 'I vant to be alone!' I know I do. I also know that almost all of us wind up in a situation where we are eating dinner all by ourselves, either by choice or because of circumstances beyond our control. Maybe you really do just want to be alone. Maybe you don't. It doesn't really matter. You've got to eat, and there is no reason you shouldn't eat well. Since eating alone is something all of us must face, it's comforting to know that it is hardly the worst thing in the world and can sometimes be one of the best things. In fact, there are many tasty dishes that can be quickly and conveniently prepared for one. And many of the recipes in this book can be altered to serve one. Add a salad and a glass of wine to complement any of these dishes, and you can experience the peace and quiet of a heaven on earth. Trust me.

No matter how many one is cooking for I hope to demystify the art of cooking by telling some of the humorous stories behind my kitchen suppers—including both the successes and the failures. Failures are important because they are seldom complete losses. Failures almost always can be turned into successes—or at the very least, valuable learning experiences.

Friends often say to me "You cook with such ease. It must be because you own restaurants." But that has nothing to do with it. In fact, the expectations that go along with owning two successful restaurants and a catering concern can put undue pressures on my cooking. My own cooking is not restaurant cooking. Unlike my chefs, I rarely do the same recipe twice. My presentations are not restaurant presentations; they tend to be larger and more bountiful than the current trend in restaurants. My emphasis here is on taste, texture, and aroma; combined, these are what make food yummy. And kitchen suppers are always yummy.

When people ask me how I know how to cook, I say it's by instinct. My husband says it's by knowledge. In truth, instinct and knowledge go hand in hand, and both should be allowed to roam free. I use cookbooks all the time for inspiration, but I usually end up creating my own recipe because the original didn't include something I wanted to eat or it was too complicated. I use my nose and my taste buds.

In the pages that follow, I share my thought processes in the kitchen: how I got from point A to point Z, how I came to change a recipe, and what I did the next time. Quite frequently I hear my friends exclaim, "Gosh, I would never have thought of that!" I think that's because the cookbooks most of my friends buy teach only the mechanics of specific recipes and do not help them understand the whys of basic techniques such as the use of thickening agents, stirring, whipping, baking, and so on. If you know the whys—and learn to trust your own nose and palate—you will have the freedom to cook almost anything. Having that freedom creates confidence. Having confidence is fun. And kitchen suppers are about having fun.

The story of how I recently saved an almost-failed strawberry-peach shortcake is a good example. I had called the pastry chef at one of my restaurants for his recipe. I had beautiful strawberries and peaches. I mixed and baked according to his instructions, though I used a slightly different pan and the wrong temperature. Well, the shortcake came out of the oven and looked beautiful, all crunchy and golden on the outside. I left it to cool. When it came time to put the dessert together, I took my bowl of fresh whipped cream out of the refrigerator. It looked like my peaches and strawberries had soaked to perfection. But when I reached for the cake, I was horrified to see that there was no longer a big golden puff. Instead, there was a big gooey doughnut-like thing. My shortcake had fallen and my heart fell with it.

Unfortunately, my pastry chef hadn't warned me about the possibility of failure, or, more importantly, what to do about it. I had to improvise—and fast— so I said to myself, "I need a crust and I need to dry out the center. What do you do when you want a crust? You toast or you broil." I took the cake out of the mold, sliced it in half, and stuck it under the broiler. Success: It came out toasty and a bit carmelized. Then I pieced it all back together, stuck the peaches inside with the whip cream, spooned the strawberries in the middle, and hid my concoction in the refrigerator. When time came to serve dessert, I opened the refrigerator door, and to my horror, saw a leaning tower of strawberry-peach mush.

Instead of wasting time getting upset, I grabbed some bowls and served the most wonderful summer "trifle." Though technically not a trifle, it worked. Did anybody know? Yes, because I told them after they had complimented me on how tasty it was. Upon hearing this, one of my guests burst out laughing. "Alison, that makes me feel great," she said. "It's good to know that you have kitchen disasters, too. But do you have to tell what you did to save them?"

The answer is no—you don't have to tell. But in this book, I do just that, because that is the secret of cooking. People only *think* they can't cook because they are scared of disaster. So what if you have a disaster? That's okay. Everybody does from time to time, including and sometimes most especially, me. Just remember, when all fails, you can always serve pasta and ice cream. And remember this, too: There is nothing that is not okay when it comes to preparing and serving kitchen suppers.

In hopes of increasing your successes and limiting your potential for disasters, I am going to show you how to develop your instinct and use your imagination. If you're already a good cook, you will be able to take my recipes and make them your own. If you're presently a timid cook, you will learn there is nothing to fear but fear itself. Kitchen suppers are fearless—and fear-free.

Over the years, I've found that planning what to cook—if you have the time and opportunity to go to the grocery store at all—is just as important as the actual cooking, and that here again, the real secret is using your instinct and your imagination. After I've looked in the kitchen to see what we already have, I plan my menu while I'm on the way to the store, and then change it once I'm in the store. When I shop, I might be inspired by something I see, like big fresh ruby beets to make borscht, for example, or portobello mushrooms to sauté and put over wilted arugula.

The finds I come across in the grocery store start the ever-changing process of my menu planning. I then decide on what flavors go with beets, what textures would complement the soup, or if I should make a thicker borscht and serve that as the main course. But by the time I get those beets back to my kitchen, my plans might change entirely. I might find when I stop by the butcher on my way home that he doesn't have the oxtails I wanted for the borscht, so I cancel my soup plans, use the beets to top an arugula salad, and use the portobello mushrooms on the side of a beef filet. The point is, kitchen suppers are about flexibility.

As a child, I loved paper cut-out dolls that you could dress different ways. It was always the same doll, but she had ten completely different "looks." You can do the same thing with recipes. This book features seventy-five recipes (including side dishes) with variations you can have fun with. You can create many more recipes and variations on your own. At the height of summer, for example, you might decide to stuff a roast pork loin with seasonal fruits and vegetables such as peaches and Vidalia onions, wrap the loin in bacon, and serve it with a fresh corn soufflé. But the same method of roasting and stuffing can be used in the winter, substituting apples, garlic, and celery root for the peaches, and roast potatoes for the corn soufflé. Or you can change the meat, stuffing, say, a loin of lamb with tomato and mint and wrapping it in leeks.

The same principles of variation and substitution apply to desserts. Tarte Tatin, for example, is a cinch, and it can be made with peaches, plums, apricots, or the traditional apples. That gives you four different desserts already. Change the ice creams or the sauces, and you have many more. The same tarte Tatin can also become a savory tart when made with caramelized leeks or Brussels sprouts and maple syrup. The fun is in creating all these variations and substitutions. And kitchen suppers are about creativity.

Kitchen suppers are also about simplicity. The recipes in this book have influences from many different countries, but all of them are recipes for country food or "peasant food." In other words, simple food. I believe simple food is the best food. And kitchen suppers are the best suppers because, by definition, they encourage you to prepare simple food.

I have been cooking for over twenty years, both for fun and as a profession, and along with discovering the virtues of simplicity, flexibility, creativity, imagination, and instinct, I've learned that the single most important ingredient in any recipe is love. My most vivid childhood memories are of what my grandmothers baked in their kitchens. That chocolate chip cookie or plum pie was so filled with love that it will always be the best. The silence that reigned as the

Christmas stollen was rising was religion. The *Joy of Cooking* was co-authored by my late relative Marion Rombauer Becker, and it was my bible.

Before entering the restaurant business, I aspired to be an actress, and between auditions, I took cooking jobs to supplement my income. For several years I worked with a now-defunct caterer in New York, who had a nervous breakdown and left me with a business that included cooking the late shift at a rock 'n roll bar. Along the way, I always cooked for friends, and I think it's the best way to enjoy one another's company. I have cooked for two people and for four hundred. The process is very similar, it just requires more food. And both situations demand love.

After closing the catering business and moving to California to pursue my acting career, I was hired as a personal chef, which I still think is one of the best jobs in the world. I began to develop recipes and have been doing so ever since. When I moved back to New York and put my acting career behind me, I started working in restaurant management. Although I am not a restaurant kind of cook, I have been very fortunate to work with some of the best chefs in the country: Jonathan Waxman of Jams and Buds, Alfred Portale of the Gotham Bar and Grill, Thomas Keller of the French Laundry, Thomas Valenti and Dan Silverman at Alison On Dominick Street, and Rick Jacobsen and Robert Gurvich at Alison By the Beach.

Because I was not working directly under these chefs, I could watch them and learn from them. I was impressed by the ease with which they tried new things, and the confidence they had just to cook with their hearts. I began to translate this into home cooking, and kitchen organization, and the results were amazing. I began to understand the whys of cooking, and I realized that there are very few hard and fast rules.

I am going to share with you the knowledge that has been passed on to me by my grandmothers and by the great chefs I have worked with—that if you trust in yourself, you can make anything happen. Like the heroine in my favorite film, *Like Water for Chocolate*, you simply diffuse the fear and make room for the love. Kitchen suppers, like all wonderful meals, are about love.

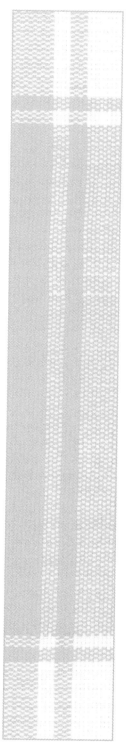

2. Why Do I Have to Do That?

2. Why Do I Have to Do That?

One of the questions my friends almost invariably ask when they come to me to discuss a highly technical, complex, or obscure step in some new recipe or cooking method is, "Why do I have to do that?" It's a question I have repeatedly asked myself. The answer I give my friends more often than not is, "You probably don't have to do that. But if you don't, you may have to do something else." At this point, they usually seem more confused than ever, and they frown at me as if they're not sure we're really friends. After all, a friend would tell you why you have to do what you have to do as straightforwardly as possible, wouldn't she?

Well, I would, and I try, but it isn't always easy to be as straightforward as you'd like to be—unless you and your friends are speaking the same language. The language of cooking, like the language of wines or the language of rocket science, can be reduced to simple terms or made extremely complicated. In the end it's a choice, and the choice depends on your overall aim and purpose. We're not trying to build rocket ships here, we're trying to cook delicious kitchen suppers—which is an adventure in its own right but one that should not make you wish you could be shot into outer space when the going gets a little sticky.

Your chances of success when you cook kitchen suppers will be much greater if you understand the basics of what you are doing in the kitchen. This is especially true if the evil kitchen witch shows up just as the good kitchen witch decides to take the night off, and it seems that the whole world is trying to keep you from cooking supper. Sometimes it's the recipe that fails you: It's either hard to follow or just plain wrong. Sometimes the recipe was created in a different country with different water and a different altitude. Sometimes the problem lies with your attempts to execute the recipe: Try as you might, nothing turns out right. Sometimes the fault lies with your equipment: You come home all excited and ready to cook, only to find that your oven is broken. Don't worry; you can still make dinner.

If it sounds like I'm speaking from experience, it's because I am. All the bad things you can possibly imagine have happened to me more than once, and then some. I remember, for example, the terrible predicament I got myself into the night after I moved into the Manhattan apartment of my dreams. I had planned a large housewarming party, but I came home from grocery shopping to discover that my oven wouldn't turn on. I had bought forty quails that I was intending to roast with onions. So, no oven, no roast quail, right?

Not necessarily. Thankfully, the top burners of the stove were working, so I decided to try pan-roasting the quail. But guess what? I discovered that the movers had misplaced a box of my cooking equipment, and I had no frying pans. No frying pans, no pan-roasted quail. Okay, there I was stumped, but only temporarily. The movers had left me with a large Creuset pot, so I quickly changed tactics. Instead of making roasted quail, I made smothered quail in the large Creuset pot, and created a dish that melted in everyone's mouth.

So, am I a kitchen magician? No, not exactly. Nor do I expect to turn you into one. But like me, you can learn how to fix a dish in a pinch by understanding certain key cooking processes, and by understanding how the essential ingredients work in whatever dish you're cooking. With this knowledge, you'll have the ability to alter a recipe or cooking method in midstream with a minimum of effort, and, perhaps even more important, you will banish fear. You'll find ways to make do with the available kitchen equipment (or lack thereof). You'll see how to eliminate steps to make cooking easier, and what to do if you inadvertently skip a step in a recipe. You will learn as you go, and you'll get the key concepts one at a time so they are as easy to digest as your food will be. In fact, after outlining what I consider to be the three keys to any cooking process, I'll go over each of the major food categories, and give specific answers to the age-old question, "Why do I have to do that?"

One further note: Never fear if you forget a key concept or make a big mistake along the way. I've included a chapter at the end of this book advising you on what to do if all else fails.

Cooking is all about heat. How's that for a concept? It couldn't be simpler, at least at first glance, but you'd be surprised how many aspiring cooks fail to grasp the true importance of heat and how to use it in cooking. There are two main ways to produce heat when you're cooking a kitchen supper at home: You can produce heat in the oven or you can produce heat on the stove top (or grill). Likewise, there are two main types of heat: moist and dry. Moist heat is what you get when you cook with liquids. Dry heat is what you get when you cook without liquids or with fat. The chart below shows which cooking techniques use moist heat and which use dry heat, in the oven or on the stove top. Don't worry, I'll provide simple working definitions of these techniques later in this chapter. But for now, I just want to give you an overview that will allow you to associate the four basic categories (dry oven/moist oven, dry stove top/moist stove top), and see how they relate to one another.

	oven	stove top
dry heat	roast bake broil	pan-roast fry sauté grill
wet heat	braise stew poach steam	poach simmer braise stew boil steam pot roast

Knowing and understanding these basic cooking methods will give you the flexibility needed to unleash your creativity—and to create contingency plans if your equipment goes on the blink, by changing methods with a minimum of fuss. Sometimes you may even choose to combine two methods of cooking, as I often do. For instance, you might braise the legs and thighs of a duck, while sautéing or grilling the breasts. Or you might start by sautéing a meat on the stove top, and then leave it to slow-cook in the oven with liquids. If you like the spices and ingredients in a poached fish recipe, what is to prevent you from sautéing it? Nothing. Instead of cooking the fish in the liquid and having a soft exterior, you will have a crustier skin. You can still use the seasonings you would use in the poaching liquid, perhaps stuffing the fish with them, or heating them in a little broth on the side and making a sauce. You will need to make allowances for different cooking times, but the point is, you can use the ingredients in many dishes and change the cooking method.

At the same time, you should be aware that not all cooking methods will work with all meats or fish. I wouldn't advise sautéing a tough piece of stew meat, for example, unless you want leather for dinner, because you need the long cooking time to break down the structure of the meat. Nor would I roast in the oven a delicate fillet of Dover sole, because there is not enough fish there to handle the high heat, and it would dry up. If you are in doubt about which cooking method to use, one of the best things to do is ask your fishmonger or butcher. Can I use this cooking method with this cut of meat or fish? If the answer is no, but you still want to use the other ingredients in the recipe, ask which cooking method would be preferable, and try to adjust the recipe to suit.

I'll get into more specifics about what cooking methods work best with which types of foods later in this chapter, but always remember, the cooking method you choose is the means to an end, not an end in itself. As far as I'm concerned, the thing that is really of utmost importance is the flavor you're after. Say you like the idea of braised short ribs with horseradish and ale, but you don't have three hours to braise the meat. You could take some ale and horseradish, and some beef stock, reduce it with whatever herbs and spices are called for, then serve it as a sauce for flank steak, which takes only ten minutes to cook. No, you are not having melt-in-your-mouth braised meat, but you will have some of the flavor you are looking for. Another example would be roasting a leg of lamb instead of making lamb stew. You could roast the vegetables alongside the leg, and season the meat with the seasonings for the stew.

Along with heat, a second key cooking concept has to do with acids. And, of course, once you start talking about acids, you have to get into alkalis. Now I know what you're thinking: "Uh-oh, here we go getting highly technical." But we're not going to, I promise. I am not a scientist, in fact, I found chemistry a bore. Maybe if they had used food as examples I might be a Nobel prize winner, but they didn't, and I'm not. What I try to remember when cooking is that acid breaks things down (as in meat tenderizing), breaks them up (as in dairy), and makes things sour or sharp (as in salad dressings). Alkali balances and neutralizes the acid to keep things together.

The third key cooking concept concerns fat content. Fat gives flavor, texture and richness. For me, there is no contest between foods cooked with fat and those cooked without. Most things cooked in or with butter or a good olive oil do taste better, although there are times a fat-free meal is great, especially in hot weather or after a long, indulgent holiday season. The question of fat in cooking, like most major questions in life, boils down to achieving a pleasing balance. But be prepared to make the necessary trade-offs between flavor and dietary considerations.

If you have to or want to remove fat from your diet, use cooking methods such as poaching, steaming, grilling, or broiling. If a food is naturally fatty, such as ground chuck, you will not need to use fat, or as much fat, when cooking with it as you would when cooking a fillet. You can roast meat without adding fat by using the juices and fats from the meat. But if you're roasting fish, I'd advise even the diet-conscious to use just a little fat because the natural juices aren't enough to do the job, and if you cook it without any added fat, your fish will turn out so dry it will be inedible.

Okay, that's it for the three key concepts concerning heat, acid, and fat. I told you I'd keep it simple, didn't I? Let's not kid ourselves, though. If cooking were really as simple as one-two-three, every recipe would fit on one of those tiny strips of paper you get in fortune cookies. There are some complexities involved even in relatively simple dishes, especially if you attempt to vary or alter them out of choice or through sheer necessity. How can you cut through the complexities and keep your head clear for creating yummy kitchen suppers?

By using these heat-acid-fat concepts to understand the essence of various cooking techniques and food preparations.

Why Do I Have to Cook That Dish This Way?

Braising

Braising creates mouthwatering, melting mouthfuls by working with moist heat. The long, slow cooking process breaks down the meat and makes the flavors meld. The meat (which can be red or white meat, game, or thick fish) is browned in fat and then placed in a pot with a small amount of liquid—I usually add about one cup for every three pounds of meat. It is then put on or in the stove in a covered pot, and slowly cooked over or in low heat until the meat is very tender. Red meat will take the longest.

The meat should fit snugly into the pot because that will help create more pressure, which helps the meat juices spread out from the center. You must have a tight-fitting lid because the steam inside the pot creates the pressure you need. If it's necessary to add small amounts of liquid during the cooking process to keep the meat moist, your lid is not as tight as it should be. If you don't have a suitable lid, seal the top with aluminum foil. A braise needs to cook for a long time to bring out the flavor in the meat and make it tender. It can be done in the oven or on the stove top, but the oven will produce a more even heat. When you're done braising, you'll have a nice, thick gravy to serve with the food.

Stewing

Braising and stewing are very similar. But for stews, you use cut-up pieces of meat rather than whole pieces. You brown the meat first, then add the stew liquid. I use more liquid in a stew, almost covering the meat, as opposed to covering it halfway as in braising. The liquid allows all the flavors to meld together. When making a stew, you add vegetables as a major part of the recipe. In braising, you add vegetables only for flavoring. You may want to use the thickeners described on pages 30–33 for the liquid in your stew, or for coating the meat before browning.

Poaching

Poaching is a faster and far more gentle cooking method than either braising or stewing and it is more suited to tender foods such as fish or chicken breasts. The food is cooked on a rack in simmering water or stock, but not in a boiling liquid. I actually do it just on top of simmering water. The liquid is flavored with herbs and aromatics. If you are poaching an oily fish such as salmon, you might also want to add wine or vinegar to cut the oil. The flavor of the liquids will be picked up by the food. But you do not serve the food in its poaching liquid. The food should not touch the bottom of the pan because, if it does, it will be cooked by the hot metal of the pan rather than the liquid, and you will have an unevenly cooked piece of fish or meat.

Fish is the most commonly poached food, but you can also poach meat, poultry, fruits, vegetables, and, of course, eggs. In all cases, remember that you are *not* boiling. The water should never get above 200 to 205 degrees. Your choice of liquid will depend on the food you are poaching. The most common combinations are: meat and stock, fish and broth, fruit and sugar syrup or wine, vegetables and water with herbs, eggs and water with a bit of vinegar to help them hold their shape.

Steaming

The soul of steaming lies in cooking the food not in a liquid but by steam; therefore, the food retains almost all its natural flavor and vitamins rather than releasing them into the cooking liquid. Steaming is similar to poaching except that the food is raised above the water in a basket and cooked by the steam of almost-boiling water. You can steam either on the stove top in a tightly covered pan or in the oven. To steam in the oven, wrap the food in parchment or foil and let the natural juices create the steam. You may add vegetables in the wrappings, which will produce flavorful juices to steam the fish in. Alternatively, you can steam in the oven by rubbing the food with a bit of oil, then placing it in a pan

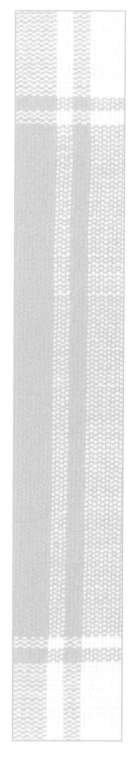

with a very tight lid. Personally, I don't like steamed meat. I recommend steaming vegetables, fish, and poultry.

Boiling

The best thing about boiling is its simplicity. Anybody can boil water, right? You just raise the heat to 212 degrees, and there you are. But you'd be surprised at who can and can't perform this simple task. Still more surprising is how little most people know about the purpose of boiling water and the purpose of boiling food or boiling a liquid in which to cook food. These methods are not always the same. The original purpose of boiling food was to rid it of any organisms that could kill. In this day and age there is little necessity for that because our food has been inspected, pasteurized, and otherwise deemed safe to eat. The purpose of boiling a liquid in which to cook the food is to shock the food and break down the outer shell quickly. Often you will be turning the heat down once the food is in the liquid, unless the food is a boiled food such as potatoes.

THINGS COOKED IN FAT OR A MINIMUM OF LIQUID (DRY HEAT)

Sautéing

Sautéing is probably the most common method of cooking with dry heat. It is relatively quick. When you sauté, you cook the food in a small amount of fat over medium to high heat using a sauté pan, which is similar to a frying pan but with higher sides. After the food is browned slightly, you might add a bit of liquid and put a loose lid on the pan to create a gravy. You want the steam to escape. The addition of liquid is more successful with meat or chicken than with fish. You can sauté anything except big hunks of tough meat, which do not sauté well because they need to be cooked through, and with sautéing the outside would be overcooked before the center was cooked through.

Frying

The fun of frying is that it tastes good. (Remember, I like fat.) The concept of frying is the same as sautéing except that it requires a little more fat and cooking over a higher heat for a bit longer. Fried food will be crisper on the outside than sautéed food. Almost any food can be fried. The exception would be tough meats that require long cooking.

Deep-frying is when the food is almost or completely immersed in fat and cooked to a dark golden brown. When deep-frying chicken, you typically use a batter or a coating in order to create a crisp and tasty "jacket" that will prevent the oil from being absorbed by the food. Deep-frying is not well suited to red meats or veal because they just don't seem to taste good cooked that way. Make sure that when you are frying you do not attempt to add any liquids at the end of the cooking process as you might do in sautéing. The addition of liquids will create a shower of splatters, which, in turn, can cause a nasty burn. If liquids get poured onto your frying pan by accident, throw salt on the pan immediately to douse the splatters.

Baking and Roasting

Baking and roasting are almost identical. It's just language—technically, you could roast a cake. The raison d'être for roasting and baking is to cook foods surrounded by even heat (although most ovens I have ever cooked in have been uneven). Anything cooked in an oven with dry heat surrounding the food is considered baked. The food can be covered or uncovered. Cakes, breads, cookies, and casseroles are always considered baked. Chicken, fish, and vegetables can be either baked or roasted. Meats are usually roasted, except for hams, which are baked.

Making a pot roast is similar to braising except it is done on the stove top. Confused? When baking or roasting meat, you use a more tender cut than if you were braising. Baking calls for the use of a consistent heat at a lower temperature. When roasting, you are likely to use a higher heat, at least to start.

Another difference between baking and roasting is that you can roast on the stove top in a Dutch oven, which is a very thick cast-iron pot with a lid. The lid should be left slightly ajar to let the steam escape, or you'll end up with braised meat. You baste, just as you do in the oven, with the juices that are released from the meat. To speed up roasting times, you can put a cover on—but then, strictly speaking, you are braising. I wouldn't worry, however, about all these technicalities. The basic idea is to have a nice even heat around what you are cooking. An oven thermometer can help you achieve this, and so can a meat thermometer, which is your best guide to what is going on inside of the meat.

Pan-Broiling

The beauty of pan-broiling is that it is quick and requires a minimum of fat. The food is cooked in a frying pan over high heat, either in its own fat or with the addition of a minimum of fat to to prevent sticking. Any fat that accumulates in the pan should be poured off. When you broil under a broiler, the fat naturally runs off. It is the heat that's cooking the food, not the hot fat.

Broiling and Grilling

The tasty satisfaction derived from grilling and broiling is the crunchy outside and the moist inside. (I like carcinogens too—but don't worry, I'm not going to kill you.) In broiling or grilling, you are cooking with direct heat—either under or over a flame. There is little difference between broiling and grilling except for the equipment used. The most important element in this method of cooking is your ability to judge how far from the heat source your food should be. My experience suggests that three to six inches is the optimum range. The thicker the food you're grilling or broiling, the farther away you should keep it from the heat source. The thinner the food, the closer it should be to the flame. Sounds contradictory, doesn't it? You'd think that thicker food would need more heat and thinner food less heat. But the thinner your food, the more chance you have of drying it out. You want it close to the flame so it cooks quickly. The thicker your food, the longer cooking time is required; you want it farther from the flame so the outside doesn't burn to a crisp before the inside is done. I've also discovered it's a good idea to use less marinade or sauce the closer you get to the flame. If you use too much marinade or sauce, the marinade will catch on fire.

Dairy

Always remember this one thing about dairy products: They react badly to acids such as citrus and vinegar. Acids make dairy products curdle. That one key fact will be the basis for understanding why you have to handle dairy products the way you do. There are no shortcuts when milk products are incorporated into acids, such as when you are making a sauce that calls for butter and lemon juice. It is best to warm the dairy product, incorporate a bit of the acid product into the milk product, and then add the milk product back into the acid product. The ratio of acid to dairy is what causes the curdling. By adding a little at a time, you will improve your chances of avoiding a curdling disaster because you'll be better able to balance out the acid/dairy ratio.

Being mindful of the temperature is also extremely important if you want your dairy to behave properly. For instance, you should chill your cream if you want it to whip properly because chilled butterfat will hold whipped cream together much better than room temperature or warm butterfat. If the cream is warm, the butterfat will be too soupy. You will inadvertently skip the whipped cream stage and wind up creating butter, because you will be beating so long and hard. This is also the reason why you cut cold butter into pastry crust. If you let it soften, you will have a tough crust. In my restaurants, we always make cappuccinos with cold milk because it produces a better foam. If your milk isn't cold, cool it with an ice cube for a minute.

Eggs

Eggs can be exasperating, but they are also one of the best flavor enhancers. Let me hasten to add a caveat about what you can and cannot get away with when using eggs. If a recipe calls for separating the eggs because you are whipping the egg whites, you must do it. You need the volume the whites will give. If the recipe asks you to separate the eggs just to put the whites in separately from the yolks, you can usually get way with putting everything in at the same time. When you are separating eggs, you must get all the yolk out of the whites or they

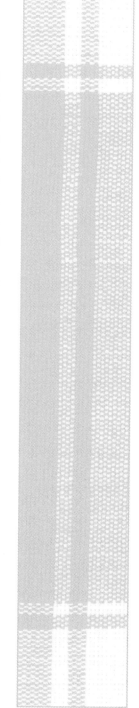

will not whip properly. Any teenie-weenie bit of fat will prevent the whites from whipping properly. The best way to get yolk out of whites is to scoop it out with an egg shell.

When whipping egg whites, they should be at room temperature to get the most volume. You do not have to own a copper bowl, although if you do, it will help stabilize the egg whites as well as emitting an electromagnetic force that helps the eggs to whip. You do not have to whisk the eggs by hand. If you are using an electric beater, try to stay with a copper or stainless-steel bowl because glass and porcelain are slippery, and the whites have a harder time staying up. Cheap aluminum will turn the whites gray. Egg whites should be beaten slowly at first, then very quickly. This will produce smaller air bubbles and make them more stable. The addition of a pinch of cream of tartar will also help stabilize the whites. If you are incorporating anything into the egg whites, such as cream of tartar or sugar, add it in the middle of the whipping process so that the whites can get a good start and reach their highest potential. If adding sugar, use confectioners' sugar. It produces the most successful results with whipped egg whites.

Egg yolks need to be brought to the proper temperature before they are added to a warm sauce so that the yolks don't become scrambled eggs. The best way to do this is to add a touch of the heated sauce to the yolks a little at a time until the yolks are warmed. Then the whole mixture can be returned to the remaining sauce.

A word of warning has to accompany any discussion of use of raw eggs. Salmonella. Salmonella is a strain of bacteria that can infect poultry (or meat) and if you are infected your tummy and digestive system can expect to spend several very uncomfortable days. Unfortunately, you cannot look at an egg and tell if it has been infected by the hen.

The only guarantee you are using "safe" eggs is to purchase pasteurized eggs, which are not easy to find (and tasteless). Beyond that, make sure the eggs you purchase are fresh. *Check the dates carefully.* Make sure the eggs are not cracked—even a hairline. Keep your eggs refrigerated in the carton or an airtight plastic container. Do not let raw eggs, or sauces that contain raw eggs or cooked eggs, sit around unrefrigerated unless you are bringing them to room temperature—and then serve immediately.

An interesting note I found in Harold Mcgee's *On Food and Cooking* says that in centuries past thyme has "been shown to be active against salmonella."

Certainly not an assured method of prevention, but interesting and tasty all the same.

Frozen Foods

The fun thing about frozen foods is that you can store things for a long period of time and not have to go to the market. One of the questions I'm most often asked is, "Do I really have to defrost frozen foods before cooking them?" Well, you should, but you don't have to. Now I know I'm treading on dangerous territory here, but I have developed my own way of cooking frozen meat or chicken. First, you should know that your cooking time must be multiplied by one and a half to two times. Second, you must start the process using low moist heat. I have a rule of thumb: The colder the meat you are starting with, the lower the heat must be at the beginning so as not to end up with raw meat on the inside and overdone meat on the outside. I gently brown the outside of my frozen meat in a casserole dish. Then I pour stock or water a third to halfway up the dish, cover it, and let the meat simmer until I can stick a skewer or a knife into the center of the food without a great deal of force; or I shove a meat thermometer into the frozen food at the beginning, and when the temperature on the meat thermometer reaches the first level of heat, I proceed with roasting or continue to braise.

If I am defrosting in the oven, I put the meat or chicken on a rack, fill the roasting pan halfway with liquid, cover the pan and the meat with tin foil, and leave it on a low/medium heat (300 to 350 degrees) until the meat thermometer begins to register an internal temperature. Then I will uncover the meat or chicken, remove most of the liquid (which I save for basting), and continue with roasting. It is at this point that I would add the vegetables to a roast or a braise.

You must make sure that the internal temperature of the meat reaches the level it is supposed to reach. This is the only way to protect yourself from meat-borne diseases. You must be patient while defrosting, but at least you can take consolation in the fact that you didn't have to change your dinner plans because you forgot to take the meat out of the freezer. If you are working with chickens, as soon as you remove the chicken from the freezer, try your best to pry out the little bag of innards that is stuck in the cavity. I have found that working with a knife placed in boiling water makes it easier. It's okay to wait until the chicken is beginning to thaw before attempting to pry out the bag, but don't forget that you must get the bag out before cooking your bird.

Fruits and Vegetables

The joy of working with fruits and vegetables is that most of them are good even raw. The only thing you can do to damage them is overcook them. Did you know that fruits and vegetables are basically the same thing? A fruit is a fruit because it houses the seed of the plant on which it is growing. A vegetable is defined as any part of the edible plant. I guess that would make seedless grapes vegetables and cucumbers fruit. Tomatoes are fruit as are many squash, but it only matters if you care. I don't. As long as it tastes good, you can call it anything you want to.

I find peeling vegetables and fruit to be the most annoying aspect of working with either. But if you just dip them in boiling water for about a minute, you will save yourself a lot of aggravation. Carrots and root vegetables will come clean easily with a vegetable peeler, but juicy things like tomatoes and peaches benefit from a good dip. The same goes for garlic and almonds.

Once you have your vegetables and fruit ready to cook, a good rule of thumb is to remember that the more acid in the vegetable or fruit, the more cooking time it will need. For instance, tomatoes will take longer than asparagus. If you are adding an acid, such as lemon juice or balsamic vinegar, this will also add to your cooking time. I use as little water as possible so as to maximize the flavor and nutrients in the vegetables. The exception is root vegetables, which require more cooking.

Now, let's say you have just taken the produce you bought yesterday out of the refrigerator and discovered to your dismay that it isn't quite as perky as it once was. Most likely, your produce got dehydrated. So what do you do? Give the produce a good soak in cold water followed by a quick damp dry, then return it to the refrigerator for an hour or so. That should make it spring back to life. If it's your mushrooms that are on the other side of fresh and you still want to serve them in salad that evening, wipe them with a damp rag sprinkled with lemon juice, then refrigerate them for an hour or so. If you're planning to cook with the mushrooms, drop them in boiling water for a minute with a squeeze of lemon juice. Do not believe that baking soda will make your vegetables better—they might look brighter on the outside, but they will be mushier on the inside because the baking soda breaks down the structure of the outside walls of the vegetable. Baking soda also destroys the vitamin C in vegetables. If you cook with the lid off, your vegetables will maintain a better color because the acid that discolors them will evaporate rather than get trapped in the pot.

Recipes call for vegetables to be chopped in various ways. You can really chop them as small as you like, but know that your sauce may not be as smooth, and that the larger the chunk, the longer the required cooking time. Your dish will simply have a different texture, but the flavor will be the same.

I chop with a knife most of the time, rather than with a food processor. I like having more control than a machine will allow. Onions often turn to mush in a food processor, as does fruit. As a rule, any produce with a high water content should be chopped with a knife. So unless you are making a puree, or are cooking large quantities, or are feeling especially lazy, chopping with a knife is what I recommend.

If you cannot find fresh vegetables or ones that look alive, use frozen vegetables. You lose a bit of texture when cooking, but if all you can find at the supermarket is brown green beans, frozen beans will be better. I have had more success with organic frozen vegetables that are packaged in bags than with the kind packaged in boxes.

Fruit is very easy to work with once it is peeled. A squeeze of lemon, lime, or orange will prevent the fruit from discoloring and turning brown. Fruit that is irrevocably on its way to kingdom come can still be salvaged for use in stewed fruit dishes or compotes.

Pasta and Rice

The pleasing thing about pasta and rice is that they are comfort foods—soft on the tummy and easy on the palate. When cooking pasta, always remember that it is critical to use enough water. If you don't use enough water, you will end up with a sticky clump. Sometimes I add oil to the water, and sometimes I don't. I have never noticed that adding oil makes any difference in the way the sauce clings to the pasta, but it does make a difference in the way the pasta clings to itself. The benefit of oil is that it makes it easier to separate the pasta—if the pasta has for some reason been allowed to cool too long, and has stuck together—before it's covered with sauce. If you want to prepare pasta in advance in order to save time and better coordinate your overall dinner preparations, half of the way through the cooking process, take it off the stove and let it soak in cold water until you're ready to resume cooking it. When you are ready to serve, bring another pot of water to a boil and finish cooking the pasta.

Risotto and other forms of rice may also be made to the halfway point. You can turn it off and then go back to it, adding hot liquid to finish it. Always add warm or hot water to rice that is warm. Cold water will change the temperature too much, and rice wants a steady temperature. I have started rice in cold water, however, and cooked it to the finish without any problems. In fact, it seems that the only time I have problems with rice is when I follow the cooking instructions printed on the package. I find that the rice takes less time than the instructions call for. My own recipe is to use two cups of liquid for one cup of rice. I add a dab of butter while cooking the rice to prevent spillover. Check the rice after ten to fifteen minutes, and add more warm liquid if necessary. With the exception of risotto, which loves attention, rice likes to be left alone. Don't stir it.

Fish

The fabulous thing about fish is the guiltless feeling you get from knowing that you are cooking food that is really good for you—at least most of the time. Just remember that all fish are not dietetic. Salmon and tuna, for example, can be extremely fatty. It is important to know the fat content of the fish you are cooking, both for dietary reasons and for creating a desirable taste. Ask the nice person at the fish counter to help you, and if there isn't one, just take a good look at the fish before you buy it. Thin fillets such as sole do not have a great deal of fat. In general, the darker the color of the flesh, the higher the fat content will be. Fattier fish also have more distinctly individual flavors than the more delicate lean fish. Knowing this will help you to determine the best cooking method for that fish, or what to substitute when the particular fish you want is not available. A lean fish such as cod will not do as well being roasted unless it is wrapped in fat or constantly basted, so cod would not be a good substitute for salmon. On the other hand, striped bass, though significantly lower in fat than salmon, could be a tasty substitute.

Fish is similar to meat in that the center cuts are richer than the end cuts. The tougher tail ends are best used in stews. Whether you are purchasing center cut or not, the fish should be gleaming and bright. If it looks dull, chances are it has been in the supermarket display case too long. Look for bright eyes in whole fish, and a bounce back feeling when you press the skin. You can keep your fish looking fresh and prevent it from becoming discolored during the poaching process by adding a touch of acid in the form of lemon juice or lime juice. If you add a lot of acid, the fish will be even whiter, though it may cause the fish to cook faster and be flakier.

Meat

What is so marvelous about meat is that it is rich and robust. There are many books on the subject of meat and as many contradictory opinions about how to cook what, whether or not to season before cooking, and so forth. I've found that the only time to salt steak is after the first sear. Salt pulls the juices from steaks, especially thin ones, and the juices sizzle away in the bottom of the pan, losing their usefulness. With roasts, it doesn't seem to matter when you salt or season because you should be basting the meat with the pan juices. If my meat turns out dry, it's usually because I didn't baste it properly, or because I over-cooked it.

I have found that cooking meat on the bone makes it cook faster because the bone acts as a heat conductor. The juices also stay in better because the heat is more consistent and the outside retains more of its juice. Cooking on the bone also produces a more flavorful roast because the bone releases flavor into the meat.

Leaving a roast to rest for five to ten minutes after cooking it helps the juices to distribute better and makes the meat easier to carve. The roast begins to firm up as the gelatin in the meat cools. If you leave your meat out to cool too long, however, you will have a tough piece of meat. If you have to stop roasting in the middle of the cooking process for any reason (perhaps because your dinner guests are going to arrive later than planned), just remove your roast from the oven and wrap it in aluminum foil. When you are ready to start again, return it to the oven at a slightly higher temperature and reduce your cooking time by ten to fifteen minutes, because the meat will have continued cooking while it was out of the oven. Make sure you baste it well.

Searing is another controversial subject, but I am a pro-searing person. I find that searing keeps the juices in and makes the outside more flavorful, which makes the drippings richer. Some people feel that the meat will dry out faster because searing causes the juices to flow out from the center of the meat to the outside too quickly. I have never found this to be true. If I am too lazy to sear, I find that I lose a bit of flavor, and the meat seems mushier.

I do not like to carve. I'm embarrassed to say that I am not that good with knives, having had a fear of them that goes back to my childhood. For many years, the only knives I would use were a paring knife and a serrated knife. I managed to get everything cut just fine. I now have proper knives, which I am not that good at sharpening, but I still reach for my paring knives and serrated knives first.

All meat should be cut across the grain. Usually the grain runs from the middle of the meat to the extremities. To know exactly how to carve, you must think about where the cut of meat came from on the animal, and how that figures into the larger picture. You can usually see if you are carving the wrong way because the meat will look stringy. Although some people say that meats not on the bone, such as London broil, are better carved on an angle, I think straight up and down is preferable. Carving on an angle will give you larger slices, but I think the cuts of meat you get are much tougher.

Another handy knife trick is to slash the fat on a steak so that it won't curl and create a funny-looking piece of meat that won't lie flat on the plate. The concept here is similar to poking little holes in sausage casings so they won't burst. The heat of cooking will cause the fat or casing on the outside to shrink faster than the inside, causing this curling and bursting and leaving you with an ugly though still edible piece of meat.

Thickeners

The true value of thickeners is to create a creamier sauce. At some point in preparing a meal, you will probably be dealing with a thickening agent, whether it be in a salad dressing, a stew, or a dessert cream. At the base of a thickener you have liquid. The type of liquid will dictate the viscosity and richness of the sauce. Cream will produce thicker outcomes than milk or stock, for instance.

There are many kinds of thickeners and the best way to choose is to know what is available. Here are the most common choices:

Arrowroot is one of the least tasty thickeners, but it is also the most delicate, and it creates a more transparent sauce than most other thickeners. Arrowroot should be blended in a little cold liquid before incorporating it into the hot liquid. It should also be used only when the dish will be served immediately and not reheated, otherwise it loses its thickening power. Use one and a half teaspoons for each cup of liquid to be thickened.

Flour is the most common thickener, and it can be used in a variety of ways. Flour paste is one of the simplest and quickest, if not quite one of the tastiest ways to thicken a sauce or stew. Use one part flour to two parts liquid, make a smooth paste, and whisk it into the boiling stock or into the drippings in the bottom of a roasting pan. The liquid you mix the flour paste into must be at least simmering if you want a smooth outcome.

Browned flour will have only half the thickening power of regular flour, but will give a better flavor. To make browned flour, spread white flour on a baking pan and put it in the oven at 250 degrees for twenty to thirty minutes, shaking frequently. Use two tablespoons of flour for each cup of liquid to be thickened.

Roux is a mix of flour and fat, and I think it is the most successful thickener because it adds a good flavor rather than a pasty one. In making a roux, the flour is browned in the fat, while constantly being stirred, until the desired color is achieved. These colors are white, blond, or brown. The roux must be blended well because the starch in the flour has to stretch evenly. If the starch doesn't, it will not be able to absorb the liquid and your sauce or base will remain thin. A roux must be cooked a minimum of three minutes to thicken properly. The time is based on the color you are looking for. What determines the color is your need. A dark roux, for example, works best when incorporated into a rich dark sauce, while a blond roux works well used in a cream sauce for veal, and a white roux works well with creamed onions.

My Roux Chart:
1 tablespoon flour and butter to 1 cup liquid = thin sauce
2 tablespoons flour and butter to 1 cup liquid = medium sauce
3 tablespoons flour and butter to 1 cup liquid = thick sauce
4 tablespoons flour and butter to 1 cup liquid = very thick sauce

If you use too much flour in a sauce or a roux, you will make a gloppy mass. It is easier to add flour in small portions, though this obviously takes time, than it is to try to save a sauce that has turned gooey because you added too much flour too quickly.

When using flour-based thickeners in sauces, remember that cooling a starch-thickened sauce increases the viscosity, so it is better to take it off the stove a bit thinner than you want. Otherwise, by the time the sauce gets to the table, it will be glue. If your sauce does turn gluey, you can remedy the situation by returning the sauce to the heat, adding a bit more liquid, and whisking it. But again, keep in mind that it is always much easier to repair a slightly thin sauce than one that has already gotten too thick.

The amount of butter you use in a sauce is determined by how rich you want that sauce to be. Butter is often whisked into sauces at the end of the cooking process to make them smooth. You can also make little butter balls of half butter/half flour (beurre manie), and stir them into a stew or a sauce. If you are using butter alone, use one tablespoon for each cup of liquid.

Cornstarch is not my favorite. I think it adds a weird translucence, and it imparts no flavor. Like arrowroot, cornstarch is mixed with cold water before it is added to the hot liquid. The liquid is then cooked over medium heat until it comes to a boil. Boil for only one minute and then serve. If you overcook the cornstarch, you will have a thin sauce.

Egg yolks, in contrast to cornstarch, impart a lovely, rich flavor. Always put the yolks in a small bowl and stir a little of the hot sauce into the bowl before you pour the yolks into the hot saucepan on the stove. That way the sauce doesn't cook the yolks and make little droplets of scrambled egg. It's best to add a touch of cream as well, for it seems to make a smoother sauce and help the eggs to blend in. Egg yolks are what help set a custard. A standard custard calls for two egg yolks for every two thirds to one cup of milk. If you're too lazy to separate the eggs, you can use the entire egg by replacing two yolks with one egg, but your custard will not be as rich. Use two yolks to one cup of liquid.

Milk has enough protein to help thicken a sauce, but I tend not to use milk because the results seem watery. If you want to use water or juice in a recipe that calls for milk, add an egg white or yolk to make up for the lack of protein. The more acid in a dish, the more protein required to thicken it, which means you'll need to add more milk or more egg yolks. If the dish has a great deal of starch, you can use less milk or fewer yolks.

Starches such as *rice* or *potatoes* grab the moisture in a dish. That's how it thickens. When a starch is exposed to heat, it stretches and more water can be absorbed.

A *reduction* is a slow evaporation of the liquid in a pot that occurs when you cook over low heat. The water content will slowly evaporate leaving an intense, viscous liquid that will be very flavorful. I have at times reduced too much, and have had to add more wine or liquid and then reduce again. The sauce still tasted good, but it was not quite as intense as it should have been.

Though not by definition a thickener, you need to know what an *emulsifier* does to help that sauce you've just tried to thicken. An emulsion is the marriage of two liquids that normally separate, a classic example being oil and water. An emulsifier will help keep the two enemies in marriage to create a smooth sauce. When you mix the two enemies, the oil is broken up. Left to its own devices, the oil will come back together. An emulsifying agent coats the broken oil drops, and prevents them from joining up. It also prevents the water from pushing the oil back into a glob. Sauces that require emulsifiers are finicky.

Contradictory as it may seem, overbeating will undermine the process, as will heat and freezing temperatures. And believe it or not, so will electrical charges, which is why you should ditch your hollandaise plans when there is lightning and thunder. Store-bought items contain monoglycerides or diglycerides and gums, which act as emulsifiers. Egg yolks are an emulsifier as are starch, some proteins, and finely ground substances such as dry mustard. You can use acids such as lemons and limes as emulsifiers, but use only a little bit. Too much, and your sauce will be out of balance and won't come together.

Some cooks use *gelatin*, which is made from animal bones, as a thickening agent. Personally, I don't like using gelatin because it gives an odd jelly-like quality to the sauce. Another option is to use *pureed vegetables or fruit*, which can naturally thicken a sauce while giving it a lot of flavor with no fat. I do this quite a bit.

Fats

I love working with butter, but sometimes oil is necessary. You might not want the flavor of butter in your dish, or you might be cooking with high heat, which will burn the butter. If I want the flavor of butter when cooking with high heat, I might use a half butter–half oil combination. For frying, you must use oil, because butter will burn before it gets to the temperature necessary for frying. A general rule is the less saturated the fat, the higher cooking temperature it can take. Butter is at the high end of the saturated fat scale (lower cooking temperature) and vegetable oil is at the low end of the saturated fat scale (higher cooking temperature).

Cooks often work with clarified butter in which the fat is separated from the non-fat elements. Clarified butter will store much longer than regular butter. It will last several weeks in the fridge and even longer in the freezer, and it is better for frying at high temperatures. But if you use clarified butter, remember that you will lose some of the rich butter flavor because you have removed the protein when you clarified it. To clarify butter, melt it over low heat and let the fat rise. Skim off the white froth and pour off the clear (that is, clarified) butter, carefully leaving the sediment behind. You can also clarify butter by melting the butter in a glass bowl, letting it cool, and then picking off the layer of fat that has solidified at the top. What is left is clarified butter.

For baking, I don't use oil. The health benefits aren't worth it, and I'd just rather not eat oil-baked food. Using oil in baked goods creates a grainy texture because the oil tries to collect rather than spreading uniformly throughout the product.

Why Do I Have to Keep Asking These Questions?

Why do I have to add salt to make water boil?
You don't have to, but it makes the water boil faster. Adding salt raises the water temperature by 2 degrees.

Why do stews and braises take so long? Why can't I just turn the heat up?
You can't just turn up the heat because the connective tissue and the muscle fibers need a long, slow cooking period to be broken down. If you cook at a higher temperature for a shorter period, the meat will cook but will remain tough because the higher heat will harden the muscle fiber. The lower the heat, the less toughening of the muscle fiber.

Why do I burn everything on the barbecue?

You might be putting on the sauce too soon, or you might be putting the food too close to the flame. Remember: The thicker the meat the farther away from the coals and the longer the cooking time with less heat. As a general rule your food should be four to six inches from the coals

Why do I have to have use wine when I'm poaching fish?

The acid keeps the fish whiter or truer to color. A lack of acid will make a gray fish because the alkali in the broth turns the fish gray.

Why do I have to scald milk?

You don't if you are using pasteurized milk. In order to thicken milk, certain elements must be broken down by intense heat. Everything in milk that needs to be broken down has already been destroyed in the pasteurization process.

Why do I have to add flavoring to whipping cream before I'm finished whipping it?

Because it hinders the bubble development. If you add the flavoring at the very end, you will have to overwhip to incorporate it.

Why do I have to marinate?

Acid breaks down the connective tissue, leaving less of that to happen when you cook. On the other hand, a marinade can make a roast drier because the acid depletes the roast's ability to retain water.

Why do I have to use certain kinds of potatoes in certain dishes?

Water content. New potatoes have more moisture and less starch. Older potatoes can stand up to longer cooking times better. For frying, Idaho potatoes, with little water content, can handle the fat better because they won't splatter.

Why do I have to fry at such high heat?

If you deep-fry at too low a temperature, the oil will seep into the food. Hot oil should seal the outside. If you crowd your pan, you will cause the temperature to drop too low, and you will get greasy food. The optimum temperature for deep-frying is 375 to 400 degrees. Start at 400 degrees.

Why do my coatings fall off the meat?

You didn't let your meat rest with the coating on it. The breading won't fall off if you give it about twenty minutes to bind to the meat.

Why does the second batch of fried or sautéed food seem better?

The second batch is always better because the oil has been seasoned by the first batch.

Why do I have problems making my yeast bread rise?

You probably subjected the yeast to too high a heat when dissolving it and killed it. Maybe you didn't add sugar: Yeast feeds on sugar, the sugar ferments and creates carbon dioxide. Maybe it was too old. Compressed yeast will not last as long as dry yeast. Or perhaps you didn't knead the bread well enough. You must knead yeast breads; if you don't, the yeast cells will not be evenly distributed.

Why do I have to sift flour before using it?

You don't. You can usually skip this step because the flour we purchase today is usually fine and not too compact.

Does the color or kind of cooking wine matter?

Only in that it affects the color of the dish. You do want to match the weight and structure of the wine with the dish you are cooking. For instance, I would not poach a gentle fish in a rustic Beaujolais. Cooking with champagne has little value other than using up dead bottles.

Why is a casserole a casserole?

A casserole traditionally is a layered dish cooked in the oven with the top on the pot.

Why does lemon or acid help prevent the discoloration of vegetables?

Because the acid slows down the oxidation process; however, in green vegetables this is not true—acid can turn them muddy gray. I usually add acid at the very end.

Why do I start soup bones in cold water?

Because hot water will seal them and defeat the purpose of having all that goodness seep from the bones

Why should I cook?

Because it's the direct line to the heart and the soul.

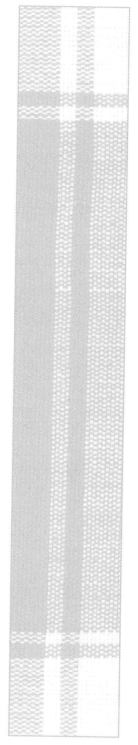

3. Pantry Pride

3. Pantry Pride

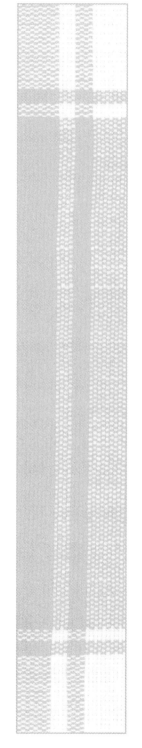

This chapter is about cheating. I admit it. I prefer to make things fresh, and usually the long way is better, but when my time is short, as it so often is, I rely on my pantry. Never be embarrassed about using some prepared foods. It would shock you to know how many great commercial chefs use prepared items occasionally—they just don't tell their restaurant customers. I could not exist without frozen puff pastry in the freezer, and several of the chefs I know could not, either. I could also tell you a few stories about chefs hiding ketchup in their kitchens, but I might get my tongue cut out.

Although my husband and I don't really have a formal pantry in our home, I have a cupboard full of helpers for those days when dinner is at 8:00 P.M. and I get home at 7:45 P.M. Maintaining a well-stocked pantry saves me a great deal of time, angst, and frantic trips to the store. And it is essential to the making of good last-minute meals. Of course, there are some dishes that require using fresh foods, but chances are I will have planned enough time to cook those dinners. Through trial and error, and being in a business where anything can go wrong usually at the last minute, I've found that it's a good idea to go shopping just for the pantry at least two or three times a year.

Since storage space is always precious, the question is what to keep in your pantry. There are a few obvious items to have on hand at all times, such as salt, pepper, sugar, oil, and vinegar. But there are also many items you might not have time to prepare from scratch that can add zing to your dishes. One good example is artichoke hearts, dried, in jars or canned. You can toss them in a salad or pasta, roast them beside lamb, or chop them and use in stuffing for chickens.

The dish is not going to be quite the same as it would be if you used fresh artichokes, but then again, you won't have to peel whole fresh artichokes, pull out the hairy stuff, and ever-so-carefully retrieve the heart, which I usually manage to mangle and lose half of anyway.

If you're traveling to different parts of the world, or even to the state next door, it's worth looking on the gourmet shelves of large markets. I'm not suggesting that you spend your hard-earned vacation scouring the local supermarkets, but a few hours might yield some yummy finds that are not distributed in your area, especially spices and condiments that fit easily into your suitcase. One of my favorite finds on a trip to Texas was jarred roux. It's a flour-butter combination that is either brown or white in color and can be used to thicken soups, sauces, and stews, and that you don't have to carefully baby-sit for hours. Now maybe jarred roux doesn't have quite the intensity of a roux you have lovingly browned on the stove. But the time it saves can be worth it, and you will no longer have to worry that the fresh roux you are trying to prepare has made the stew look like dishwater and that the tablespoon of flour you added in desperation is floating around in little clumps.

In the following lists you will find all the special goodies I like to see in my pantry. Not all of them are used in the recipes in this book, but in many cases, they can be substituted for items the recipes do call for. I have also included the obvious basics, because these are the ones most likely to be forgotten when you are searching for that something special.

I buy most of my nut oils, balsamic vinegar, and honeys through Rosenthal Wine merchants. The quality cannot be beat. If you call 1 (800) 910-1990, Kerry will be happy to tell you where you can purchase these items in your neighborhood.

Please note: I have had to make a rule for myself, and you may want to follow it, as well. In my purchasing euphoria, I have been known to overdo it, coming home with bags full of groceries that take up lots of pantry space and never get used. That being the case, my rule is, anything that sits on the shelf until a week before its use-by date, or for two years, whichever comes sooner, either gets used immediately or goes to the local church. Like the canned sardines I carted home one day not long ago. I don't even like canned sardines, and neither does my husband, but I bought them thinking I might use them in a dish to be named later. I finally tossed the sardines in the food processor, added sour cream and onions, and made a cold pasta sauce. It was quite tasty. But as a general principle, don't buy what you don't like just because it seems like an item you ought to have in the pantry. Even if you might be intending to try a recipe that calls for that particular item, you can usually substitute something else you do like.

THE BARE MINIMUM:

Salt
Pepper
Garlic
Onion
A variety of herbs and spices
Chicken broth
Canned tomatoes
Mustard
Sugar
Honey
Oil
Vinegar
Butter
Sour cream (or yogurt)
Cooking wine

IN THE PANTRY

Salt

I keep kosher salt, sea salt, and iodized salt in my pantry. If I could have only one I would keep kosher salt in the house. I prefer the coarse texture, and it is not as salty as iodized salt so you are less in danger of oversalting. It is also hands-down best when used in roasting. How much salt to use is a very personal issue. In almost all my recipes I have instructed to "salt to taste." Start with a little and go easy.

Pepper

Pepper can be purchased in different grinds, or as whole peppercorns (if you prefer to grind them yourself), and in black, white, pink, or green. In the case of

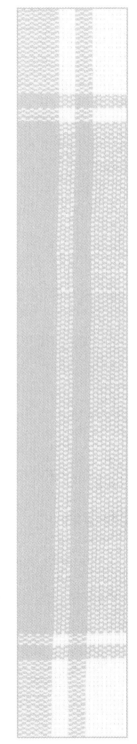

pink or green peppercorns, you usually have to buy them whole. The curious cook may want to investigate the subtle flavors in different kinds of pepper from around the world. I tend to stick with coarse ground black pepper for everyday use—sometimes referred to as restaurant grind.

Herbs and Spices

I prefer fresh herbs because the flavor is truer and livelier, and this is one item I feel is worth the effort to shop for. I rarely use dried ones; they seem to just sit on the shelf collecting dust. These days, fresh herbs are readily available, so unless you live way away from civilization, or are too tired, there is no reason to resort to dried. I do look for any unusual combinations I might find in my travels, such as pimento or curry powder from Jamaica. Or at the supermarket, Taste of Thai makes a wonderful red curry paste for an instant curry dinner. I choose what herbs to cook with by smell. Things that smell good together usually taste good together. As for fresh herbs, think about what's in season, and you'll usually get the best flavor. By the way, dried herbs are not very useful or tasty after they have been on the shelf for more than a year. If you can find frozen herbs, buy these instead.

DRIED HERBS

Oregano
Herbes de Provence

FRESH HERBS

Rosemary
Thyme
Dill
Basil
Oregano
Marjoram

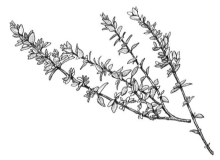

SPICES

Cajun spice
Cumin
Cinnamon

Nutmeg
Chili powder
Curry Powder
Dried hot peppers
Celery seed
Lemon pepper

Other Flavorful Finds

Garlic spray (One of my most recent finds from Garlic Valley Farms in Glendale California. It's actually garlic juice in a pump spray bottle. A spritz here, there, when sautéing, or in sauce.)
Onion spray (See above!!!)
Dried mushrooms
Dried artichokes
Sun-dried tomatoes
Tomato paste
Crushed tomatoes
Whole tomatoes
Chicken, vegetable, and beef broths (My favorite brand is from Pacific Foods of Oregon. It is organic and comes in a carton with a lid. I buy it at the local King Kullen. Next in line I prefer the canned versions because they seem to have fewer chemicals than the cubes. You can also find extract bases in jars that are excellent, if a bit harder to find.)
White beans
Black beans
Artichoke hearts
Black and green olives

Condiments, Sauces, and Dressings

You can save a dish that's missing an appetizing taste or simply seems a little dull with a tablespoon of mustard or a shot of Tabasco. If a recipe calls for an ingredient you don't like, think about why it is used. Although I like to use mustard

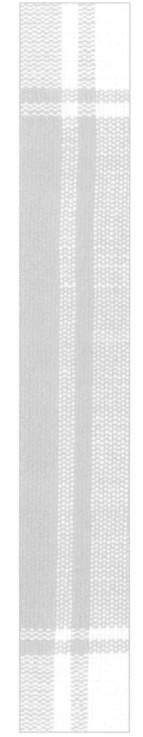

to add a bit of tang, it may not appeal to *your* taste buds. In that case, you can usually substitute a bit of lemon, vinegar, or horseradish cream. Just remember that the flavor and composition will be different depending on your choice of substitute, so go slowly and sparingly until you arrive at a flavor and composition you like.

Mustards, whole grain and Dijon (There are many flavored mustards—such as garlic—on the market, but I usually find that you can flavor your own. Then again, if time is a factor and pantry space isn't, go for broke and buy all the flavored mustards you desire.)

Worcestershire sauce; Tabasco; hot sauce (These are the little-dab-will-do-you trio. In the case of Tabasco and hot sauce, you run the obvious risk of making your mouth feel like it's on fire if you use too much. But using too much Worcestershire sauce exposes you to the not-so-obvious risk of making your dish taste "worster"—pardon the pun—rather than better.)

Soy sauce; teriyaki sauce (I don't use these items very much because they don't happen to tantalize my taste buds, but if you like them, both soy and teriyaki are very good flavor enhancers.)

Ketchup (Does this need an explanation? A dab in the dressing, slathered on meatloaf, or on a "leftovers" sandwich.)

Maple syrup; honey (I rely on these basic sweeteners as alternatives to sugar. I often use maple syrup with pork, and honey with lamb. Buy only real maple syrup, grade A. There are many honeys on the market, and the sheer range of choices can be dizzying. If you can only have one, stay with a basic clover or acacia. But if you have the time and patience, it makes sense to look for more exotic honeys that suit your tastes. I've found that thyme honey, for example, is fabulous on chicken.)

Salad dressing (For those nights you just can't make one. I adore the Brianna's salad dressings. They come in several varieties, including such basic types as French, Vinaigrette, and Blue Cheese. I love them all.)

Horseradish and horseradish cream (I feel that almost any beef dish can be improved with horseradish. I have also used it with chicken, and on certain vegetables such as potatoes and beets. Horseradish cream provides a bit of heat without being overbearing. You can make your own horseradish cream by mixing a tablespoon of horseradish with two tablespoons of cream, sour cream, or crème fraîche.)

Dairy

I love dairy products, the real thing. I don't believe in substitutes because they never seem to taste right and can be full of chemicals. As far as I'm concerned, if you cannot have the real thing, then don't bother. There are so many great foods that can be made without dairy products. Why make yourself eat artificial dairy substitutes?

Butter (I love butter and tend to reach for it unless I am cooking over very high heat and the butter will burn. Butter tastes better. I do not use any margarine and would substitute olive oil if my diet did not permit me to eat butter. Buy grade AA butter—either salted or sweet.)
Clarified butter (See page 34.)
Eggs (I always use extra large. I buy brown eggs if I can find them. Make sure to use fresh eggs. Old eggs will not bind properly; they will not help things to rise. The whites will not whip into shape. And as with any "old" food, they can make you sick.)
Mayonnaise (Making fresh mayonnaise in a food processor is quite simple, but when you only have five minutes to dinnertime, finding a jar of Hellmann's in the refrigerator will make you happy.)
Sour cream (I prefer regular sour cream because it doesn't have the chemicals the lower-fat versions have, but I do use low fat quite a bit because my thighs prefer it.)
Crème fraîche (also known as French sour cream)
Fromage blanc (a lower-fat version of crème fraîche)
Yogurt (a good low-fat substitute, and a nice condiment with spicy foods such as curries.)
Cream cheese (I blend cream cheese into dressings and sauces for a bit of added flavor and creaminess. It can also be an instant pasta sauce.)
Ricotta cheese

Sorbets; ice creams (I know these are really freezer items, but I include them on the list because they serve the same function as well-chosen pantry items. Just as a tangy condiment can save a meal from tastelessness, a good sorbet or ice cream can save a dessert from disaster. More on that point in a later chapter.)

Coconut milk (Mixed into potatoes or carrots with a little curry, poured over chicken while roasting, or added while sautéing shrimp, it's just yummy.)

Basic Oils

Olive (for almost anything)
Safflower (for a light oil in dressings)
Peanut (for high-heat cooking)
Crisco (If you can eat fried foods, I believe Crisco is the only way to go because it fries food better than anything.)

Specialty Oils

These items are not a necessity but they're awfully nice to have on hand to improve a salad dressing or perk up a poultry dish.

Lemon oil
Sesame oil
Almond oil
Hazelnut oil
Walnut oil

Staple Staples

I love rice, it's so easy to make. You can sauté cooked rice with vegetables, other grains, or nuts, and make an interesting side dish or salad out of leftovers. Add a little dressing and you have rice salad.

Long-grain rice (fluffiest when cooked)

Aromatic rices (ones with a slightly floral scent such as Texmati or Jasmine)

Short- or medium-grain rice (The rice has a stickier texture, such as that found in Japanese rice. It is a creamy rice suited to rice pudding as well.)

Arborio rice (a classic short-grained, soft rice from Italy, which you *must* use to make a proper risotto)

Wild rice (Not really a rice, it is a seed from lake grass. True wild rice is very nutty. Much of what you purchase today is not wild, however, but farmed. It is still quite good and has a lovely texture. I find when cooking real wild rice according to package instructions that the rice comes out a bit watery. So start with a little less water—you can always add more.)

Converted rice (steam-processed to seal the outer layer)

Brown rice (Simply rice with its outer shell left on, it is said to be more nutritious and is more flavorful, I think, than white rice.)

Pastas, in good variety (You must have pastas because if all fails you're probably going to serve pasta. Make sure you have something you like in the house at all times—with plenty of back-up.)

Grains (This is another area where you can find some exotic and tasty varieties to complement your usual staples. In the Mexican section of the local supermarket, for instance, I found a black bean and rice combination I have used in salad and with chicken. Just be sure to look at the ingredients listed on the outside of the package. If almost everything is natural, try it. Another true time-saver is cooked polenta found in little rolls in the refrigerator section. You just slice and sauté.)

Vinegars and Cooking Wines

Salad dressing depends on the quality of the oil and the vinegar. It makes sense to buy the best you can so you don't have to spend time doctoring your dressing with spices. You can change the weight of the dressing by changing the vinegar. For a light cucumber salad, a rice wine vinegar is perfect. For a heav-

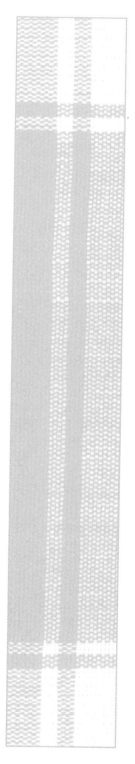

ily composed salad, a deep red wine vinegar would be more appropriate. How do you know what to choose? Taste and smell your options using what I call the "cucumber comparison test." Compare a piece of cucumber dipped in the rice vinegar with a piece dipped in red wine vinegar. Do the taste and aroma of the vinegar overpower the food it's planned for, or do they complement it? The answers will be apparent, and so will your choice of vinegars. Make sure you buy the best quality you can find (and afford.) Quality will make the biggest difference in flavor.

As for cooking wines, I use whatever drinking wine is left over from the night before. And if there's nothing left, I use the least expensive bottle of wine I can find that I would still drink. There are no hard and fast rules governing my choice of red or white wine for cooking. I have used red wine in dishes calling for white, and vice versa, without any major problems except a little discoloration that does not really affect the taste of the dish. Mainly, it's a matter of commonsense, and having a feel for the weight or body of the wines you are considering. For example, you can usually get away with substituting a full-bodied white wine for a red wine, and a light red for a white. But it's probably not a great idea to use a big Cahors when the recipe calls for a light Pinot Blanc. I'd also advise against using white wine in a tomato-based spaghetti sauce because it just wouldn't add enough body.

VINEGAR

Good balsamic vinegar (It should have the proper Modena stamp on it.)
Red wine vinegar
Rice wine vinegar (a light white vinegar that is wonderful for cucumbers or rice salad)
Sherry vinegar
Verjus (This fancy-sounding French word is a term for sour grape juice made from the first growth of grapes not used in the wine-making process. It's basically just a cross between vinegar and wine. Verjus is now being produced in this country and is becoming more readily available. I like to use it with fish.)

Baking Supplies

I keep just the simplest items in the house because I seldom venture into very complicated recipes. The baking basics are flour, fat, sugar, and leavening in one form or another.

Flour (I prefer all purpose unbleached flour because it will work for almost any recipe.)
Sugar: white, brown, and confectioners'
Cornmeal
Baking soda
Baking powder
Chocolate chips and squares
Pure vanilla extract
Almond extract
Cream of tartar
Frozen puff pastry (a must for tartes Tatins)
Crepe shells (great filled with ice creams or fruits for an easy dessert)

Fruits and Nuts

Almonds, blanched and regular (Yes, you can blanch them in boiling water, rinse and cool them down, then squirt the almonds from their peels yourself, if you want to spend the time. But why bother if you can get fresh nuts already blanched?)
Walnuts
Pecans
Raisins
Dried apricots
Dried cherries

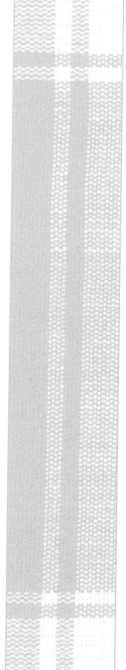

Jellies and Jams

I frequently use jams and jellies to glaze meats, to top desserts, and to add weight and flavor to salad dressings and marinades. They add a bit of viscosity to a sauce, as well as sweetness. The trick is to add them teaspoon by teaspoon so that you don't create a cloying mess. Look for exotic items on travels to places outside your home state and in foreign countries. I found a great mango jam in the Caribbean islands that became a major component of my barbecue sauce. And recently I found a sorrel jam that is dynamite with chicken.

Mint jelly
Currant jelly
Jalapeño jelly (for a touch of heat and sweet)
A variety of fruit jams

You don't need to go out and purchase all this right now—and maybe some of these items will never make an appearance in your pantry. Less is more when you are trying new tastes. Buy only what you like—if you don't like it, you won't cook with it. Experimentation doesn't mean you have to suffer. Have fun, enjoy, and keep stirring the pot.

4. Table Talk

4. Table Talk

I'm not a homemaking guru, much less a spiritual guru, but I do believe that a handsome table presentation makes food taste better. My husband tells me it's all in my mind, and he's probably right. There is no scientific reason why the way you set and decorate your table should affect the taste of the food you eat there. But I swear it does. Maybe it's a case of mind over matter, or vice versa. All I know is, the atmosphere and physical surroundings in which food is served can't help influencing my enjoyment of it. Even if it's all in my mind, the table presentation matters to me.

Although composing an attractive table presentation for a kitchen supper takes a little extra time and imagination, it is well worth the effort. At the very least, you can think of it as a kind of insurance policy for your guests and yourself. If the recipes you're trying turn out to be a disaster because of errors you've made while slaving over the stove, or not slaving over it enough, you can take consolation in the fact that the table looks pretty. Best of all, you don't have to own fancy china or fine linen to produce an attractive table. When it comes to kitchen suppers, you can rely on the same guiding principles you apply to food. Just as simple food is the best food, simple table presentations are usually the best presentations.

In hopes of taking the fear out of table presentation traumas, I have tried to do what famous gurus in other fields do. You may have heard of concepts like the "Seven Chakras of Spirituality," or Dante's "Seven Circles of Hell" (which I feel like I'm in the middle of when I have guests due at 8:00 and start cooking at 7:45). Well, what follows are "Seven Thoughts About Table Presentation." So

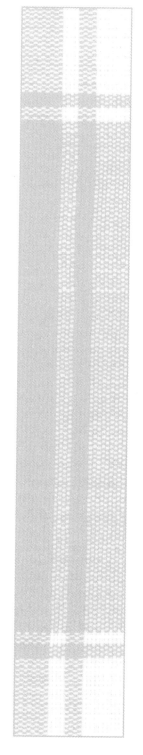

draw a deep breath, say "Ommm," and let your mind take control over such matters with love and joy.

Thought #1: Stains on the tablecloth are okay—they are signs of a meal thoroughly enjoyed.

I try to buy tablecloths on sale because they always end up stained and usually cannot be fixed. My most recent batch of tablecloths came to an untimely end the night before Thanksgiving. During our annual flurry of anxieties and disagreements ("The turkey is going to be on time this year, isn't it?"), my mother knocked over her wineglass with a monstrous metal wrist brace she had been fitted with following an injury in an ice-skating accident. I had layered my kitchen table with several cloths to cover various other stains, but this spill was a big one, and four cloths now have dull red ovals in various places.

Several weeks later, as I was looking through the linens at an after-Christmas sale, I ran into a friend who commiserated with me about my tablecloth tragedy and offered some encouraging words. She reminded me that in Europe the cloths are always stained, and that it is considered the sign of a great meal. I still proceeded to purchase new tablecloths, but they soon acquired stains of their own, which got me thinking. Why not take a tip from the Europeans and treat tablecloths the way they do? Instead of regarding stains as a shame, why not consider them marks of distinction?

Let me hasten to say that I am not advocating filth or sloth. Far from it. But a just-washed tablecloth with a few indelible stains is not a dirty tablecloth. If you regard the mere sight of stains as totally repugnant, you can always place the food platters and the salt and pepper shakers over the unsightly spots. And if you do your spot-hiding artfully enough, you might even find yourself creating a fabulously eccentric table presentation. Another simple alternative is to use placemats, the kind you can shake out!

Thought #2: Use cloth napkins.

No matter what you are serving or where you are serving it, using cloth napkins always makes table presentations look better. Paper napkins all nasty and wadded up on the table at the end of dinner make the table look like a trash can. What I am about to say may seem a bit contradictory, as I have lent my support to stained tablecloths, but it's not. Stained tablecloths are clean; they are just stained. Stained napkins are another matter because they are meant to be used to wipe your mouth. When we are serving guests, I always use napkins that are stain-free. I reserve the stained ones for Harry and me.

Now I know that paper napkins may seem to be easier, if not completely hassle free. But paper products are expensive, and using them is bad for the trees. What's more, cloth napkins are really not much trouble. When they get soiled, you just throw them in the washing machine, and fluff or hang them out to dry.

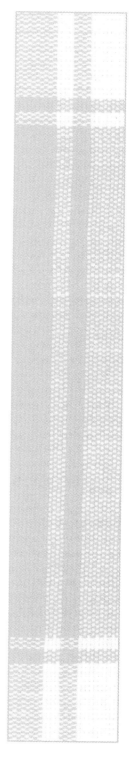

Then they're ready to go unless you insist on ironing them because you love to iron, which I do not. I don't buy expensive linens and fine napkins that require a starchy, flat look; the sets I own that require such care were inherited from my late mother-in-law, and are used perhaps once a year and sent out to the laundry. Besides, I usually fold my napkins into the wineglasses as part of my table presentation, and that wrinkles them anyway.

Thought #3: If you don't have enough matching glasses or the "right" glasses, mix them up. In other words, if it holds liquid, use it.

When my husband and I got married, we had full sets of wonderful glasses. That was six years ago. We now have partial sets of wonderful glasses. If we do not have enough glasses when I set the table for guests (meaning more than four glasses that match), I put matching glasses at every other place. Then we stick the napkins folded into the glasses (remember, this way you don't need to iron), using a different colored or patterned napkin at every other place, and the table looks ready for a jolly meal. It is what goes into the glass that counts—other than the napkin of course.

Which brings us to the right glasses. There is nothing wrong with champagne in a wineglass, or wine in a juice glass, or beer in a champagne glass, except that it is technically incorrect. I do find using porcelain for alcoholic beverages a little odd, although I once had a set of porcelain cups from Portugal that were made for wine. I loved those Portuguese wine cups, and wish I still had them. In any event, you could spend a lifetime and a fortune collecting the right glasses for the right wines. But I happen to feel that with whom you raise your glass is more important than the glass itself. And if a person really minds that your white burgundy is in a red Bordeaux glass, you have to stop and ask yourself, Do I really want that person at my dinner table?

Of course, it's nice to have a wide range of choices in glassware just as it is in food items. And sometimes the choice dictates itself. If you are intent on serving a truly elegant dinner, for example, you will probably want your glasses to match. And if you place a premium on being strictly proper, you will also want to make sure that both you and your guests know which glasses are for what. For this reason, I am including the easy-to-use glassware guide illustrated here.

| Red Wine | White Wine | Brandy | Champagne | Sherry/Port | Anything Else |

Thought #4: Thought #3 applies to plates as well.

If you are blessed with one or more full sets of beautiful dinner plates, use them by all means. But if your plates, like my plates, have suffered the fate of my embattled glassware, don't be afraid to mix and match. As a general rule, you don't want to put chipped plates on the table, unless they are very old and very valuable. And if you have plates like that, you probably won't be using them for kitchen suppers. Besides, very old and very valuable plates have to be hand washed with extreme care. If you're forced to mix and match, try to stay with a theme in overall color scheme or design. If you don't have soup plates or bowls, use mugs or coffee cups.

Thought #5: Use your imagination.

You don't have to spend a fortune to have a nice table. One of my favorite tablecloths was found in a discount fabric store when I was trying to create a pic-nic table "look" for an event that Alison On Dominick Street was catering, and I had no money to spend. There in the bin of odds and ends was a beautiful piece of wool crepe in a dark red and green plaid. The ends were slightly fringed from the cut, which gave it the perfect picnic table feel. All I had to do was add a wicker basket filled with daisies and breads and a bottle of wine, and our table looked great. I still use this tablecloth five years later. In the meantime, I have also used bolt ends and other close-outs to make tablecloths, and to cut napkins and strips for napkin rings.

Plates, glasses, and flatware can be found in warehouse outlets, second-hand stores, and flea markets. I have a friend who buys everything in blue and white. She has many mismatched plates and glasses, but her table presentations look great because the blue on the plates and the blue on the glasses somehow pull it all together. If you don't have time for any of this, I recommend that you buy basic whites, and pick up color for your table from the flower shop, your garden, or elsewhere.

Even if you're desperate, try to avoid making "distress" purchases you'll later regret and/or seldom use. Look around your home for that odd bowl, dish, plate, or platter that might make an imaginative serving piece. I have several platters that haven't seen daylight since I bought them because I thought they would be the only way to serve a particular dish and purchased them even though I didn't really like them. Just think about what it is you really need the serving piece to do, and you can usually find something to fulfill that need. Cans stripped of their labels and tied with a ribbon make great vases. Mustard jars can become votive candleholders. I spent a wasted day searching for a soup tureen that I thought I had to have, and couldn't find one that was affordable or that I liked. I came home ready to change the menu when I spied a very pretty cachepot that we had received as a wedding present. It wasn't holding a plant, so it became a soup tureen, and a wonderful soup tureen at that.

Thought #6: Candles, flowers, and centerpieces should illuminate, not dominate, your table.

I can't count how many times I have moved a centerpiece that I had slaved over for hours because once I found a place for it on the table, it was in the way of the food and the sightlines of my guests. Don't get me wrong. I love flowers as much if not more than anyone else. A fresh bunch of daisies in a jelly jar, or

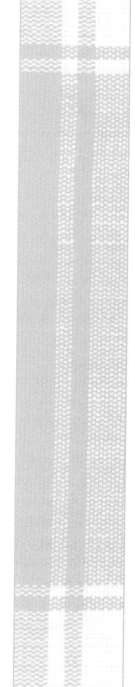

a bouquet of tulips from a local farm stand trimmed short enough can be beautiful on the center of any table. At the same time, though, it's important to plan your menu so that your creation doesn't sit forlornly in the corner waiting to take center stage again when everything is cleaned up. What's the point?

I believe in useful centerpieces. Sometimes the food itself is the best choice of all. A beautiful loaf of bread on a bread board or a first course salad that will be replaced with a main course stew are fine table decorations in their own right. So are bowls of fruit such as grapes, apples, and pears, and handsomely shaped and labeled bottles of wine. Here again, if you remember to keep it simple, you will almost never go wrong.

Although kitchen suppers may be informal by definition, I believe they should be eaten by candlelight. There is nothing more romantic or more sensual than a candlelit meal. Whether you put votives at each setting, place a large cylinder in the middle of the table, or arrange tall tapers in traditional candlesticks, you can create a special atmosphere with relatively little effort or expense. But if candles are going to be your sole centerpiece, it helps to be inventive. If you are using rosemary in one of your dishes, for example, you might wrap a couple of sprigs around the base of the candle to give the meal a theme. Another of my favorite tricks is to press flower heads into the melted wax where the candles join their holders.

A word of caution is in order: There is no such thing as a truly "dripless" candle. A "dripless" candle will drip if it is in any kind of draft. I know this from years of first-hand experience because we use "dripless" tapers at Alison On Dominick Street. Some tables have very few wax drippings, but on tables where the air vents are blowing, the candles burn in half the time and create gargoyle-like sculptures over the bases. The good news is that many people, including myself, enjoy playing with candle wax, and it usually does wash out of your tablecloths provided you peel off the initial clump while it's still soft. If you encounter some really obnoxious and hard-to-remove drippings, place a spare piece of fabric on top of the wax, and iron it with a hot iron; that should make the wax attach to the spare piece of fabric.

I seldom put placecards on my table unless I am serving a dinner for more than eight people. When I do resort to placecards, I try to find something prettier and more creative than ordinary strips of paper. Many of the best placecards can be easily made with items from the kitchen or items that are lying around the house. I like to use fruit that's in season, for example, or at Thanksgiving, gourds and pumpkins. Sometimes I simply write the names of my guests on votive holders, or on pieces of ribbon wrapped around the napkins. Our good friend Eleanora Kennedy, *the* hostess with the mostest, makes placecards from shells and stones she finds on the beach, and keeps them on her mantel to use when her guests return. An ordinary felt-tipped pen will write on almost anything that is suitable for use as a placecard, but if you're the artistic type, you might try using paint pens, which come in a variety of elegant colors including gold, silver, and copper.

Thought #7: If it causes anxiety, don't do it.

If you find that your stomach is getting tied in knots from worrying over your table presentation, take a deep breath and try to relax. Then strip down your presentation, and make it simple. It's the food and the conversation that are going to make the dinner, not the table decorations or the color of the napkins. So what if your husband's golfing partner and his socially ambitious wife think you don't have nice linen. If they can't get over it, they are not likely to be sitting at your dinner table again, anyway. As long as you have utensils to eat with and vessels to drink from, everything will be okay. Kitchen suppers are about eating with friends who appreciate a meal that has been cooked from the heart. The European attitude toward stained tablecloths applies to the overall presentation, as well. A messy table is one where fun was had.

NOTE: Serve from the left and clear from the right, except for cocktails, which get served from the right.

5. Simple Food Is the Best Food

5. Simple Food Is the Best Food

Kitchen suppers are, by definition, simple, and preparing them should require relatively simple cooking procedures and simple ingredients. My overall aim and purpose here are to show you how to make cooking a little bit easier and a lot more enjoyable. My way is not the way restaurant cooks go about cooking, nor is it the way certain very serious gourmands go about cooking. There's nothing wrong with the methods of restaurant cooks or very serious gourmands, but their approaches are often very complex and highly technical because they are trying to cook very complex dishes that require following highly technical recipes. For them, cooking is a business. Cooking kitchen suppers is meant to be fun.

The biggest mistake people make when cooking is adding too many ingredients and creating complications. For a professional chef trying out new dishes, this is part of the job, but for the home cook it is certainly not necessary. A well-prepared simple meal with balanced courses will be appreciated much more than a complicated supper that might be marred by too many flavors and too much going on.

My husband Harry often steps into the kitchen as I am preparing dinner. He likes simple foods with a great deal of flavor. He will say, "You're not putting too much in that, are you?" as he glances over the massive quantities of food I have out on the counters. And he is right to remind me. It is fun sometimes to let your imagination run wild, and certainly in this book there are recipes that could not be considered simple and pure. Most of the time, though, I have learned to use ingredients I like, to not add too many of them, and to have respect for the flavor of the food I am serving.

If you buy the best ingredients, you do not want to cover their natural flavors with all sorts of spices and sauce. A tomato at its peak cannot be made better by a heavy dressing. A bit of fresh basil and maybe a drop of balsamic vinegar are enough. There is nothing wrong with roasting a chicken with a bit of salt, pepper, lemon, and garlic. It's going to be good as long as the chicken was good. Do not confuse simplicity with boredom.

If time is a concern, this is a blessing in disguise. You won't have the time to think too much and be overly zealous with your creations. If you have lots of time, use it to make something that requires a long, slow cooking process instead of emptying your entire pantry into one meal. I have learned this the hard way and found that too many ingredients often hide one another and result in a dish that tastes undefined.

When in doubt, cook with a kiss: and "Keep it simple, silly." That way, you will always have a successful kitchen supper.

Appley Pork Chops

I make this in a very large skillet that will hold all of the chops at once. If you don't own one, just divide the chops between 2 medium skillets, using just enough additional oil to cook them. Serve these with hash browns (page 189) for a supersimple supper. This is a beer supper—try to find a light-bodied Belgian ale.

1/4 cup high-quality apple butter (made from apples only, no sweeteners)

2 tablespoons Dijon mustard

8 center-cut loin pork chops (about 1 inch thick)

1/4 cup olive oil, or more as needed

2 medium apples, such as McIntosh, cored and chopped into 1/2-inch pieces

1 medium onion, chopped

2 garlic cloves, chopped

1 cup hearty dry red wine

1/2 cup fresh apple cider

Makes 4 servings

1. In a small bowl, combine the apple butter and mustard. Slather the mixture all over the pork chops.

2. In a very large skillet, heat the 1/4 cup of oil over medium heat. Add the apples, onion, and garlic and reduce the heat to medium-low. Cook, stirring often, until the apples are barely softened, about 6 minutes. Transfer the apple mixture to a bowl and set aside. Do not clean the skillet.

3. Return the skillet to the stove. (There should be enough fat glazing the skillet to sauté the pork; add a little more oil if needed.) Add the pork chops and cook, turning once, until they're just cooked through (the insides should be pale pink) and both sides are browned, 15 to 20 minutes total. Adjust the heat as needed so the outside glaze doesn't burn.

4. Transfer the pork to a plate and increase the heat to high. Add the wine and apple cider. Using a wooden spatula, scrape up the good bits in the bottom of the pan. Return the pork and any juices collected on the plate to the pan, and top with the apple mixture. Reduce the heat to medium and cook for 5 minutes. Serve immediately.

Jellied Blood Orange Pork Chops with Roasted Vegetables and Red Cabbage

This is an extremely hearty dish, which I made for a winter celebration.

Makes 4 servings

We had just come home from a Caribbean vacation, but without our luggage, which somehow the airline had never put on the plane. In fact, the entire plane's load of luggage had been left in Nevis. Harry and I had packed our coats, figuring that we would take them out at the baggage claim before going into the freezing weather when we returned. Wrong. To make matters worse, the car I had arranged to pick us up at the airport never arrived. It was midnight. Luck befell us, and some very nice people we met in the baggage complaint area, who happened to live near us, also happened to have their car at the airport. So, the next day, still cold from the night before, I made the heartiest dinner I could think of to celebrate the return of our luggage (at 7 A.M.), and to say thank you to our dinner guests, our rescuers.

FOR THE ROASTED VEGETABLES:

16 small potatoes, scrubbed but unpeeled (about 1 pound); or use 4 medium potatoes, cut into 1-inch cubes

One 10-ounce container Brussels sprouts, cleaned

$\frac{1}{4}$ cup olive oil

1 teaspoon kosher or sea salt

FOR THE WILTED RED CABBAGE:

2 tablespoons olive oil

2 tablespoons balsamic vinegar

$\frac{2}{3}$ cup fresh blood or Valencia orange juice (2 oranges)

1 small onion, thinly sliced

$1\frac{1}{2}$ cups packed shredded red cabbage (about 8 ounces)

FOR THE PORK CHOPS:

2 tablespoons olive oil

2 tablespoons pure maple syrup

1 garlic clove, minced

2 blood or Valencia oranges, peeled and cut into segments

1 tablespoon chopped fresh rosemary

½ cup currant jelly

Four center-cut pork chops, cut
  2 inches thick

1 cup dry white wine, as needed

1. To roast the vegetables, preheat the oven to 475°F. In a large roasting pan, toss the potatoes and Brussels sprouts with the oil. Roast until tender, checking often, about 40 minutes. Season with the salt.

2. To prepare the cabbage: In a medium, heavy-bottomed, non-reactive saucepan, whisk the oil and vinegar together. Whisk in the orange juice. Add the onion and bring to a simmer over medium-low heat. Cover tightly and simmer for 5 minutes. Add the cabbage and mix well to coat with the orange juice. Cover tightly and braise until tender and soft, about 35 minutes.

3. To prepare the pork chops: In a very large skillet, heat 1 tablespoon of the oil over medium heat. Add the maple syrup and the minced garlic. Add the oranges and stir well to coat with the syrup. Stir in the rosemary. Add the currant jelly, reduce the heat to medium-low, and cook until the jelly melts, about 5 minutes.

4. Add the pork chops to the skillet. Increase the heat to medium-high. Cook until the undersides are nicely browned and caramelized, about 5 minutes. Turn and cook until the other side is caramelized, about 5 more minutes. Baste with the jelly mixture. Cook, turning often, until the pork is slightly pink when pierced at the bone, about 20 minutes. If the jelly mixture evaporates, stir in up to ½ cup of the wine, as needed.

5. To serve, combine the roasted vegetables with the cabbage and place on a large platter. Arrange the pork chops over the vegetables. Stir the remaining ½ cup of wine into the skillet and bring to a boil. Cook until thickened, about 2 minutes. Pour over the pork chops and serve immediately.

Eye of Round with Orange Cream and Horseradish

Mashed potatoes or wide egg noodles are a must with this dish to absorb all the sauce. If the beef gets dry in the pot, add more liquid—wine or beef stock—because you want a lot of sauce.

Makes 6 to 8 servings

3 tablespoons unsalted butter

3 tablespoons olive oil

3 garlic cloves, chopped

2 tablespoons coarsely cracked ("butcher grind") black pepper

1 cup chopped fresh flat-leaf parsley

One 4-pound eye of round beef roast

Salt, to taste (I use 1 teaspoon kosher salt)

1 cup fresh orange juice

1 cup hearty dry red wine, or more as needed

1 cup heavy cream

4 medium leeks, white part only, thinly sliced

¼ cup peeled and grated fresh horseradish, or 2 tablespoons prepared horseradish

1 tablespoon honey

1. In a large Dutch oven, heat the butter and oil over medium heat. Add the garlic and cook until fragrant, about 1 minute. Stir in the pepper and ½ cup of the parsley. Push the parsley mixture to the sides of the pot.

2. Add the roast to the pot, sprinkle with salt, and cook, turning occasionally, until seared on all sides, about 10 minutes. Stir in the orange juice, 1 cup of wine, and the remaining ½ cup of the parsley. Bring to a simmer and cover. Reduce the heat to medium-low. Simmer, allowing 18 to 20 minutes per pound, until medium rare (about 130°F. on the meat thermometer), about 1 hour, 20 minutes. If the cooking liquid evaporates, add more wine.

3. Meanwhile, in a medium saucepan, bring the cream and leeks to a simmer over medium heat. Reduce the heat to low and simmer until the leeks are

meltingly tender and the cream is reduced by about half, about 20 minutes. Stir in the horseradish and honey and simmer for 2 minutes. Remove from the heat and keep warm.

4. When the roast is tender, transfer it to a serving platter. Stir the leek and cream mixture into the cooking juices. Simmer for 5 minutes to combine the flavors. Slice the roast and serve hot, with the sauce.

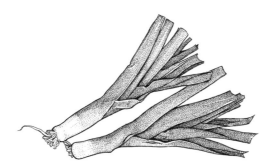

Gemelli with Salted Capers and Tomatoes

I hesitated to include this recipe because it is so simple. But it is too good to leave out. It is also flexible. I have added 2 cups of sliced chicken breasts to create a heavier dish. I added 2 cups of shrimp one evening and it was also good. When you add a protein, you may need to use a bit more oil and ¹/₂ to 1 cup more wine. The leftovers make a great salad—take a look at Auntie Pasta Salad on page 205.

Makes 4 to 6 servings

¹/₄ cup olive oil, preferably high-quality extra-virgin

2 garlic cloves, chopped

12 ripe plum tomatoes, coarsely chopped (don't bother to peel or seed them)

¹/₂ cup salted capers (see Note)

1 pound gemelli, cavatelli, or bow-tie pasta

1. In a large skillet, heat the oil over low heat. Add the garlic and cook until soft and fragrant, about 3 minutes. Stir in the tomatoes and capers. Bring to a simmer. Reduce the heat to low and simmer, stirring occasionally, for 15 minutes. Keep the sauce warm.

2. Meanwhile, bring a large pot of lightly salted water to a boil over high heat. Add the pasta and stir. Cook until the pasta is barely tender, about 10 minutes.

3. Drain the pasta well. Transfer to a warm serving bowl. Add the sauce and stir well. Serve hot.

NOTE: I first discovered salted capers when Peter Guzy (who, with Edward Asfour, so beautifully designed Alison On Dominick Street) brought some back from a trip to Tuscany. Big, fat buds preserved in layers of coarse salt, they are plumper and more intensely flavored than the typical variety packed in vinegar. I use them as they come, but some cooks brush or rinse off the salt first. You can find salted capers at Italian grocers, specialty food stores, and some supermarkets. They often come in bottles, but also in bulk and in vacuum-packed bags. You may have to ask for them at the delicatessen counter.

If you can't find salt capers, try to find dried capers and add a teaspoon of coarse salt. If you can't find dried capers, use regular capers, drained and dried. Toss them with a teaspoon of coarse salt.

Salmon with Onion and Celery Root

This is the only salmon dish my husband will eat, and he loves it. Simple potatoes roasted in olive oil and a spinach and arugula salad complete this meal for us.

Makes 2 servings

2 small knobs celery root (celeriac), peeled
2 tablespoons butter
½ cup finely chopped shallots (about 2 shallots)
1 small red onion, chopped
1 clove garlic, sliced paper thin

¼ cup chopped fresh flat-leaf parsley
1 tablespoon chopped fresh dill
Freshly ground black pepper to taste
Two 12-ounce skinless salmon fillets
2 tablespoons fresh lemon juice; or 1 lemon, cut in half

1. Cut each celery root in half and trim away any woody or spongy parts from the center. Using a sharp knife, a food processor fitted with the julienne blade, or a mandoline, cut the celery root into long ⅛-inch-thick strips.

2. In a large skillet, heat the butter over low heat. Add the celery root and shallots. Cook, stirring occasionally, until the celery root is tender, about 15 minutes. Stir in the red onion, garlic, parsley, and dill. Mix well. Cook until the onion is tender, about 3 minutes. Season with the pepper. Using a slotted spoon, leaving as much of the cooking juices as possible in the skillet, transfer the celery root mixture to a plate and set aside.

3. Increase the heat to medium-high. Lightly season the salmon with pepper. Place it in the skillet and squeeze the lemon juice over the fillets. Cook, turning once, until medium-rare, about 4 minutes total. Return the celery root mixture to the pan, smothering the salmon. Cook until the celery root is reheated, about 1 minute. (If you like your salmon more well done, cook for a minute longer.) Serve immediately.

6. Nightmares of the First Course

6. Nightmares of the First Course

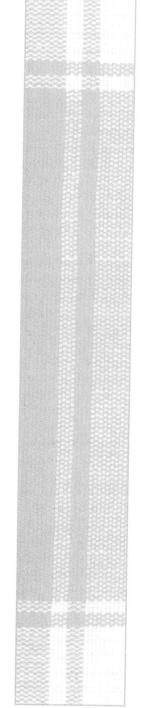

What is an appetizer? My dictionary says it is "something taken before a meal to create appetite," which, in turn, is defined as "a desire for food, drink, rest, etc." My husband puts it in more prosaic terms. He says an appetizer is like foreplay: It is supposed to stimulate excitement and desire for the meal ahead by teasing the taste buds and the tummy. I like his analogy, just as I like kissing and cuddling. I just wish I could feel the same way about appetizers.

To me, the very concept of an appetizer used to be a nightmare, which my dictionary defines as "a terrifying dream." For many years, I wouldn't even learn to spell hors d'oeuvre, the French term for appetizer, believing that if I couldn't spell it, I wouldn't have to make any. I worried that preparing a first course would make me late with the rest of dinner. And that made me worry that the main course would be ruined. On occasion, my fear would produce a frantic phone call to one of my restaurants in hopes that the chef could offer some soothing words of advice. All this fear and drama were usually unfounded and unnecessary, but they were part of my "cook's growing pains."

In retrospect, I realize that a big part of my problem was that I tried too hard. I would attempt to copy the intricately complex, extremely delicate appetizer recipes that are more suitable to a restaurant than to a comfy home kitchen. Those attempts would turn my terrifying dreams into terrifying (or at best mediocre) realities, which, like a classic Catch 22, only exacerbated the fears I had in the first place.

I am happy to report that I have since discovered a way to overcome my appetizer nightmare. I call it "the night light trick." Like a night light in a strange hotel room, it was sitting there right in front of me the whole time, I just didn't know where to look for it. I had been turning outside in search of comfort, paging through cookbooks and consulting my restaurant chefs. At long last, I realized that I had to turn inside to exorcise my nightmare. I had to rely on what my husband calls "knowledge" and I call my own "instinct" for cooking. Eventually, inspiration switched on just like a night light.

I do have to give credit, however, to my friend Cheryl Merser for helping me screw in the bulb. Cheryl is the author of several books on cooking and gardening, and she loves appetizers. Where I feared them like a nightmare, she regards them as a hostess's dream come true. She believes that serving a well-prepared and especially generous first course takes the pressure off the main course. She also claims that first courses actually save her time and extra effort because she doesn't have to bother making canapés to offer hungry guests while they wait for dinner.

Whenever I get downhearted about making appetizers, I try to remember Cheryl's reassuring words. If my night light doesn't glow brightly at first, I've found that it helps to work backward—to choose the main dish and then decide upon an appropriate appetizer. When we are planning menus for parties at the restaurant or catering a wedding, I leave the canapés and hors d'oeuvre for last to avoid repetitions and taste conflicts. We balance the menu with weight and flavor. Needless to say, I've read many "rules" for balancing a menu, and all of them seem contradictory to me. Some balancing rules call for you to serve heavy appetizers with light main courses, and light appetizers with heavy main courses. Others prescribe heavy with heavy and light with light. Personally, I don't think it really matters as long as you and your guests have enough room to finish the meal and the first course doesn't wipe out the taste buds for what is to come.

What does matter to me is that the flavors flow into one another, and that the overall meal suits the season of the year. If it's cold outside, a hot soup or a warm tart will melt the icicles and improve the conversation. If it's a warm summer evening, a chilled poached fish or a composed salad will refresh an appetite dampened by heat. But I wouldn't serve an overpowering dish of chili peppers before a delicate fish, and I wouldn't serve a dense country pâté before a thick, juicy pot roast. Instead, I would "balance" the fish with a vegetable tart or a risotto, and complement the meat with a celery remoulade or a poached fish.

An almost fool-proof approach is to make appetizers that feature one or more of the key ingredients in the main course. After all, the purpose of an appetizer is to make your guests beg for the next course, not because they want you to get the appetizer out of their sight but because the appetizer has tantalized their anticipation of what is to come. Sometimes it is fun to serve a "theme" menu such as a mushroom tasting that starts with a mushroom salad or a braised portobello mushroom, followed by a wild mushroom risotto. Like decorating a room with a monochromatic color scheme, you run the risk of being boring and repetitious, but you also have the virtue of simplicity in your favor, and even the slightest variation from one course to the next will stand out boldly.

Another, even simpler approach is to derive your appetizers directly from the main course. In the south of France, for example, they often serve the broth of the bouillabaisse first, then the fish. You might want to expand on this idea and serve the broth of a braised meat or a chicken as a first course. I think a salad of duck breasts makes a perfect appetizer for a main course of braised duck stew made with the legs and thighs.

A third approach is to think about what you might normally serve as a side dish to a particular entrée and create an appetizer around that. A ratatouille appetizer, for instance, can provide a mouth-watering prelude to a roast lamb. So can a vegetable soufflé made in individual ramekins. Roast beets served with a vinaigrette and sprinkled with crumbled goat cheese are always delicious, but the beets can be even tastier if you roast them alongside the chicken you are serving for your main course.

Just remember, if all else fails, there is always an elegantly simple way to solve your appetizer problems. Skip the appetizer course entirely, and serve a salad and cheese course *after* the main course. I admit this seems like a cop-out or a full-fledged retreat, but sometimes it's better to cut your losses and regroup to fight another day. When the good kitchen witch is asleep on the job and the wicked kitchen witch is racking your brain with her broomstick, a green salad and a wedge of runny Brie will make the evil spell go away so you can get on with cooking the rest of the dinner.

Over the years, I've found that the appetizer recipes that follow are the ones that work best for me regardless of which witch happens to be lurking in my kitchen. I've also learned that it makes sense to stick with a few things that do the trick (unless you have plenty of time to experiment, which I seldom do). You can easily alter a couple of the ingredients and some of the seasonings to create a variety of appetizers from the same basic recipe.

Portobello Mushrooms

2 large portobello mushrooms, stems
    discarded (you can save them to use
    in a stock, soup, or pasta sauce)
⅓ cup olive oil, plus more as needed
3 tablespoons balsamic vinegar
2 teaspoons finely chopped fresh
    rosemary

1 garlic clove, minced
Salt and freshly ground black pepper, to
    taste
4 slices brioche bread, challah, or
    crusty peasant bread, warmed

Makes 4 servings

1. Slice the mushroom caps into ¼-inch-wide strips. In a medium bowl, toss them with 1 tablespoon of the oil, the balsamic vinegar, and the rosemary. Let stand for 30 minutes.

2. In a large skillet, heat the remaining oil over low heat. Add the garlic and cook until tender and fragrant, about 1 minute. Add the mushrooms and season with salt and pepper. Cook, stirring occasionally, until the mushrooms are hot and juicy, about 5 minutes. The mushrooms should be in a fair amount of liquid—add a little more oil, if needed.

3. Place the warm brioche slices on individual plates. Spoon the hot mushrooms and their liquid over the brioche, and serve immediately.

Asparagus with Warm Dijon Dressing

In the fall when white asparagus appears in the market, I often use a combination of white and green asparagus. It looks lovely on the plate. A very simple way to dress up a simple supper.

Whatever color you decide to use, this is a welcome first course (or side dish).

Makes 6 to 8 servings

2 pounds asparagus, woody ends
  trimmed and discarded
¾ cup (1½ sticks) butter
2 shallots, chopped (about ⅓ cup); or
  4 garlic cloves, chopped

3 tablespoons Dijon mustard
¼ cup rice vinegar
2 teaspoons balsamic vinegar

1. Lay the asparagus in a large saucepan and add enough water to come about one third up their sides. Bring to a boil, lower the heat to a simmer, and cover. Cook until the asparagus are barely crisp-tender, 3 to 5 minutes.

2. Meanwhile, in a large skillet, melt the butter over low heat. Add the shallots and cook, stirring occasionally, until they're translucent, about 3 minutes. Whisk in the mustard, then the vinegars, and heat through for 1 or 2 minutes. Whisk until smooth.

3. Arrange the asparagus on a large platter or individual plates. Pour the dressing over the asparagus and serve immediately.

Blue Cheese Soufflé

Soufflés are not hard. You just think they are. If you can master this easy recipe you will have several more variations at your fingertips. Substitute Cheddar cheese and port for the blue cheese and vermouth. You may also replace some of the milk with sour cream, but then add an extra tablespoon or two of flour.

Makes 4 to 6

servings

FOR THE PAN:

2 tablespoons butter, at room
temperature

¼ cup fine cracker crumbs, preferably
Ritz crackers or saltines

FOR THE SOUFFLÉ:

4 tablespoons (½ stick) butter, at room
temperature

¼ cup all-purpose flour

1½ cups milk

4 large eggs, at room temperature,
separated

8 ounces blue cheese, crumbled (about
1½ cups)

1 tablespoon dry vermouth

Freshly ground black pepper, to taste
(not more than a teaspoon)

1. Preheat the oven to 400°F. To prepare the pan: Coat the inside of a 2-quart soufflé dish with the butter. Sprinkle the crumbs in the dish and tilt to coat the dish with the crumbs.

2. To make the soufflé: In a medium saucepan, melt the butter over medium heat until it's foamy. Whisk in the flour until the mixture is smooth. Whisk in the milk and bring to a simmer, whisking occasionally, to make a thick sauce. Remove from the heat and let stand until slightly cooled, about 5 minutes.

3. In a medium bowl, whisk the egg yolks. Gradually whisk in about 1 cup of the hot milk mixture. Stir the egg yolks into the sauce in the saucepan. Add the blue cheese and vermouth, whisking until the cheese is almost completely melted.

4. In a clean medium bowl, whisk the egg whites until stiff peaks form. Stir a large spoonful of the egg whites into the cheese mixture to lighten it. Using a rubber spatula, carefully fold the remaining egg whites into the cheese mixture. Do not beat the mixture or it will deflate and you will have messed everything up before you even had a chance. Season with the pepper. Pour the mixture into the prepared pan.

5. Bake for 15 minutes. Reduce the oven temperature to 350°F. and continue baking until the soufflé is puffed and golden, 15 to 20 minutes more. Serve immediately.

Mimi's Tomato Bisque

When my good friend Mimi first gave me this recipe, she said, "Never tell people it's the gin; they are going to beg you, but don't. It took me two years to beg the chef to reveal the ingredients—ingredient by ingredient. I had to guess, and when I guessed one correctly he would give me the next one. Finally, when I told him I was exasperated because my soup didn't taste like his, he said with a Cheshire cat grin—'C'est du gin.'"

Over the years, Mimi made some changes of her own to the recipe—and it is extraordinary. I give you this recipe with her blessing—it's too good to keep secret. And sadly the chef is no longer with us.

Makes 4 to 6 servings

3 cups milk

½ cup fine dry bread crumbs

1 medium onion stuck with 9 whole cloves

2 teaspoons sugar

1 sprig parsley

1 bay leaf

2 cups chopped ripe fresh or drained, canned tomatoes

½ teaspoon baking soda

2 to 3 tablespoons gin, to taste

4 tablespoons (½ stick) butter

1 cup sour cream

Salt and freshly ground black pepper, to taste

For garnish: Lemon slices, pickled onions each stuck with a whole clove, chopped fresh parsley, or dollops of sour cream

1. In a medium pot, combine the milk, bread crumbs, onion, sugar, parsley, and bay leaf. Bring to a simmer over very low heat, then simmer for 5 minutes. Discard the bay leaf. Remove and reserve the onion.

2. Stir in the tomatoes and baking soda. Bring to a simmer, then cook gently for 15 minutes. In batches, transfer the soup to a food processor or blender and puree.

3. Pour the pureed soup back into the soup pot. Return the onion to the soup. Stir in the gin. Bring to a gentle simmer over very low heat. Cook gently for 20 to 30 minutes.

4. Discard the onion and whisk in the butter. Stir in the sour cream. Season with salt and pepper. Increase the heat to medium and cook, stirring constantly, until the soup is very hot but not boiling. Serve immediately, garnishing each serving as you wish.

Beet, Red Onion, and Roquefort Salad

Makes 6 servings

Most guests in either of my restaurants love it when we serve a beet and goat cheese terrine. But because I usually think of these things too late, I have turned the terrine into a salad. I prefer the Roquefort to goat cheese—but you can certainly substitute one for the other. If you want to make a more substantial salad, or turn this into a luncheon dish, the addition of steamed new potatoes or white beans would do the trick; and for protein, sliced chicken breast poached in the juice from the beets produces a pretty purple chicken (that tastes good too!). I have used romaine lettuce in this recipe, but certainly try arugula or any wild or bitter greens that look good.

FOR THE WALNUT VINAIGRETTE:

¹/₂ cup olive oil

¹/₄ cup walnut oil (or additional olive oil)

¹/₄ cup sherry vinegar

¹/₄ cup white wine vinegar

1 garlic clove

20 walnut halves, coarsely chopped

1 tablespoon chopped red onion (from sliced red onions, below)

Salt and freshly ground black pepper, to taste

FOR THE SALAD:

4 medium beets, trimmed, scrubbed, but unpeeled

1 head romaine lettuce, torn into bite-sized pieces, washed, and dried

Salt and freshly ground black pepper, to taste

2 small red onions, thinly sliced

4 tablespoons crumbled Roquefort cheese

2 tablespoons chopped fresh dill

1. To make the vinaigrette: In a blender or food processor, pulse the olive and walnut oils and the sherry and wine vinegars and the garlic until combined. Add the walnuts, chopped onion, and pulse 2 or 3 times until the walnuts are coarsely chopped. Season with salt and pepper. Set aside.

2. To make the salad: Place the beets in a medium saucepan and add enough cold water to cover. Bring to a boil over high heat. Reduce the heat to medium and cook until they're tender when pierced with the tip of a sharp knife, 20 to 30 minutes. Do not overcook. Drain and cool. Peel the beets with a small knife and cut them into $1/2$-inch cubes or $1/4$-inch-wide sticks—whichever you prefer.

3. Place the lettuce and beets in a large bowl. Add about 1 cup of the dressing and toss well. Season with salt and pepper.

4. Divide the salad among 6 plates (or serve on a large platter). Top with sliced red onion and crumbled cheese. Sprinkle with the dill and drizzle with the remaining dressing.

Belgian Endive Salad with Hazelnut Dressing

Makes 4 servings

FOR THE HAZELNUT DRESSING:
2 tablespoons red wine vinegar
2 tablespoons sherry vinegar
1 tablespoon Dijon mustard
½ cup olive oil
1 tablespoon hazelnut oil (or additional olive oil)
1 tablespoon sour cream
25 shelled hazelnuts, preferably peeled (see Note), finely chopped

Salt and freshly ground black pepper, to taste

FOR THE SALAD:
4 Belgian endives, trimmed and wiped with a moist paper towel
2 tablespoons fresh lemon juice
2 tablespoons minced fresh thyme or chives, for garnish (optional)

1. To make the dressing: In a medium bowl, whisk together the wine and sherry vinegars and the Dijon mustard until the mustard dissolves. Gradually whisk in the olive oil, then the hazelnut oil and sour cream. Stir in the nuts and season with salt and pepper.

2. To make the salad: In a food processor fitted with either the 2- or 4-millimeter slicing blade, feed the endives through the tube to slice them crosswise. (Or slice with a large sharp knife.) You should have about 4 cups sliced endive. Place the endive in a bowl and separate the slices into thin rounds. Toss with the lemon juice.

3. Toss the endive with half of the dressing. Arrange on individual plates, drizzle with the remaining dressing, and sprinkle with the thyme or chives, if desired. Serve immediately.

NOTE: Hazelnuts are now available peeled. If yours still have their brown skins, here's how to peel them: Spread the hazelnuts on a baking sheet. Bake in a preheated 350°F. oven, stirring occasionally, until the skins are curling and the hazelnuts are lightly toasted, about 10 minutes. Wrap them in a clean kitchen towel and let them stand for 10 minutes. Rub the hazelnuts in the towel to remove most of the skins (some will remain, and that's fine.) Cool completely.

Warm Duck Breast and Lentil Salad

Okay, so there seem to be a lot of steps here. It's really not too bad—and if you want you can just keep putting everything together in one bowl, toss as you go along, and call it salade composé. *This is a great cool weather luncheon, or it could be a supper served with a cheese course or egg noodles and some crusty bread.*

Makes 4 servings

FOR THE LENTILS:

1 cup small French lentils, preferably *lentilles de Puy*, but any lentils will do

3 cups chicken broth, preferably homemade

2 garlic cloves, chopped

2 sprigs fresh rosemary (optional)

FOR THE DUCK BREASTS:

2 tablespoons butter

2 garlic cloves, chopped

4 boneless Long Island (Peking) duck breasts, skin removed (just pull it off in one piece, or have the butcher do it)

FOR THE DRESSING:

8 ounces slab bacon, rind removed, cut into ¹/₂-inch cubes

1 large leek, white part only, well washed, patted dry, and cut into ¹/₂-inch dice

¹/₄ cup balsamic vinegar

¹/₄ cup fresh orange juice

¹/₄ cup walnut oil

1 tablespoon hazelnut oil (or additional walnut oil)

FOR THE MUSHROOMS:

2 tablespoons butter

1 large portobello mushroom, trimmed and thinly sliced

¹/₄ cup balsamic vinegar

¹/₄ cup fresh orange juice

3 medium beets, cooked, peeled (see page 87), and cut into thin slivers

1¹/₂ pounds fresh spinach leaves, tough stems removed, well washed and dried

Salt and freshly ground pepper, to taste

1. To prepare the lentils: In a wire sieve, rinse the lentils under cold water and sort through them to remove any stones. In a medium saucepan, bring the lentils, broth, garlic, and rosemary (if using) to a boil over high heat. Reduce the heat to low and simmer, uncovered, until the lentils are tender but not soft, about 30 minutes.

2. Meanwhile, prepare the duck breasts: In a large skillet, melt the butter over medium heat until foamy. Add the garlic and cook until it's fragrant, about 1 minute. Add the duck breasts and cook until the undersides are golden, about 3 minutes. Turn and cook until the duck breasts are medium, about 3 minutes more. (The duck will feel slightly resilient when pressed in the center, and will look slightly rose-colored if pierced with the tip of a knife. Cook a little longer if you like, but don't cook to well done, or it will be tough.) Transfer the duck breasts to a platter and cover them loosely with aluminum foil to keep warm.

3. To prepare the dressing: In the same skillet (do not wash it out), cook the bacon over medium heat until browned but not crisp, about 5 minutes. Using a slotted spoon, transfer the bacon to the plate with the duck breasts, leaving the bacon fat in the skillet.

4. Add the leek to the skillet and cook over medium heat until softened, about 1 minute. Add the balsamic vinegar and orange juice and bring to a boil, scraping up the browned bits in the pan. Reduce the heat and simmer until the leek is tender, about 3 minutes. Remove from the heat and whisk in the walnut oil and hazelnut oil. Pour the dressing into a small saucepan and set it aside.

5. To prepare the mushroom: Wipe out the skillet with paper towels. Add the butter and melt over medium-high heat. Add the mushroom, balsamic vinegar, and orange juice. Cook until the mushroom is tender and has absorbed some of the liquids, about 5 minutes. Move the mushroom to one side of the skillet. Place the shredded beets on the other side, just to warm them through. (Try to keep the beet juices from coloring the mushroom, but don't worry if it happens. If you like, you can also toss the mushroom and beets together and cook for a minute to heat through.

6. To assemble the salad: Drain the lentils and remove the rosemary sprigs. In a large bowl, toss the warm lentils with the spinach, then transfer them to a

(continued)

large platter. Using a sharp knife, cut the duck breasts on the bias into $1/2$-inch-thick slices. Season the duck with salt and pepper. Arrange overlapping slices of duck down the middle of the platter, then sprinkle with the bacon. Spoon the mushroom and beets around the duck breasts.

7. Bring the dressing to a full boil over medium heat. Pour it over the salad and serve immediately.

Cucumbers with Dill and Red Onion

Here's a simple salad for a quiet night. It's best in the summer, when the herbs are very fresh, the cucumbers are hours old, and the onions are tender. In the winter, I will happily substitute a sliced ripe avocado for the cucumber. This is the simplest of all salad dressings—mellow white balsamic vinegar, which, unlike wine vinegar, doesn't really need any oil to cut the acidity.

Makes 2 servings

1 Kirby cucumber, scrubbed; or
   ½ medium cucumber, peeled
½ teaspoon sugar
2 tablespoons white balsamic vinegar
   or rice vinegar
1 teaspooon finely chopped fresh dill

Kosher or sea salt and freshly ground
   black pepper, to taste
½ small red onion, very thinly sliced

1. Slice the cucumber into ¼-inch-thick rounds. Spread on a plate.

2. Sprinkle with the sugar, then the vinegar, then the dill. Season with a pinch of salt and a pinch of pepper. Top with the red onion. Serve immediately.

7. A Chicken Isn't

Just a Chicken

7. A Chicken Isn't Just a Chicken

Chicken again? Yes! It's one of the most versatile, economical proteins there is. I have used chicken in recipes calling for game or other poultry (they are all birds to me). The flavor may not be quite as rich, but when there is only half an hour to shop, the search for quail might be a problem; chicken you can purchase in almost any food store. And chicken is great for leftovers: The carcass can be used for soup, and the meat can be pulled off and used with pasta or in a pot pie or a salad.

There are countless ways to cook a chicken, depending on season, time, budget, and the chicken. In order of bird age, the main varieties of chicken are: poussins (dinner for two), fryers (also good broiled), roasters (I think the most versatile), capons (the most flavorful roaster, but harder to find), hens (best used in dishes calling for long simmering), and cocks (best used in soup). There are also Cornish game hens for individual servings. And there are free-range chickens, which are supposed to have been allowed to roam free and given a special diet to make them tastier. Whatever kind of chicken I choose for a particular dinner, I always buy grade A. I also make sure to follow any instructions on the package concerning salmonella. I wash my hands and the surface I am working on before and after preparing the chicken, a practice I strongly urge you to adhere to as well.

Chickens usually come complete with livers, necks, and giblets for gravy and stuffing. Almost any herb or spice can be used in its preparation. Chicken can be cooked whole, in pieces, skin on, skin off, boned, or not. It can be fried, braised, sautéed, broiled, stewed, or my favorite—just plain roasted. I usually

have a chicken to roast in the freezer at all times. I can think of few things better than a roast chicken all crackling fresh from the oven—except for Ivy's perfect fried chicken.

Ivy is a spry, seemingly ageless Jamaican woman who has worked for my parents for over two decades. One year when my husband and I were hosting our annual Memorial Day weekend barbecue, I found out that twice as many people as we expected were going to arrive. In a panic, I realized that we were going to run out of pork barbecue, so I decided that I needed to have some of Ivy's perfect fried chicken on hand. The problem was that Ivy had recently retired for the fourth time and, I thought, was hiding down in Miami. I asked my Mom to contact Ivy and have her call me immediately. Ivy called, and this is how the conversation went:

"Ivy," I asked in a tone of desperation, "please tell me, how do I make your fried chicken?"

"Well, Miss Alison," Ivy replied with a mischievous giggle. "You just fry it."

"How?"

"You take the chicken and soak it in juice."

"What kind of juice?"

"Well, you can use lemon juice."

"I've got a hundred and fifty people coming, Ivy. That's an awful lot of lemons to squeeze."

"Well, you can use orange juice."

"It doesn't matter?"

"No, just use juice."

"So I could use grapefruit juice?"

"Yup."

"Could I use apple juice?"

"Maybe."

"How much juice?"

"Well, I don't know—enough to soak it in."

"For how long?"

"Long enough."

"Okay, so what do I do after soaking the chicken in the juice?"

"You shake it in flour and salt and pepper."

"How much?"

"Enough to coat it well."

"Do you use any herbs?"

"Sometimes."

"Which herbs? Thyme? Dill? What?"

"Anything you want."

"Ivy, come on. I need to know what kind of herbs to use. Please—tell me!"

"Miss Alison, you just do it with whatever it is that you have around."

At this point, I could tell that Ivy was getting rather annoyed with my questions, and I realized that I would have to figure out the answers on my own.

"So, Ivy, what do I fry the chicken in?"

"Crisco," she replied.

Finally a direct answer!

"How much Crisco do I use?"

"Miss Alison, I don't know. Enough to brown the pieces. You just keep adding more with each batch if you need it."

"How long do I brown it for?"

"Until it's cooked through."

That was a big help, I thought to myself, but pressed on anyway. "What heat do I cook it at—high?"

"Nope."

"Medium?"

"Just about."

Finally, I was too exasperated to ask any more questions. "Ivy, will please you come up and help me?" I begged, adding, "I'll even send you an airplane ticket in the overnight mail."

"Nope," she said.

And that was that.

So there I was, about to make my first attempt at cooking my version of Ivy's perfect fried chicken with 150 guests due to arrive in twenty-four hours. I had forty pounds of pork barbecue cooking, sweet bars baking, and various salads to assemble. I figured that I'd better leave the chicken for the next day, which turned out to be a very wise decision.

I had ordered twenty chickens from the butcher, asking him to cut them in small pieces to get ten to twelve pieces out of each chicken. He must have been hard of hearing. The twenty chickens arrived whole and uncut, and the breasts were enormous. I don't like butchering too much—you get a little too friendly with the bird—but I had to do the dirty deed myself or it would not get done properly if at all. So I pulled out my trusty kitchen scissors, and started clipping away. It was not a perfect job, but I figured that anyone who would inspect the pieces that closely and voice a critical opinion, could just go home unfed.

With my butchering accomplished, I looked at this mountain of chicken and wondered what to soak it in. My bowls were already in use for the salads. All my roasting pans, including the extra disposables I usually keep on hand, were filled with pork barbecue. A garbage bag seemed unwieldy, and, I thought, wouldn't be strong enough for all the chicken and the juice. Then I remembered that I had bought a large plastic sweater box I hadn't used yet. Of course, the sweater box was in the very back of my broom closet, and I had to pull everything out to get to it, but it did the trick.

Since the local market sells fresh-squeezed orange juice, that's what I chose to use. (I have since used pasteurized, and it works almost as well, especially the orange-tangerine mix. I have also mixed in a little honey, which adds a crunchy sweetness, and a special jalapeño honey that is extra yummy.) With five hours to go until party time, I rinsed out the plastic sweater box, put in all the chicken pieces, and poured in five gallons of orange juice, which happened to be just enough (I had figured on a quart per chicken). I also threw in a handful of thyme sprigs, and two whole heads of garlic, quartered (I didn't peel, I just sliced). I don't know how much flavor this gave to the chicken (I've done it without and it's been just as good), but it certainly looked pretty. I left the chicken to soak for an hour or so.

Then I started looking around for something to toss the chicken in. All I had left were very large lawn and leaf garbage bags, so that was one decision that decided itself. I poured flour, salt, and pepper into one of the bags. Since Ivy had refused to specify the proper amounts, all I could do was guess. My husband later told me that he overheard me having conversations with myself every time he passed through the kitchen that day, but I was too flustered and too caught up in my work to remember what I said to myself or why I said it. In any event, I ultimately concluded that I should use about half a cup of flour per piece. Since I was getting thirty pieces from every five pounds of chicken, I poured forty pounds of flour into the garbage bag (a little extra for good measure). I then figured one tablespoon of salt and one tablespoon of pepper per chicken, which I rounded off to two and a half cups of salt and two and a half cups of pepper. But using those amounts only made the flour look speckled. Rather than wasting precious time redoing my calculations, I decided I would simply taste the first batch after it was done, and add more salt and pepper if I needed it.

I put the chicken pieces in the bag handful by handful, and tossed them around in the flour. The problem, I quickly realized, was that there was not going to be enough room for all the chicken with the flour in the bag. Unfortunately, this was not one of those ready to make "shake and bake" recipes you see advertised on TV. I got out a second garbage bag and put the already coated chicken pieces in that. By this point, I was sitting on the kitchen floor, with the plastic sweater box on one side, a garbage bag full of flour between my legs, and another garbage bag full of chicken pieces between me and the stove. Every surface in the kitchen was covered with bowls and pots, and I was covered with flour. Thankfully, I had matted the kitchen floor with old newspapers, so it didn't matter what landed on it. Maybe I should have tried this a first time with fewer people to feed, but I had no choice but to go on. And so I proceeded with my little improvised production line.

Half an hour later, all the chicken was coated. I ended up putting half the pieces in the first garbage bag and half in the second bag, and tossing the flour back and forth. I had used too much flour, twice as much as necessary, in fact. It was a mess—but a happy mess.

I got three frying pans ready to go with the Crisco. Having no idea how much I needed (I had never used Crisco before), I had bought three extra large containers. I put one cup of Crisco in each pan, which was going to hold about between seven and fifteen pieces. I put the heat on high and let the fat melt down, then turned down the heat slightly and put the pieces in. The first thing I realized was that the pieces were going to take different cooking times. The wings and legs would take about fifteen minutes and the breasts would take twenty to twenty-five. I started to get scared to death of a mass poisoning due to undercooked chicken. One pan of this first batch came out with cut marks all over it from my knife-poking tests. I also found that the pieces fried in my cast-iron pan had a darker coating.

Even so, everything was now pretty much going along just hunky-dory. My three pans were sizzling away. I turned each of the chicken pieces and prodded them. They were all getting nice and golden. I stole a moment away from the stove to run outside and set the buffet tables and play with flowers. It was beginning to look very pretty. I was feeling quite proud until I looked at the clock. I had estimated a half hour per three batches. At this rate I wouldn't be done until an hour after the guests arrived—oops. And I still had to take a shower.

Time to reorganize. I took the first batch out to lay on paper towels to dry and then went searching through the gloppy garbage bags for all the wings, legs, and thighs, because they were small and I could fit more in the pan. I added more Crisco to bring the level back up to about three quarters of an inch deep, and with a slotted spoon I removed the droppings from the first batch. I stuffed all the small pieces I could in the pan. I knew I had to leave some room, but I was beginning to feel an anxiety attack coming on. The second batch thankfully cooked more evenly, probably because the pieces were the same size, and like pancakes, the second batch was more golden brown and better.

The clock kept ticking, and I kept turning. Finally, when there were no more small pieces, I had to get in the shower. It's one thing to be cooking when the guests arrive, and another to greet them half dressed in pajamas covered with flour. I considered putting the breasts in the frying pans because they needed about ten minutes a side, and I could probably get in and out of the shower quickly enough to turn them. But a strong desire not to burn the house down won the battle with my now full-fledged anxiety attack.

After my shower, I dressed in a clean set of cooking clothes (I have learned to wait until the last possible moment to put on my party clothes when I'm both the hostess and the chef), and raced back to the kitchen. I heated the fat in the pans and put in the first batch of chicken breasts. I had about eighty pieces left. I put the chili on the back burner. Yelled for Harry to get the grill going. Put the oven on to begin warming the barbecue. Last year I had waited until the last minute to take the barbecue from the fridge; at least I had done it right this year and it was already at room temperature rather than being one huge cold gelatinous hunk of pork.

I went to find my biscuit recipe, borrowed from my pastry chef, Michael Morehouse. It was not to be found, which was not surprising because the kitchen was in a state. It is not good to have an anxiety attack when cooking—somehow the kitchen has one too, and everything is a mess. So I went searching for a solution, turning the chicken in the nick of time, stirring the chili as the first scent of burn wafted in the air (I saved it in time). I could just skip the biscuits. But no. I went to get out the second large container of Crisco from the cupboard and way in the back my little cooking angel had hidden an extra large, restaurant-sized box of Bisquick, purchased on a Sam's Club shopping spree. Yay for the pantry! I could have biscuits—they wouldn't be Michael's, but they would be almost fool-proof and tasty all the same.

The nieces arrived and I handed them the Bisquick and a big plastic bucket that I would later use for ice. I had bought disposable sheet pans, so we were set. At the last minute we would take the barbecue from the oven and then bake the biscuits so they would be fresh and hot.

I went back to the chicken. Changed to the next batch. Each batch seemed more golden and crisper than the previous one. I kept scooping out the droppings, leaving a few because I am convinced they help season the new oil, which is why the later batches are better. I have no scientific reason for this. I just know that it works this way when I do it. I straightened up the kitchen. Brought the salads to the buffet, put the sweets on platters. Sliced the corn bread and put it in a large basket. There was still no place to put anything, but now everything looked pretty. After I put the last batch of chicken in, I rolled up the newspapers and had an instantly almost-clean floor.

The phone had been ringing most of the day, but I had let the machine or Harry answer it. It rang again. Feeling settled, I picked it up.

"Hello?"

"Miss Muff?"

"Ivy!"

"Just wanted to check on you."

"It came out perfect! No help from you. How's Miami?"

"Who knows? I'm at your mother's house."

"You mean you could have come and helped me?"

"I could have, but I wouldn't. You think I want to clean up after that damn thing for two hundred people, Jeez."

"Ive! I'm all cleaned up. Will you come now?"

"Yup, we're all coming."

"I still have a batch left to do."

"Okay, Miss Muff."

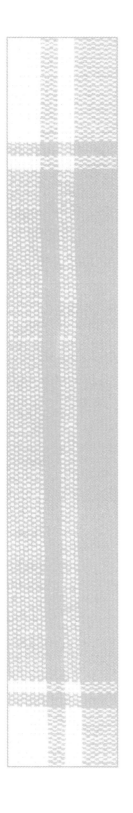

"Ivy, I love you."

"You see?"

"See what?"

"Miss Muff, you want to eat it, you just have to do it. And you can do it."

"Thanks, Ivy."

"You're welcome."

Ivy's Fried Chicken

2 whole chickens, cut up (or 16 pieces)

2 quarts orange juice

4 garlic cloves, peeled and cut in half

2 tablespoons honey (optional)

1 tablespoon fresh thyme, chopped (optional)

2 pounds all-purpose flour (8 cups)

1 to 2 tablespoons salt

1 to 2 tablespoons freshly ground black pepper

1 to 2 cups Crisco

Makes 8 servings

1. In a large baking dish or bowl, combine the chicken pieces with the orange juice and garlic. If using the honey, mix it with the juice before adding the juice to the chicken. Sprinkle with the thyme, if using it, cover, refrigerate, and leave to marinate for 1 to 2 hours.

2. In a large bowl or a small garbage bag, combine the flour with the salt and pepper. Dredge all the chicken pieces in the flour mixture so that they are well coated.

3. In a frying pan, with the heat on medium-high to high, melt enough of the Crisco to come ³/₄ inch up the sides of the pan.

4. Add the chicken—in batches if necessary (if you crowd the pan the chicken will steam instead of frying)—to the pan and fry for about 10 minutes. When the bottom is just turning brown, turn and fry on the other side for another 10 minutes, until the second side is golden brown. Keep turning to prevent the chicken from becoming too dark, and fry until all the pieces are cooked through. The smaller pieces, such as wings and legs, will take a total of 20 to 25 minutes; thighs will take 25 to 30 minutes; and breasts 30 to 40 minutes.

*Homey Roast Chicken Wrapped in Bacon
with Celery Root Stuffing*

One cold spring night, I wanted a special meal to serve to my parents and my husband. We hadn't seen each other for a bit and I wanted to make a supper that would exude the feelings of home, warmth, and companionship. We made a simple green salad with a Dijon dressing and served everything all at once. A crusty peasant bread was added to help scoop things up. And dessert was a runny apple tart. For wine, we drank Beaujolais.

FOR THE STUFFING:

1 cup wild rice

1 stalk lemongrass, split lengthwise

2 tablespoons butter

1 small onion, chopped

2 small knobs celery root (celeriac), peeled and cut into thin slivers (use a food processor or mandoline, if you wish)

4 medium leeks, trimmed, well-washed, dried, and cut into $\frac{1}{2}$-inch-thick rounds (use $\frac{3}{4}$ of the stem)

1 cup wild rice

2 tablespoons fresh lemon juice

Salt and freshly ground black pepper, to taste

FOR THE ROAST CHICKEN:

One 5-pound chicken, giblets removed and saved for another use

2 garlic cloves

2 lemons, cut in half

$\frac{1}{4}$ cup chopped fresh thyme leaves

6 to 8 thick bacon slices

16 small red-skinned potatoes

6 carrots, cut into 2-inch lengths

1 cup dry white wine (optional)

1 tablespoon all-purpose flour (optional)

1. To make the stuffing: In a pot with a cover, cook the wild rice, with the lemongrass, according to the package instructions. Discard the lemongrass and set the cooked rice aside.

2. Meanwhile, in a large skillet, heat the butter over medium heat. Add the onion and cook until it's soft, about 5 minutes. Add the celery root to the skillet and cook until the slivers have softened, about 5 minutes. Stir in the leeks and cook them until tender, about 8 minutes. Add the wild rice and lemon juice and mix well. Season with salt and pepper.

3. To make the chicken: Preheat the oven to 450°F. Rinse the chicken and pat it dry with paper towels. Rub it all over with the garlic cloves, and place the garlic in the body cavity. Squeeze the juice from the lemons all over the chicken, inside and out, and place one of the lemon halves in the body cavity. Spoon the stuffing into the chicken. Close the body cavity with metal skewers. Tie the drumsticks together with kitchen twine. Sprinkle the thyme over the top of the chicken. Wrap the bacon strips around the chicken to almost cover it completely. You may poke additional twigs of thyme in the bacon strips—it looks very pretty. Place the chicken, breast up, on a rack in a large roasting pan, preferably non-stick. Surround the chicken with the potatoes and carrots.

4. Roast for 20 minutes. Reduce the oven temperature to 350°. Cook, occasionally stirring the vegetables, until a meat thermometer inserted in the thickest part of the thigh reads 170°, about 90 minutes. Transfer the chicken to a large serving platter and let it stand for 5 to 10 minutes.

5. To serve, remove the bacon from the chicken (if it sticks, let it stay) and set it aside. Using a sharp knife, carve the chicken. Spoon the stuffing out of the cavity onto a platter. Serve the chicken with the bacon, stuffing, carrots, and potatoes.

6. If you want to make gravy, set the roasting pan over a low flame and deglaze the pan with 1 cup of wine. Whisk in a tablespoon of flour and whisk like mad over a low flame until all the flour is combined. Simmer for 1 minute.

VARIATION: For Wild Rice, Parsnip, and Orange Stuffing, substitute 1 pound parsnips, peeled and cut into 1/2-inch dice, for the celery root. Substitute 1/4 cup fresh orange juice for the lemon juice. Lime juice tastes good, too.

Chicken Breasts with Ricotta

Serves 4

When our son Harrison was born, I began to truly appreciate the nights when the house was quiet and I could cook a little something for myself without all the fanfare of cooking for more than one. (I probably would also have appreciated being waited on at a fancy restaurant in spite of the funny looks, but that wasn't an option anymore given my diaper-changing duties.) On one such evening, the baby had dozed off earlier than expected, and my husband was off on a golfing assignment. The house was calm, and I was hungry for something delicious. I needed to be quick because I was enjoying stolen time.

I opened the refrigerator and pulled out a chicken breast left from the day before. I had planned to make chicken salad that day, but had never gotten around to it. On the shelf above the chicken breast, there was some skim milk ricotta cheese that would take care of my urge for something creamy. There was also some red wine in a bottle opened two days prior. I cut up the chicken breast and sautéed it with just a bit of garlic, added the ricotta cheese, the red wine, and a little salt and pepper. I made a cup of squiggly pasta and a small green salad to complete my dinner menu. A glass of wine and I experienced that little peace and quiet of a heaven on earth. It was so simple, so good, and so soothing. It was my own kitchen supper.

2 tablespoons butter

2 tablespoons safflower oil

1 garlic clove, chopped

4 skinless and boneless chicken breasts, (1½ to 2 pounds), cut into 2-inch chunks

1 cup fresh ricotta cheese

1 tablespoon coarse ground black pepper

1 cup red or white wine

1. In a deep sauté pan, melt the butter with the safflower oil.

2. Sauté the garlic in the melted butter and oil until fragrant, about 2 minutes.

3. Add the cut-up chicken breasts and brown lightly on all sides, about 10 minutes.

4. Stir in the ricotta cheese, the pepper, and the wine.

5. Simmer for 5 minutes, until the mixture is all nice and bubbly and the chicken breasts are cooked through.

Tuscan Stewed Chicken Thighs

Makes 4 servings

My friend Mimi gave me this recipe. She got it from a friend who got it from an Italian chef, who got it from his father in Abruzzi, Italy. This recipe is as good as its ingredients. It starts as really yummy and goes to extraordinary if you can use home-made stock and fabulous tomatoes. I use canned tomatoes most of the year because the plum tomatoes are generally not very good, and the canned ones seem to be sweeter. I have used other vegetables with successful results, and I have slightly altered the original recipe, which didn't have enough tomato for my liking. I have recently found organic chicken broth in the supermarket that has a fabulous flavor. it comes in a box not a can, but the canned version or cubes will work just fine. No matter what you use—except white meat, which becomes stringy—this simple dish is a melting mouthful.

I serve it with a celery root and ricotta risotto and the whole combination reminds me of the cream of celery soup with chicken that I grew up with as a child. A Pinot Noir from Oregon goes beautifully with this dish.

5 tablespoons olive oil or butter

³⁄₄ cup chopped shallots (about 6 shallots)

4 garlic cloves, chopped

12 chicken thighs

1 cup all-purpose flour

1 medium onion, chopped

3 medium celery ribs, chopped

2 medium carrots, chopped

One 14¹⁄₂-ounce can tomatoes in juice, drained and chopped; or 6 to 8 ripe plum tomatoes, chopped

4 medium red-skinned potatoes, peeled and cut into 1-inch chunks

1 medium red bell pepper, seeded and cut into ¹⁄₄-inch-wide strips

3 to 4 cups chicken broth

1 tablespoon freshly ground black pepper

1 teaspoon salt

1. In a Dutch oven, heat the oil or butter over medium-low heat. Add the shallots and garlic and cook, stirring constantly, until they're softened, about 2 minutes. Push the shallots and garlic to the sides of the pot.

2. Dredge the chicken in the flour, shaking off the excess flour. Increase the heat to medium. In batches without crowding, add the chicken to the Dutch oven. Cook, turning occasionally, until the skin is lightly browned, about 5 minutes. As the chicken is browned, transfer it to a plate.

3. Return all the chicken to the Dutch oven along with the onion, celery, and carrots. Reduce the heat to medium-low. Cook, stirring occasionally, until the mixture begins to smell good, about 10 minutes. Stir in the tomatoes, potatoes, and bell pepper. Stir in 1 cup of the broth. Season with the pepper and salt.

4. Stir the pot to get all the ingredients nicely mixed together, cover, and simmer for approximately 1 to 1$\frac{1}{2}$ hours. Gradually stir in the remaining broth every 10 minutes or so, as it is absorbed. When done, the chicken should show no sign of pink when pierced at the bone and the potatoes will be melting into the sauce. The sauce should be stew-y, not soupy, so add more or less broth as needed.

Transfer to a deep platter and serve hot (or serve it right out of the pot).

Roast Cornish Game Hens with Peach, Bacon, and Potato Stuffing

Makes 4 servings

I like to serve this dish with wilted dandelion greens cooked in olive oil with slivered red onions. You don't need another course (other than a great dessert) because Cornish hens are large, but I have served this with a light salad such as cucumber with red onion. For dessert, we had fresh berries and brownies. As for wine, I have splurged and served a white Châteauneuf-du-Pape, but an inexpensive white Rhône tastes good too.

3 medium white or red new potatoes, cut into ³/₄-inch cubes

Four 1¹/₂-pound Cornish game hens

4 slices bacon, coarsely chopped

1 large onion, finely chopped

1 tablespoon chopped fresh thyme

2 tablespoons olive oil, as needed

4 ripe medium peaches, pitted, and coarsely chopped

Freshly ground black pepper, to taste

1 cup fresh orange juice

¹/₂ cup chopped fresh flat-leaf parsley

4 tablespoons (¹/₂ stick) butter, melted

2 garlic cloves, minced

1. Preheat the oven to 500°F. Lightly oil a large roasting pan.

2. In a medium saucepan, cover the potatoes with lightly salted water and bring to a boil over high heat. Reduce the heat to medium and boil until the potatoes are partially cooked, about 5 minutes. Drain and rinse under cold running water. Set aside.

3. Meanwhile, remove the giblets from the hens. Coarsely chop the livers and set them aside. Save the other giblets for another use, such as stock or soup. Rinse the hens under cold water, and pat them dry with paper towels.

4. In a large skillet, cook the bacon over medium heat until it gives off its fat, about 3 minutes. Add the onion and chopped livers. Cook until the onion is soft, about 2 minutes. Add the potatoes and thyme. Cook, stirring often, until

the potatoes are almost tender, about 10 minutes, adding the oil to the skillet if the mixture looks dry. Stir in the peaches and cook until they're heated through, about 2 minutes. Season with the pepper.

5. Stuff the hens with the potato mixture. Close the body cavities with toothpicks or tie the drumsticks together with kitchen twine to hold the stuffing. Place the hens in the prepared roasting pan.

6. In a small bowl, combine the orange juice, parsley, melted butter, and garlic. Pour the mixture evenly over the hens. Place the pan in the oven and reduce the oven temperature to 450°. Roast for 20 minutes. Reduce the oven temperature to 350°, and continue roasting for another 30 minutes. Increase the oven temperature to 500°, and roast until the hens show no sign of pink when pierced at the thigh, 5 to 10 minutes longer. Throughout the roasting period, baste the hens every 15 minutes with the pan juices. Let the hens stand for 5 to 10 minutes before serving.

7. To serve, remove the toothpicks or twine. Place each hen on a plate. Spoon some of the stuffing out of each bird to spill out onto the plate. Serve immediately.

Pot-Roasted Chicken with Egg Noodles

Makes 4 servings

I first made this dish on a boat. There was no way to roast a chicken, and we wanted roast chicken, so this is what came out of the galley. You are welcome to add any vegetables you choose. The seasonings are easily adjusted. I have experimented with chopped basil and added chopped tomatoes, leaving out the thyme and rosemary. I have garnished it both ways with Parmesan shavings. A crusty peasant bread and a crisp Pouilly-Fumé will certainly make a lovely supper.

4 tablespoons (¹/₂ stick) butter

2 garlic cloves, finely chopped

One 3¹/₂- to 4-pound chicken (with the liver and neck)

3 quarts water (or 2 quarts water and 1 quart chicken broth)

2 medium onions, or 4 leeks (white parts only), thinly sliced

1 stalk lemongrass, peeled and split lengthwise

1 tablespoon freshly ground black pepper

1 bouquet garni (4 sprigs thyme, 4 sprigs rosemary, 8 sprigs parsley tied together)

3 cups cleaned, sliced spinach or other dark green leafy vegetable

1 pound broad egg noodles

¹/₂ cup shaved Parmesan cheese, or more to taste

1. In a heavy Dutch oven large enough to hold the chicken, melt the butter. Add the garlic and sauté over low heat until fragrant, about 3 minutes.

2. Put the whole chicken in the pot and brown it on all sides over medium heat. Add the liver and the neck.

3. Add the water, onions or leeks, lemongrass, pepper, and the bouquet garni. Bring the liquid to a boil, then turn down the heat to medium-low. Sim-

mer, covered, for 1 to 1½ hours. The meat should be almost, but not quite, falling off the bone.

4. Remove the neck, bouquet garni, and lemongrass. Remove the chicken to a cutting board.

5. Add the spinach to the pot and simmer, uncovered, for 5 minutes.

6. Cook the egg noodles according to package directions.

7. To serve, put the cooked egg noodles in the bottom of a soup plate. Place generous slices of the chicken on top. Ladle the broth on top of the chicken and the noodles making sure each portion has a nice portion of spinach.

8. Garnish with the Parmesan shavings.

Red Hot Chicken Soup

This version of chicken soup is chockful of vitamin C. It has cured many a cold and warmed a lot of bitter winter nights. The beets create a lovely color, while adding an additional element to regular chicken soup—which I also love. In fact, you may use this recipe as a base for chicken soup, substituting more carrots or potatoes, or substituting celery for the beets. Turnips are also yummy.

Makes 8 servings

4 tablespoons butter or olive oil
8 garlic cloves, chopped
One 4-pound stewing chicken
2 onions, quartered
2 large tomatoes, chopped
5 quarts water
Juice of 4 large lemons
2 cups red or white wine
Four 3-inch beets, cut into 1¹/₂-inch
    cubes
3 carrots, chopped into 1¹/₂-inch chunks

2 tablespoons fresh rosemary
1 teaspoon chopped fresh sage
2 tablespoons coarse-ground black
    pepper
1 teaspoon coarse salt
¹/₂ cup chopped fresh flat-leaf parsley
1 dried Jamaican hot pepper, or
    1 tablespoon hot sauce (You can use
    more. Harry always adds more to his
    bowl so that it burns.)

1. In an 8-quart pot, melt the butter or heat the oil and sauté the garlic until fragrant, about 3 minutes.

2. Add the chicken, onions, tomatoes, water, lemon juice, and wine. Bring to a boil, then turn the heat down and simmer, covered, for 30 minutes.

3. Add the beets, carrots, rosemary, sage, pepper, and salt. Simmer the soup, covered, for an additional 2 hours.

4. When the meat in beginning to fall off the bone, remove the carcass to a board. Skim any weird-looking elements (such as the neck) out of the broth. Remove the meat from the bones and return it to the pot At this point you may hold the soup, refrigerate it, or freeze it.

5. When ready to eat, add the hot pepper or sauce and bring the soup to a high simmer for 15 minutes; add the chopped parsley, and serve.

Split Game Hens with Almonds and Rose Petal Jam

This dish was inspired by the movie Like Water for Chocolate, *in which rose petals play a large part. I had rented the film to share with Harry, and the very next day, much to my delight, I happened on rose petal jam in the store. I originally made this dish on the grill in the height of summer. It was yummy, but the jam does cause a bit of burn (which I like). If you are going to grill, keep the food high above the flame and baste it with the jam mixture rather than putting most of it on at the beginning. I have since roasted the hens and substituted chicken with equally tasty results.*

Makes 4 servings

We have served this with a simple tomato and onion salad. If you must have your greens, add some basil or arugula into the salad. It's also great with the Wild Rice and Corn Pilaf on page 194. Because I wanted the table full of food, we also had a cheese board, and then beautiful summer berries for dessert.

Four 1½-pound Cornish game hens, rinsed and patted dry
1½ cups rose petal jam (see Note)
½ cup fresh lime juice (about 4 limes)
2 tablespoons almond or olive oil
3 garlic cloves, finely chopped

1 teaspoon kosher or coarse sea salt (not table salt)
1 teaspoon freshly ground black pepper
1 tablespoon chopped fresh thyme
½ cup slivered almonds

1. Preheat the oven to 450°F. Lightly oil a large roasting pan.

2. Using a heavy knife, cut each hen down one side of the backbone. Open up the hens and press on the breastbone to flatten them. Place the butterflied hens in the prepared pan, skin side up.

3. In a small bowl, combine the jam, lime juice, almond oil, garlic, salt, and pepper. Brush the hens generously with the jam mixture.

(continued)

4. Roast in the preheated oven for 10 minutes. Reduce the oven temperature to 350° and continue roasting, basting occasionally with the pan juices, until there is no sign of pink when the hens are pierced at the bone, about 45 minutes. Sprinkle the fresh thyme and the almonds over the hens during the last 10 minutes of roasting. Serve hot.

NOTE: Rose petal jam can be found in Mexican, Greek, and Middle Eastern markets, specialty food stores, and some supermarkets.

8. A Toast to Roasts

8. A Toast to Roasts

I love roasting. You can roast anything. You put the pan in the oven at a high temperature. You baste occasionally. Everything sizzles and crisps, and out comes a masterpiece with a minimum of fuss. I learned just how much I love roasting one late summer evening when my perfectly timed plans and multicourse menu were altered by nature.

On this particular occasion, we had invited friends to dinner at our home in Sag Harbor, so I set out early from the city, planning to spend a couple of hours shopping. If I arrived home by 6:00 P.M., I would be ready to serve our guests at 8:00. I wasn't sure what I was going to make, but I felt like roasting something, serving it with a summer fruit compote and a couple of side dishes to take advantage of the height of summer bounty, and some kind of rustic dessert. I figured I would find the "something" to roast at Sam's Club, where I was headed to purchase some large-quantity items I needed for up-coming events to be catered by Alison On Dominick Street, and I would create the menu around it.

There was no traffic and, giddy with expectation (each aisle at Sam's Club is a gleeful adventure), I pulled into the parking lot right at 3:00 P.M. I grabbed an oversized cart and off I went, up and down the aisles, picking up various house items in giant sizes, making my way to the paper goods, eyeing a little wagon I wanted for gardening. The clock was ticking as I was distracted by some large cotton kitchen towels and plastic containers that I have found to be indispensable.

Finally, I made my way over to the food section, where I made an unplanned score of roasted peanuts in the shell for one of the big events. One hundred pounds of roasted peanuts in the shell translated to twenty enormous bags, which meant that I didn't have room for the little red wagon I coveted, and I had better concentrate on dinner or there would be no room for that either.

It was now 4:30.

Over at the meat counter, dinner presented itself in the form of beautiful pork loins, three to a pack. Each loin would make a perfect dinner for four, so two could go in the freezer for future use. Then a large pack of meaty bacon found its way into the cart. I decided to wrap the bacon around the pork loin to keep it moist. The produce department provided me with beautiful strawberries and blueberries, and an oversized bag of nectarines, which I needed for an English Summer Pudding I was making for a buffet over the weekend. I selected ten fine looking quarts, and made my way to the register with my two overloaded carts, but not before grabbing an extra-large bag of Vidalia onions, thinking I would make an onion tart to start that evening's feast.

It was now 5:15

I was thinking about the fruit compote I was going to serve with the pork as I stumbled across the parking lot with my purchases loaded on a dolly, when the hundred pounds of roasted peanuts toppled, causing a domino effect that ended with my berries spilling. Total disaster was averted with the help of two little girls who helped me scoop up the berries, reminding me that they could be washed. Their mother, who seemed silently to question my sanity as she looked over the size of my purchases, brought out some Scotch tape to ensure it wouldn't happen again. The girls were so happy to have saved the day that they insisted upon helping me load the car and then wouldn't take any payment. They restored my dwindling faith in the world, and I drove away filled with hope and expectations of a grand meal.

It was now 5:45.

Back on the Long Island Expressway, my thoughts returned to dinner. With the Pepperidge Farm puff pastry I always keep in the freezer, I was going to make an onion tart to start. Then I would roast the loin of pork, and make a fruit compote to go with it, borrowing from the nectarines I had just purchased. At the vegetable market on the way to the house, I would purchase corn (which I would take off the cob and sauté, with wild rice), salad greens, and bread. Then I decided to make a lemon pound cake, which I would slice thin to make strawberry and whipped cream "sandwiches." All this could be done in about one and a half hours.

It was now getting on 6:30.

The setting sun was particularly beautiful, all golden and rosy, but there was one big, curious-looking billowing cloud in the perfectly clear sky. At first I thought the cloud might have broken off from a recent hurricane and floated our way like a lost sheep. But as I came closer, it loomed larger and appeared quite dark and surreal. All of a sudden, it mushroomed, like the pictures you see of a nuclear explosion. I realized this ominous looking thing was no rain cloud. As I turned onto the final leg of highway, I saw flames in the distance. Fire trucks sped by me with sirens blaring, and a police barricade formed in front of me.

Wild fires had broken out across eastern Long Island, and they were jumping the highway. The smoke grew thicker and thicker. The confusion created by lack of visibility was made worse by policemen pointing in every direction. I felt like Dorothy in Oz. There were people and cars everywhere, and this was becoming like driving in New York City with a blindfold on. I wanted to stop and call home, but I was developing an unsettling fear that if I stopped I might be roasted with the pork.

It was now 7:00.

My dinner guests were due in an hour, so I decided against the onion tart.

That proved to be a good decision. It took another thirty minutes before the smoke subsided and the traffic began to move. At ten minutes to eight, I pulled up to the vegetable market. It was closed, and had been since 7:30. For some insane reason I became even more determined to pull this dinner off.

I hit the highway again, intending to go to any market that was open. As luck would have it, a small farm stand was just closing, and seeing my desperation, they let me raid the shelves. There was no corn, but they had potatoes, they had a pound cake, one piece of foccacia, arugula and broccoli, cheese and sour cream. I took it all, and spying some fresh flowers in the back, purchased those as well. If dinner was going to be an hour and a half late, we deserved fresh flowers on the table.

It was now almost 8:30.

I arrived at our house to find my husband entertaining our guests, who had been there since 7:30. My husband offered to take us out to a restaurant, but I had come this far, and was so proud of myself for packing the things we would need for dinner in the front seat, that I said, "No, we will be eating in one hour, and by the time we find a restaurant that can take us and get there and order,

we won't be eating until nine-thirty anyway." Our guests agreed, and we pulled out the cheese.

Never have I had to cook an entire dinner after the guests have arrived. This was a whole new pressure. How was I going to make all my little dishes, keep the kitchen clean, and have dinner before midnight? I wasn't. This was going to become a one-pan dinner—everything was going to be roasted.

I took one of the pork loins out of the wrapper and split it. I sliced some of the nectarines and onions that were supposed to be a part of my compote, and sandwiched them inside the pork. Then I slathered the loin with honey mustard, put some rosemary twigs on top, and wrapped the whole thing in bacon strips.

I put the loin in the roasting pan and into the oven at a high heat. I washed the small potatoes, doused them with olive oil, opened the oven, and added them to the roasting pan. I broke up the broccoli, rinsed it, opened the oven, and put them into the roasting pan.

Dinner was forty-five minutes away.

I washed the arugula, made a simple vinaigrette, washed the strawberries, mixed some brown sugar into the sour cream, and sat down for a glass of wine with our guests, who by this time were thankfully amused and amazed by the process. I shared in their amazement. I had never made roasted broccoli.

At 9:30, the roasting pan came out of the oven. The onions and nectarines had softened inside the pork, so we had compote after all. The bacon had kept everything moist and imparted a smoky flavor. The broccoli was crunchy on the outside, and soft on the inside and has become a favorite of my husband. And roasted potatoes with rosemary are always a winner. Nobody knew about all my other plans, we had a grand dinner, and it was easy. I only wished I had roasted the strawberries, too.

Roasted Veal Chops with Orange Juice, Rosemary, and New Potatoes

I have served these chops with spinach sautéed in olive oil and garlic, finished with a touch of cream. We have started with portobello mushrooms and finished with a chocolate cake. For wine: a Provençal Chardonnay.

Makes 6 servings

1½ cups fresh orange juice
¾ cup dry vermouth or white wine
2 tablespoons Dijon mustard
2 tablespoons chopped fresh rosemary
3 garlic cloves, chopped and mashed to a paste
1 teaspoon freshly ground black pepper
6 thick-cut loin veal chops (see Note)

2 pounds small red-skinned new potatoes, scrubbed but unpeeled; or 2 pounds medium potatoes, cut into 1-inch chunks
½ cup olive oil
1 tablespoon kosher or sea salt (not table salt)

1. Preheat the oven to 500°F. In a blender or food processor, process the orange juice, vermouth, mustard, rosemary, garlic, and pepper until well combined. Pour the mixture into a large ceramic or glass baking dish. Add the veal chops and turn to coat them. Cover tightly with plastic wrap and set aside.

2. Toss the potatoes with the oil and salt. (I like these potatoes on the salty side.) Place the potatoes in the roasting pan and roast, stirring occasionally, until they are about half-tender when pierced with a knife, about 20 minutes.

3. Arrange the veal chops over the potatoes, and pour the marinade over all. Reduce the oven temperature to 350°. Roast, basting occasionally, until the veal chops show only a slight tinge of pink in the center when pierced near the bone, 20 to 30 minutes (see Note). Transfer the veal to a serving platter, arrange the potatoes around the chops, and pour the cooking juices over all. Serve immediately.

NOTE: Veal chops need to cook for 18 to 20 minutes per pound, or about 6 minutes per inch. I use 14- to 16-ounce loin veal chops, each cut 1½ inches thick.

Roast Leg of Lamb with Roasted Figs, Onions, Peppers, Potatoes, and Eggplant

Makes 6 servings

Carving a leg of lamb is not easy, but then again, it really doesn't matter. I have found it best to just start carving—it all tastes the same anyway. The easiest direction to start in is parallel to the bone.

To begin, we serve a salad of wild rice, fresh corn, and tomato, simply tossed with balsamic vinegar and oil, on a bed of arugula. Dinner is followed with a chocolate bread pudding. The wine is a California Cabernet.

One 6- to 8-pound leg of lamb, more if you want leftovers

8 garlic cloves, peeled

1 cup olive oil

1 tablespoon salt

1 tablespoon freshly ground black pepper, or more to taste (I use more because I am a pepper freak.)

Handful of fresh rosemary, chopped (about 1/4 cup), and a few whole sprigs

18 small new potatoes

3 red bell peppers, seeded and quartered

6 small Japanese eggplant, split; or use 1 large eggplant, cut in 4 lengthwise slices, each slice cut lengthwise into thirds

3 large Spanish onions, quartered

18 small fresh figs; or 9 large ones, cut in half (If you want to use dried figs—simmer them in a cup of port or red wine for 15 minutes. You can reuse the port in the recipe.)

1 cup port or red wine (port is better)

1. Preheat the oven to 450°F. With a paring knife, make 8 small slits in the lamb at even intervals and insert the garlic.

2. Place the lamb in a roasting pan and brush the leg with a generous amount of the oil. Sprinkle it with the salt and pepper and the chopped rosemary.

3. Toss the vegetables with ½ cup of the remaining oil, and place them, with the whole rosemary sprigs, around the lamb.

4. Turn the oven up to 500° and roast for 30 minutes. Then turn the heat down to 350° and roast for another hour to 1 hour 20 minutes. Occasionally baste the lamb with any juices from the pan, and turn the vegetables over. Check the vegetables to make sure they are not getting too soft. If they are approaching mushiness, take them out of the pan and set them aside. If they are dry, add some more olive oil. One hour from the start of cooking, brush the figs with some olive oil and add them to the roasting pan. A leg of lamb should be cooked 15 to 18 minutes per pound. A spring lamb will require the shorter cooking time, an older lamb the longer. And then your preference will take over. I use a meat thermometer.

5. When the lamb is done (you can make a small cut to check it), take the pan from the oven and remove the lamb to a cutting board. Place the vegetables and figs on a platter and keep warm.

6. While the lamb rests, place the roasting pan on the stove top. Put the burners on low and pour the port into the pan to deglaze it. Scrape all the good stuff off the bottom. Simmer slowly until the sauce is reduced to a consistency you like, 5 to 10 minutes. The longer the simmer, the more viscous a sauce you will have.

7. Carve the lamb and place it on a platter with the vegetables and the figs alongside, surrounding, or in the middle of the meat. Pour any juices from the carving board into the sauce in the roasting pan. Bring the sauce to a rolling boil and turn off the heat. Ladle some of the sauce over the lamb, and put the rest into a gravy boat. Serve.

Roasted Lemony Loin of Lamb with Baby Artichokes and Purple Potatoes

Makes 6 servings

The sauce in this recipe can be improvised. I have added a tablespoon of mustard for a less sweet sauce. I have not had mint jelly, so have used ¼ cup of sugar and more fresh mint. I have also added store-bought mint sauce. If you don't like mint, you can just use mustard and 2 tablespoons of honey, and you can substitute red wine for the vinegar.

We have served this with an endive and Roquefort salad with hazelnut dressing to begin, and for dessert we had a Ginger and Caramelized Pear Cake (page 228). For wine, we chose a Pinot Noir from California.

One 5-pound loin of lamb (4 if you're on a diet, 6 if you want leftovers), tell the butcher to leave the outer fat intact
8 small garlic cloves, peeled
¾ cup garlic-flavored olive oil (see Note)
6 sprigs fresh rosemary
6 medium lemons
Salt and freshly ground black pepper, to taste

18 baby artichokes
18 small purple potatoes or any potato you prefer, scrubbed but unpeeled
½ cup high-quality balsamic vinegar, white balsamic vinegar, or red wine
½ cup mint jelly
¼ cup chopped fresh mint
1 tablespoon chopped fresh rosemary (optional)

1. Preheat the oven to 450°F. Using a small knife, make 8 slits in the lamb and insert a garlic clove into each slit. Brush the lamb with about 2 tablespoons of the oil. Lay the rosemary sprigs over the lamb.

2. Slice 4 of the lemons into ¼-inch-thick rounds. Using toothpicks, secure the lemons all over the lamb. The lamb will be covered with lemon slices with

some rosemary peeking out. Place the lamb in a large roasting pan, drizzle it with another 2 tablespoons of the oil, and season it with the salt and pepper.

3. Using kitchen shears or a sharp knife, trim the tips and stems off the artichokes. If the outer leaves seem tough, pull them off until you reach the tender, pale green leaves beneath. Toss the artichokes with ¼ cup of the remaining oil, and arrange them in one end of the pan.

4. Toss the potatoes with another ¼ cup of the oil and a pinch of salt. Place them in the opposite end of the pan. (I keep the potatoes and artichokes separate in case the artichokes are done before the potatoes and need to be removed from the pan.)

5. Roast in the preheated oven for 20 minutes. Reduce the oven temperature to 350° and continue to roast, occasionally basting the lamb with the pan juices and stirring the vegetables, until a meat thermometer inserted in the thickest part of the loin reads 130° for medium-rare lamb, about 25 minutes. Allow 8 to 9 minutes per pound, about 45 minutes total cooking time. Transfer the vegetables to a serving platter and cover them with foil to keep warm. Place the lamb on a carving board and let it stand while making the sauce.

6. Squeeze the juice from the remaining 2 lemons. You should have about ⅓ cup. Set it aside. Place the roasting pan across 2 burners over medium heat. When the pan is hot, pour in the vinegar and stir with a wooden spoon to scrape up the good stuff in the bottom of the pan. Now add the lemon juice and stir in the mint jelly, fresh mint, and chopped rosemary, if using it. Bring to a simmer, reduce the heat to low, and simmer, stirring often, until slightly thickened, about 2 minutes.

7. Carve the lamb and place it on the platter with the vegetables. Pour any juices from the carving board into the sauce and bring to a boil. Spoon some of the sauce over the lamb, pour the rest into a sauceboat, and serve.

NOTE: Garlic-flavored oil can be found in most supermarkets, or you can make your own. Combine 1 cup olive oil with 4 chopped garlic cloves and let stand for 1 hour. Strain, discard the garlic, and use the oil.

Roast Duck with Almonds and Chestnut Honey with Honeyed Acorn Squash

Makes 4 servings

The first time I made this dish, my husband and I both had the flu. A friend came over for a midwinter flu-athon dinner, and I was not quite prepared. The duck was still partially frozen, so I covered the sauté pan during the initial browning, and everything came out just fine. If you can't find chestnut honey, you can use any good honey. The almond oil is important, though you could use walnut, and put walnuts on top.

I wasn't in the mood to make another vegetable. What I did do was to add some scallions to the roasting pan a few minutes before the duck was done. They were a perfect foil for the honey and looked pretty, too. For dessert, I made my favorite tarte Tatin, because it's easy. We drank a Provençal Merlot.

³/₄ cup fresh orange juice

¹/₄ cup almond oil

5 tablespoons full-flavored honey, preferably chestnut

2 garlic cloves, chopped

One 6-pound Long Island duck

6 tablespoons (³/₄ stick) butter

2 teaspoons chopped fresh rosemary

Salt, to taste

1¹/₂ teaspoons freshly ground pepper, plus additional to taste

2 medium acorn squash, cut in half, seeds removed

¹/₂ cup (2 ounces) slivered almonds

8 whole scallions, washed and dried

1. Preheat the oven to 425°F. Arrange 2 racks in the oven to hold 2 roasting pans, one for the duck and one for the acorn squash.

2. In a small bowl, combine the orange juice, almond oil, 1 tablespoon of the honey, and 1 garlic clove. Set aside.

3. Using kitchen shears or a sharp knife, trim off any excess fat and skin

from the duck. Cut the duck into 6 pieces: 2 breasts (with the wings attached), 2 thighs, and 2 drumsticks. Cut each breast crosswise to give 2 pieces—one should be slightly smaller than the other with the wing left attached. You now have 8 pieces.

4. In a large, deep skillet, melt 2 tablespoons of the butter over medium heat until foamy. Add the remaining garlic clove and the rosemary. Cook, stirring often, until fragrant, about 1 minute. In batches without crowding, add the duck and cook, turning occasionally, until it's browned on all sides, about 10 minutes. Transfer the browned duck to a large roasting pan.

5. Pour the orange juice mixture into the skillet and bring to a boil, scraping up everything from the bottom of the pan with a wooden spoon. Pour the juice over the duck and season with salt and pepper to taste. Roast for 20 minutes.

6. Meanwhile, place the acorn squash, cut side up, in another roasting pan. Place 1 tablespoon of butter and 1 tablespoon of honey into the cavity of each squash half, and sprinkle with the $1^{1}/_{2}$ teaspoons of pepper. Pour enough water into the pan to come 1 inch up the sides.

7. After the duck has roasted for 20 minutes, reduce the oven temperature to 375°. Sprinkle the almonds over the duck. Place the acorn squash on the lower rack. Roast both the squash and the duck for 20 minutes. Scatter the scallions over the duck and continue to roast until the duck shows no sign of pink when pierced at the bone and the squash is tender, about 30 minutes longer. The total cooking time is about 1 hour, 10 minutes.

8. Arrange the duck and scallions on one platter and the acorn squash on another. Skim any yellow fat from the duck roasting pan and pour the brown juices over the duck. Serve immediately.

Roasted Sea Bass Stuffed with Fennel and Red Pepper with Roast Baby Vegetables

Makes 6 to 8 servings

I have used wild rice in the stuffing and it is also wonderful. Just use 1 cup cooked wild rice and reduce the fennel and red peppers to one each. I have served this fish with a simple fettuccine with olive oil, butter, and garlic; an arugula salad; and a Plum Tart (page 221). The wine was a Quincy from the Loire Valley.

2 medium bulbs fennel, with top stalks and fronds

3 stalks lemongrass, split lengthwise

8 whole garlic cloves, peeled

2 tablespoons butter

2 medium red bell peppers, seeded and cut into ¼-inch-wide strips

½ cup fresh orange juice

Salt and freshly ground black pepper, to taste

One 6-pound sea bass, scaled and gutted, (leave head and tail on)

4 tablespoons olive oil

20 baby yellow squash

20 baby zucchini

1. Preheat the oven to 450°F. Lightly oil a roasting pan large enough to hold the fish. Cut off the stalks and fronds from the fennel and place them in the roasting pan, along with the lemongrass and garlic.

2. Cut the fennel bulbs crosswise into ½-inch-thick slices. In a large skillet, heat the butter over medium heat. Add the fennel and red peppers. Cook, stirring occasionally, until the vegetables are softened, about 5 minutes. Stir in the orange juice and reduce the heat to medium-low. Simmer until the vegetables are very soft and the juice is almost completely evaporated, about 10 minutes. Season with salt and pepper.

3. Rinse the fish inside and out with cold running water and pat it dry with

paper towels. Fill the body cavity with the vegetable mixture. To hold in the stuffing, tie a long piece of kitchen twine around the tail, wrap it in a spiral around the fish to reach the head, and knot it at the head end. Place the fish in the pan and brush it with 2 tablespoons of the oil. In a medium bowl, toss the baby vegetables with the remaining 2 tablespoons of oil and season them with salt and pepper. Scatter the vegetables around the fish.

4. Roast for 10 minutes. Reduce the oven temperature to 350° and continue roasting until the fish looks opaque when flaked in a thick part with a fork, about 20 minutes longer. The total roasting time is about 30 minutes.

5. Using 2 large metal spatulas, transfer the fish to a large serving platter. Spoon the vegetables and cooking juices around the fish, discarding the lemongrass. Serve immediately.

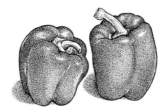

Roast Pork Stuffed with Rosemary, Garlic, and Leeks, with Apple and Plum Compote

Makes 8 servings

You can reheat the fruit compote if you wish, and you can substitute pears for the apples, or peaches and apricots for the plums. I have served this recipe with Popovers (recipe follows) filled with Acorn Squash Puree (page 152), and put a dollop of the fruit compote on top. We then had a simple green salad and cheese, followed by a store-bought pecan tart. For wine, we had an inexpensive red Burgundy.

FOR THE PORK:

5 tablespoons unsalted butter

2 garlic cloves, chopped

6 medium leeks, white part only, well
washed, dried, and sliced into
1/2-inch-thick rounds,

2 tablespoons chopped fresh rosemary

1 tablespoon light brown sugar

2 large onions, sliced

3 cups red wine

One 4-pound boneless loin of pork

FOR THE COMPOTE:

1 tablespoon butter

1/2 cup chopped shallots (about
6 shallots)

3 garlic cloves, minced

1 cup fresh orange juice

1 cup dried sour cherries

3 medium McIntosh apples, peeled,
cored, and cut into 1-inch pieces

3 medium red or black plums, pitted
and cut into 1-inch chunks

1. To prepare the pork: In a large skillet over medium heat, melt 3 tablespoons of the butter until it's foamy. Add the garlic and cook until it's fragrant, about 1 minute. Stir in the leeks and rosemary. Cook, stirring occasionally, until the leeks are soft, about 10 minutes. Set aside.

2. Meanwhile, in a large saucepan, melt the brown sugar over low heat. Add the sliced onions and the remaining 2 tablespoons of butter. Cook, stirring often, until the onions are softened and caramelized, about 15 minutes. Watch carefully to be sure the onions don't burn. Add the red wine and bring to a boil over high heat. Reduce the heat to medium and cook until the liquid has reduced by half, about 20 minutes. Set the wine and onion mixture aside.

3. Preheat the oven to 350°F. Using a large sharp knife, cut the pork in half lengthwise. Spread the leeks over the bottom half, and replace the top. Tie the loin crosswise in several places with kitchen twine. Place in a roasting pan and spoon about half the wine and onion mixture over the top of the pork.

4. Roast, allowing 20 minutes per pound, basting occasionally with the pan juices, until a meat thermometer inserted in the center of the roast reads 150°, about 1 hour and 20 minutes. (If the pan juices evaporate, you can baste the roast with a few spoonsful of the red wine from the onion mixture, as needed; do not use all of the wine, because it will be turned into the sauce for the roast.)

5. To make the compote: In a medium saucepan, heat the butter over medium-low heat. Add the shallots and garlic and cook, stirring occasionally, until they're softened, about 3 minutes. Add the orange juice and dried cherries, bring to a simmer, and cook for 5 minutes. Add the apples and plums, and simmer until the fruit is soft, but not mushy, about 10 minutes. Remove from the heat, transfer to a serving bowl, and cool. (If desired, set the compote aside in the pan and reheat it over low heat before serving.)

6. Transfer the roast to a serving platter and let it stand for 10 minutes before carving. Place the roasting pan over medium heat. Add the remaining wine and onion mixture and bring to a boil, scraping up the browned bits in the bottom of the pan. Lower the heat and simmer for 1 to 2 minutes. Turn off the heat.

7. Remove the kitchen twine from the roast and carve it crosswise into thick slices. Pour the wine and onion sauce over the roast. Serve with the apple compote passed on the side.

Popovers

There is almost nothing better than a luscious, warm, golden toasty popover. You may add a couple of tablespoons of any herb for additional flavor. I like mine plain. You can break them open and fill them with stew or vegetables, or serve them as you would a roll. They are best served straight from the oven, so time your dinner accordingly. I have had the most success with my popovers popping when I have heated the fat in the bottom of the tin first.

Makes 12 regular or 6 extra-large

1 tablespoon bacon fat, melted butter, or vegetable oil, for the tin
3 eggs
1¼ cups flour
½ teaspoon salt

1¼ cups milk (for extra richness use 1 cup milk and ¼ cup cream)
½ teaspoon sugar or honey
2 tablespoons butter, melted

1. Preheat the oven to 400°F. Distribute the bacon fat evenly among the cups of a 12-cup (or 6 extra-large) muffin tin. Place the tin in the oven.

2. In a mixing bowl, combine the eggs, flour, salt, milk, sugar, and melted butter. Blend well.

3. Remove the muffin tin from the oven and pour the batter evenly among the muffin cups. They should be one half to three quarters full.

4. Place the tin back in the oven. Reduce the heat to 375° and bake until the popovers are plump and golden, 25 to 30 minutes. Try not to open the oven during baking! Serve immediately.

Roast Duck with Cinnamon Stuffing, Tangerine Juice, and Honey Wine Sauce

I like to carve at the table, but if you don't, slice the duck beforehand. Mound the stuffing in the middle of the platter and arrange the slices and legs around it. Pour the sauce over all and serve.

Makes 4 servings

All you need with this dish is a dark green vegetable such as spinach or broccoli rabe. The last time I served this we had broccoli rabe and slivered beets sautéed with shallots, olive oil, and balsamic vinegar. We started with a Blue Cheese Soufflé (page 82) and ended with a Pear Tarte Tatin (page 220). A good crusty peasant bread, and red Côte du Rhone completed the meal.

One 6-pound Long Island duck
8 small garlic cloves
3 tangerines
8 tablespoons (1 stick) butter
1 medium red onion, chopped
2 medium parsnips, peeled and cut into
  1-inch dice
2 medium turnips, cut into 1-inch dice
1½ cups raw wild rice, cooked
  according to package instructions

4 slices cinnamon-raisin or white
  bread, toasted and cut into ½-inch
  pieces (see Note)
1½ cups hearty dry red wine
¼ cup full-flavored honey, preferably
  chestnut or thyme
1 tablespoon chopped fresh thyme
1 teaspoon freshly ground black pepper

1. Rinse the duck inside and out with cold running water, reserving the neck and liver. Trim the excess fat and skin from the duck. Pat the duck dry with paper towels. Using a small sharp knife, make 8 incisions in the duck breast and

(continued)

thighs, inserting a garlic clove in each incision. Refrigerate the duck until ready to stuff.

2. Cut the tangerines in half and squeeze the juice. Set the juice and the tangerine halves aside.

3. In a large skillet, melt 3 tablespoons of the butter over medium-low heat. Add the onion and cook until it begins to soften, about 1 minute. Add the duck liver. Cook, stirring occasionally, until the liver is firm, about 8 minutes. Remove the liver and chop into $1/2$-inch dice; return the chopped liver to the skillet with the onion.

4. Add the parsnips and turnips to the skillet with $1/2$ cup of the tangerine juice and 2 tablespoons of the remaining butter. Cook until the vegetables are barely tender, about 8 minutes. Stir in the wild rice and the remaining 3 tablespoons of butter. Stir in the bread cubes. Cook, stirring often, until the flavors are well blended, about 5 minutes.

5. Preheat the oven to 400°F. Prick the duck skin all over with a fork, but don't pierce the meat. Rub the duck inside and out with the tangerine peels. Fill the body cavity with the stuffing. If desired, close the body cavity with metal skewers and twine to keep the stuffing in. (I don't always do this because I don't mind if a little stuffing falls out into the pan.) Tie the legs together with kitchen twine. Place the duck, breast side down, on a rack in a roasting pan.

6. Roast for 20 minutes. Turn the duck breast side up and baste it with the fat in the pan. Reduce the oven temperature to 350° and continue roasting, basting occasionally, until a meat thermometer inserted in the thickest part of the thigh reads 170°, about $1 1/2$ hours longer. The total roasting time is about 1 hour, 50 minutes.

7. While the duck is roasting, make the sauce base: In a small saucepan, bring the reserved duck neck, the wine, honey, thyme, and pepper to a boil over high heat. Reduce the heat to very low and simmer gently until the liquid is reduced to 1 cup, about 15 minutes. Remove and discard the duck neck.

8. Transfer the duck to a serving platter and let it stand for 10 minutes before carving. Meanwhile, pour the fat and cooking juices into a large glass measuring cup. Let stand until the clear yellow fat separates and rises to the top.

Pour or skim off the yellow fat, which can be cooled, covered, and refrigerated to use as a cooking fat. Pour the brown juices back into the roasting pan, and place the pan over medium heat. Add the sauce base and bring to a boil, scraping up the browned bits on the bottom of the pan. Pour the sauce into a sauceboat.

9. Untie the duck. Using a spoon, spill the stuffing out of the duck onto a platter. Carve the duck (it's just like a chicken or turkey), and serve with a spoonful of the stuffing, and the sauce passed on the side.

NOTE: If using white bread, add ½ teaspoon ground cinnamon and 1 tablespoon raisins to the stuffing.

Roasted Fillet of Beef with Orange, Cloves, Leeks, and Horseradish Cream

Makes 6 to 8

servings

I think plain spinach is best with this recipe because you can spoon some of the horse-radish cream on top, and it tastes great. Mashed potatoes are a good choice for a starch; however, roast potatoes are easier, as you can throw them in with the fillet. If you choose to roast the potatoes, toss them in a little oil and coarse salt and put them in the oven about 10 minutes before the fillet. Everything can go in the same pan. I served the Dark Chocolate Cake with Almonds and Orange on page 222 with this dinner, and an inexpensive St. Emilion. We started dinner with a white and green Asparagus with Warm Dijon Dressing (page 81).

One 5-pound beef fillet, trimmed
1 cup fresh orange juice
1 cup hearty dry red wine
½ cup chopped fresh flat-leaf parsley
3 garlic cloves, chopped
2 tablespoons coarsely cracked
   ("butcher grind") black pepper
3 tablespoons olive oil

1 tablespoon whole cloves
6 medium leeks, white and pale green
   parts, well washed, dried, and thinly
   sliced
1 cup sour cream
½ cup freshly grated horseradish, or
   2 tablespoons prepared horseradish
1 tablespoon honey

1. Fold the thin part of the fillet under the roast and tie it with kitchen string so the roast is the same thickness throughout. Place it in a shallow glass or ceramic dish.

2. In a medium bowl, whisk together the orange juice, wine, parsley, garlic, and pepper. Pour the mixture over the beef. Let it marinate at room temperature, turning occasionally, for 30 minutes.

3. Meanwhile, preheat the oven to 500°F. Remove the beef from the marinade, reserving the marinade, and place it in a large roasting pan. Rub the beef all over with the oil. Sprinkle the cloves over the beef.

4. Roast, allowing 8 to 10 minutes per pound, until a meat thermometer inserted in the center reads 130° for medium-rare meat, a total of 40 to 50 minutes. Transfer the roast to a platter and cover it with aluminum foil while making the sauce. (Be sure to cover the meat to keep it warm and moist.)

5. Place the roasting pan across 2 burners and turn the heat to high. Add the reserved marinade and bring it to a boil, scraping up the browned bits on the bottom of the pan. Add the leeks and return to a boil. Reduce heat and cook until the sauce has reduced by one third, about 5 minutes. Whisk in the sour cream, horseradish, and honey. Heat through, but do not boil again.

6. Slice the beef and pour a little sauce over the slices. Pour the remaining sauce into a sauceboat. Serve immediately.

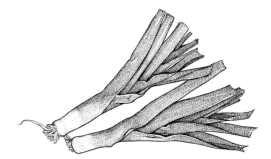

9. Everything in a Pot

9. Everything in a Pot

I love one-pot cooking. The fact that the kitchen is easier to clean up after supper is just one of many reasons. The aromas of food cooked in one pot are always so rich and various, and an entire meal or an entire main course served in one pot always seems so dramatic. Although I sometimes have to use more than one pot during the actual cooking process, all the ingredients eventually wind up in the same place. When the foods and the flavors meld together in one pot, I'm able to create wonderfully warm and comforting meals that seem to snuggle against the palate.

My seminal experience in one-pot cooking began on a late afternoon in January when despair seemed to blanket our house like the snow drifts covering the backyard. My husband was upstairs in bed with the flu, and I wanted to make something that would cure his ills, warm our souls, and help me shake the beginning of the New Year's blues while I put off making all the well-intentioned resolutions I knew I would never really keep. It was in this dark and dreary mood that I decided to make shepherd's pie.

In days of yore, shepherd's pie was made with leftovers from the large Sunday meal, making use of the roasted meat, the gravy, and various table scraps. Today, we think of a classic shepherd's pie as a dish made with lamb or mutton (which is basically a grown-up lamb), but there is no reason not to substitute beef, veal, or pork. In essence, shepherd's pie is a stew combined with mashed potatoes. You can fill out the stew portion of the recipe with vegetables such as carrots and peas, or you can leave out the vegetables altogether. If you're using pork instead of lamb, for example, you might substitute apples and onions for the carrots and peas.

On this particular afternoon, I was in the mood to make the classic shepherd's pie, so I went off to the grocery store to pick up some stewing lamb. The town was quiet, still sleeping off its post-holiday stupor, and there was no butcher on duty, so I purchased lamb shoulder chops and cut the meat off the bone myself. If you decide to try making shepherd's pie and your local butcher is on duty when you arrive at the store, he may give you a funny look if you ask for "stewing lamb." Just tell him you want lamb trimmed from the leg or the shoulder, it doesn't really matter which. What you do not want to use is rib, loin, or sirloin. Those better cuts of meat dry out during the stewing process because there is not enough fat on them. If you can use the bones when you're cooking, do so by all means. You will have a much richer stew, especially if you scrape the marrow from inside the bone and stir it into the sauce.

When I returned from my trip to town, my husband was still tossing and turning in the upstairs bedroom, and I was chagrined to find that the kitchen seemed drearier than ever. Determined to brighten up this depressing scene, I peered into the vegetable bin to see what I had to fill out my stew. There were two plum tomatoes on the verge of turning bad, some leeks and carrots, and some fresh peas I'd bought on a whim the day before. Removing the peas from their pods would require extra time and work, but it seemed like a fitting activity on such a disheartening winter's day, as well as a perfect opportunity to muse about life, liberty, and the pursuit of happiness.

Sure enough, by the time I had shelled the peas, browned the lamb, and started the sauce bubbling in its pot, the kitchen warmed up, and what had seemed like a hopeless afternoon suddenly became an afternoon brimming with possibilities. My husband loves mint jelly and mustard whenever he eats lamb chops or lamb shank, so I put a little of both in the stew. I also added a bit of honey for an extra-sweet twist. My stew now began to take on a delightfully distinctive shape, texture, and aroma.

Then it came time to face the task I secretly dreaded—making the mashed potatoes to top off my shepherd's pie. My husband and I shared a not-so-funny running joke about the first (and, until now, last) time I'd tried to make mashed potatoes in our Sag Harbor kitchen. I'm sure that anyone who has succeeded in making good mashed potatoes knows that you cannot do the mashing in a food processor because the speed of the machine whips them too fast and brings out the gluten, which quickly turns into gooey globs. I had nevertheless decided that I might be able to use the food processor to whip the potatoes with several sprigs of basil if I was very careful and went very slowly. Boy, was I wrong! What I had gotten from that ill-fated experiment with the food processor was a sickly green mess that had the taste and consistency of bathroom caulking. My loving husband tried to eat two forksful before telling me what I already knew—I had failed mashed potatoes miserably!

But my craving for shepherd's pie now overpowered my fear of another failure, so I took a deep breath, and vowed to produce a properly prepared batch of nice white mashed potatoes. I peeled off the skins and boiled the potatoes in a pot. When I could easily poke them with a fork, I put them in a bowl and added generous helpings of butter and sour cream. Still too stubborn (or perhaps, too lazy) to labor with a hand mixer, I transferred my potato concoction to my KitchenAid mixer and set the motor on low speed. To my immeasurable relief, it worked! I churned out a batch of the loveliest, creamiest, tangiest mashed potatoes I'd ever seen. I have since experimented with adding buttermilk and cream cheese to my mashed potatoes, and have discovered that as long as I add small amounts until I get the consistency I want—while keeping the mixer on *low* speed—I can produce great mashed potatoes.

When the stew was cooked, I put it into a small copper pot, spread my newly created mashed potatoes on top, and slid the pot into the oven. By now, my once cold and forbidding kitchen was absolutely toasty, and the aromas of the shepherd's pie baking in the oven seemed to make it bustle with new life. At last, there was hope and anything was possible—even mashed potatoes! I went upstairs to see if my flu-afflicted husband had risen from the dead. When I entered our darkened bedroom, he propped himself up on the pillows and crinkled his nose, sniffing and sniffling at the same time. I could tell that the delectable aromas of lamb and mint wafting up from the kitchen were penetrating his stuffy head and his heart. "Honey one," he said nuzzling me with a nose infatuated by the scent of shepherd's pie, "this is true love!"

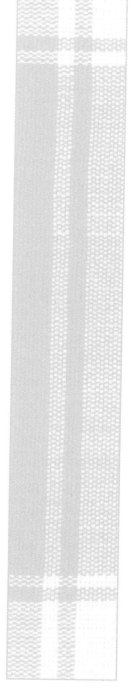

Lamb Shepherd's Pie

Makes 6 servings

FOR THE LAMB FILLING:

2 cups hearty dry red wine, plus more as needed

$1/2$ cup chopped plum tomatoes, or use drained canned tomatoes

$1/2$ cup chopped fresh mint

3 tablespoons fresh lemon juice

2 tablespoons Dijon mustard

4 tablespoons ($1/2$ stick) butter

4 garlic cloves, coarsely chopped

2 pounds boneless stewing lamb, such as neck or shoulder, cut into 1-inch cubes

1 pound lamb bones (optional)

2 tablespoons all-purpose flour

2 medium carrots, cut into 1-inch lengths

2 medium leeks, white part only, well washed, dried, and cut lengthwise into 1-inch pieces

$1/4$ cup bottled mint sauce (or make Fresh Mint Sauce, page 185)

2 tablespoons honey

1 tablespoon chopped fresh rosemary

$1/2$ cup fresh or frozen peas

Salt and freshly ground black pepper, to taste

FOR THE TOPPING:

3 large russet or Idaho potatoes, peeled and cut into 2-inch chunks

1 large egg

2 tablespoons sour cream

3 tablespoons butter, melted

1. To prepare the lamb filling: In a large saucepan over medium heat, bring the 2 cups of wine, to a simmer with the tomatoes, mint, lemon juice, and mustard. Reduce the heat to medium-low and simmer while you brown the lamb. If your butcher has been kind enough to give you the lamb bones, put them in the pot too.

2. In a large Dutch oven or flameproof casserole, melt the butter over medium heat. Add the garlic. In batches, without crowding, add the lamb, and brown it on all sides. As the lamb browns, transfer it to a plate. Return the lamb to the pot, sprinkle it with the flour, and stir well. Stir in the wine mixture (bones removed if you have used them), bring to a simmer, and cover loosely.

Cook until the meat is beginning to become tender, about 1 hour. Stir in the carrots, leeks, mint sauce, honey, and rosemary. Continue simmering for 15 minutes, until the vegetables are tender. Stir in the peas (I like my peas almost mushy. If you want yours crisp, add them at the last 5 minutes). Simmer for another 15 minutes. Season with salt and pepper and remove from the heat.

3. While the stew is simmering, make the mashed potato topping: Preheat the oven to 350°F. Place the potatoes in a large saucepan with enough lightly salted water to cover. Bring to a boil over high heat. Reduce the heat to medium and cook until the potatoes are tender, 15 to 20 minutes. Drain and return them to the pot. Using a potato masher or an electric mixer on low speed (but not a food processor, which will turn the potatoes into gelatinous glop), mash the potatoes. In a small bowl, combine the egg and sour cream. Mash the mixture into the potatoes, along with 2 tablespoons of the melted butter. You can leave the potatoes chunky, or mash them smooth, as you prefer (I like them chunky for this recipe).

4. Spread the potatoes evenly over the top of the stew. Drizzle the topping with the remaining tablespoon of butter. Bake until the topping is browned, about 30 minutes. The juices will be just bubbling up trying to get through the potatoes. If the top starts to dry out while baking, dot it with a little more butter. Serve hot.

Bouillabaisse Kilkare

This recipe is dedicated to our good friends Michael and Eleonora Kennedy. It was first made by me in their kitchen at Kilkare—their beautiful seaside cottage. One late spring day I decided I had to make gumbo. We were going for dinner at the Kennedys', but I was cooking, and I had promised gumbo. I searched for okra everywhere, but every store had just sold the last of it. I had all my other ingredients. I looked at them and they looked at me, and gumbo became bouillabaisse Kilkare. It was fabulous. So it does not matter if you can't find the okra. If you don't want to make the fish stock, you can purchase it at many fish stores, or just simmer the clam juice, wine, and vegetable broth without the fish bones.

There are as many versions of bouillabaisse as there are people who make it. All over the south of France, one will find "the true bouillabaisse." I have shortened the cooking time, as well as reducing the number of steps. Traditionally, the soup is served before the fish—however, this is my bouillabaisse and we loved it.

Makes 8 generous servings

FOR THE FISH STOCK:
2 pounds assorted fish bones and heads (without gills) from white-fleshed fish such as cod, bass, snapper, flounder, or halibut
4 cups bottled clam juice
2 cups dry white wine
One 13 ³/₄-ounce can vegetable broth
¹/₃ cup water, plus more as needed

FOR THE BOUILLABAISSE:
4 tablespoons (¹/₂ stick) butter
1 cup olive oil
1 large onion, chopped
3 medium celery ribs, chopped
2 medium carrots, chopped
¹/₄ cup chopped fresh flat-leaf parsley

8 medium plum tomatoes, peeled, seeded, and chopped; or use 3 cups drained and chopped canned tomatoes
1 quart reserved fish stock
2 cups canned or bottled clam juice
A few pinches crushed saffron threads
3 pounds codfish steaks, cut 1 inch thick
8 small potatoes (any kind), scrubbed but unpeeled
8 lobster tails
32 mussels, well scrubbed and debearded
32 cherrystone clams, well scrubbed
¹/₂ cup anise-flavored liqueur, such as Pernod (optional)
3 tablespoons chopped fresh chives

¼ cup chopped fresh basil

3 tablespoons chopped fresh dill

Salt and freshly ground black pepper, to taste

8 large slices French bread, toasted

2 garlic cloves, peeled

FOR THE ROUILLE:

10 large garlic cloves, peeled

3 large egg yolks, at room temperature

1 teaspoon Dijon mustard

1½ cups olive oil

1 large red bell pepper, seeded and coarsely chopped

1. To make the fish stock: Rinse all of the bones well under cold running water. Place them in a large pot and add the clam juice, wine, vegetable broth, and water. Bring to a simmer over high heat. Reduce the heat to medium-low and simmer for 30 minutes. Strain and measure the stock. Add water, if necessary, to make 1 quart.

2. To make the bouillabaisse: In a large soup pot, heat the butter and olive oil over medium heat. Add the onion, celery, carrots, and parsley. Cook until they're softened, about 10 minutes. Stir in the tomatoes, then the fish stock, clam juice, and saffron. Add the cod and bring to a simmer. Reduce the heat to medium-low and simmer for 15 minutes. Add the potatoes and simmer for another 15 minutes.

3. Add the lobster tails, mussels, and clams. Simmer until the clams and mussels open, about 8 minutes. Using a large slotted spoon or a skimmer, transfer the fish and potatoes to very large bowl and cover with foil to keep warm. Add the liqueur to the broth, if using it, along with the chives, basil, and dill. Season with salt and pepper. Simmer for 3 minutes.

4. Meanwhile, make the rouille: In a food processor, with the machine running, drop the garlic cloves one at a time through the feed tube and process until very finely chopped. Add the egg yolks and mustard (see page 24). With the machine running, add the oil in a thin stream and process until thickened. Add the red pepper and process until pureed. Transfer to a bowl.

5. To serve, rub each toast with the garlic and place one in the bottom of each soup bowl. Spoon the fish and shellfish into the bowls and ladle in the broth. Serve immediately, with the rouille passed on the side. Be sure to have plenty of napkins and bowls for the shells.

Braised Short Ribs with Acorn Squash Puree

This dish is a rich, homey winter treat. The soft ribs melt into the smooth puree and it becomes pure comfort food—but better! If you don't have one or another alcohol in the house, you can substitute more wine—but do try to use the ale and vermouth, they add that special flavor.

Makes 4 to 6

servings

FOR THE SHORT RIBS:
4 tablespoons vegetable oil
$\frac{1}{3}$ cup chopped shallots (about
   2 shallots)
2 to 4 garlic cloves, chopped (How
   much do you like garlic?)
4 tablespoons light brown sugar
6 medium carrots, 2 cut into $\frac{1}{2}$-inch
   dice, 4 cut into $\frac{1}{2}$-inch-long pieces
2 medium turnips, cut into $\frac{1}{2}$-inch dice
4 pounds meaty beef short ribs
1 large onion, chopped
1 cup fresh orange or tangerine juice or
   apple cider

1 cup raisins
4 cups ale, preferably Belgian
   farmhouse-style
1 cup sweet vermouth
2 cups dry red wine, approximately
4 medium parsnips, halved lengthwise
   if thick, and cut into 1-inch lengths

FOR THE ACORN SQUASH PUREE:
2 medium acorn squash
2 garlic cloves
1 cup sour cream, low-fat or regular
1 teaspoon dark brown sugar

1. To prepare the short ribs: In a large Dutch oven, heat the oil over medium-low heat. Add the shallots, garlic, and 2 tablespoons of the brown sugar. Cook until the shallots soften, stirring often to help the sugar melt evenly, about 3 minutes. Add the *diced* carrots and the turnips, and mix well. Transfer to a plate and set aside.

2. In batches, add the short ribs and cook, turning occasionally, until browned on all sides, about 10 minutes. As the ribs are browned, transfer them to a plate.

3. Add the onion to the pot and cook until softened, about 5 minutes. Stir in the orange or tangerine juice and raisins. Bring to a simmer and cook until the onions are tender, about 5 minutes. Return the short ribs and the vegetables to the pot. Add the ale, vermouth, the remaining 2 tablespoons of brown sugar, and enough wine to barely cover the ribs. Bring to a boil over high heat and cook until the liquid reduces by about one third, about 10 minutes.

4. Preheat the oven to 300°F. Tightly cover the pot and bake until the short ribs are very tender, about 2½ hours. During the last hour, stir in the *sliced* carrots and the parsnips. Add more wine if needed to keep the short ribs barely covered with liquid. The dish is ready when the meat begins to fall off the bones.

5. To make the acorn squash puree: Place the whole acorn squash in a baking dish and cover them with aluminum foil. (You can just place them whole in the oven if you don't have room for the baking dish). After the short ribs have baked for about 1½ hours, place the acorn squash on the lower rack. Bake until the squash is tender, 45 to 60 minutes.

6. In a food processor, with the machine running, drop the garlic through the feed tube to chop fine. Protecting your hands with a folded kitchen towel, cut the squash in half, scoop out the seeds, and spoon out the flesh, transferring it to the food processor. (You may also peel the acorn before seeding. The skin usually peels quite easily.) Add the sour cream and brown sugar and process until pureed.

7. To serve, spoon the squash puree onto dinner plates. Spoon the ribs, with the sauce and vegetables, over the squash.

Duck Stew with Prunes and Apricots

I serve everything on one big platter. I put all the duck pieces on the perimeter, pour the sauce with the veggies over it, then put the noodles in the middle. It's just fine if some of the duck juice runs under the noodles, and it makes a great presentation. If you don't have a platter large enough, just clean up the outside of the casserole, serve the stew in that, and put the noodles in a bowl. Drizzle with the truffle oil just before serving.

Makes 8

large servings

Two 5-pound Long Island ducks, cut into 8 pieces each, excess fat and skin trimmed, necks and livers reserved
8 cups (about 2½ bottles) hearty dry red wine, or more as needed
3 large onions, sliced into ¼-inch half-moons
3 medium carrots, sliced into ¼-inch-thick rounds
1 large head garlic cloves, peeled
2 bouquets garni (see Note)
¼ teaspoon freshly ground black pepper, plus more to taste

20 dried apricots
20 pitted prunes
2 cups hot, strongly brewed tea, such as Orange Pekoe
2 tablespoons butter
1 tablespoon peanut or vegetable oil
2 tablespoons all-purpose flour
1 cup chicken broth, preferably homemade, or more as needed
Swiss Chard Noodles (page 192), or 1 pound dried egg noodles, cooked according to package directions, for serving

1. At least 6 hours before making the stew, marinate the duck. In a large, non-reactive (stainless or porcelain or pottery) bowl, combine the ducks with 6 cups of the wine, the onions, carrots, garlic, 1 bouquet garni, and the ¼ teaspoon of pepper. If needed, add more wine to cover the duck. Cover tightly with plastic wrap and refrigerate (or leave in a cool place) for at least 6 and up to 10 hours.

2. Meanwhile, in a small bowl, steep the apricots and prunes in the hot tea until they're plump and softened, about 30 minutes. Drain, and place the fruit in a medium saucepan. Add enough of the remaining wine to cover (about 2 cups). Bring to a simmer over medium heat, then reduce the heat to low and simmer for 8 minutes. Drain the fruit, and add the drained wine to the marinade. Set the fruit aside.

3. Position a rack in the center of the oven and preheat to 350°F. Remove the duck from the marinade and pat it dry with paper towels. Reserve the marinade. In a large Dutch oven, heat 1 tablespoon of the butter with the oil over medium-high heat. In batches, without crowding, brown the duck on all sides, about 8 minutes per batch. As each batch is browned, transfer the duck to a large platter and pour the rendered duck fat into a heat-proof bowl. Return 2 tablespoons of fat to the Dutch oven to brown each subsequent batch. If desired, use a separate large skillet to brown some of the duck and speed up the process.

4. After all the duck is browned, return $1/4$ cup of duck fat to the Dutch oven. (The remaining duck fat can be used in other recipes as a cooking fat; cover and refrigerate it for up to 2 weeks, or freeze it in an airtight container for up to 3 months.) Strain the marinade into another bowl, reserving both the vegetables and the marinade. Add the vegetables to the Dutch oven, along with the duck necks and livers. Cook over medium heat until the vegetables soften, 10 to 15 minutes. Discard the duck necks. Stir in the remaining tablespoon of butter. Sprinkle the vegetables with the flour and stir until they are well coated, about 1 minute.

5. Add the reserved marinade and bring to a boil over high heat. Reduce the heat to medium-low and simmer for 5 minutes. Stir in the broth. Return the duck to the Dutch oven with the remaining bouquet garni. (If the duck isn't completely covered, add more broth.) Bring to a boil. Cover tightly and bake in the preheated oven until the duck is tender, 45 to 60 minutes. Using tongs, transfer the duck to a large platter and cover it with foil to keep warm.

6. Skim the fat from the surface of the sauce. Discard the bouquet garni and bring the sauce to a boil over high heat. Cook, stirring often, until reduced by half, 15 to 20 minutes. During the last 5 minutes, add the reserved prunes and apricots. Taste and season the sauce with salt and pepper. Return the duck to the sauce and simmer over low heat until reheated, about 3 minutes.

7. To serve, place the noodles on a large, deep platter. Arrange the duck over the noodles. Spoon the vegetables, fruit, and sauce over all.

NOTE: To make each bouquet garni, tie 3 small celery ribs, 8 sprigs of fresh parsley, 6 sprigs of thyme, and 1 dried bay leaf into a bundle with kitchen twine.

Lemon Veal Shanks with Dried Artichokes

If you have any leftovers, take all the meat off the bones and freeze it to turn into the Veal Pasta Sauce on page 209.

Makes 6 servings

$^{1}/_{2}$ cup dried artichokes (see Note)

1 cup boiling water

4 tablespoons olive oil, plus more as
    needed

4 medium leeks, white and pale green
    parts, well washed, dried, and cut
    into 1-inch lengths

6 garlic cloves, coarsely chopped

6 veal shanks, cut crosswise into 2-inch
    lengths as for osso buco (3 to
    4 pounds)

$^{1}/_{2}$ cup all-purpose flour

1 cup dry sherry

4 large white mushrooms, sliced

4 tablespoons fresh lemon juice

1 tablespoon chopped fresh rosemary

Salt and freshly ground black pepper, to
    taste

$1^{1}/_{2}$ cups bowtie pasta

1. In a small bowl, cover the dried artichokes with the boiling water and set aside until the artichokes are softened, 20 to 30 minutes.

2. In a Dutch oven, heat the oil over medium heat. Add half the leeks and the garlic. Cook, stirring occasionally, until the leeks soften, about 4 minutes. Transfer the leeks to a plate. Do not wash the pot.

3. In batches without crowding, dredge the shanks in the flour, shaking off the excess, and brown them on all sides, about 10 minutes. (If necessary, add more oil to the Dutch oven to brown the shanks.) Transfer the browned veal to the plate with the leeks. When all the meat is browned, return the meat and leeks to the pot.

4. Add the artichokes with their soaking water and the sherry to the Dutch oven. Bring to a boil. Reduce the heat to very low, cover, and simmer for 1 hour.

5. Add the remaining leeks, the sliced mushrooms, 2 tablespoons of the lemon juice, and the rosemary. Season with salt and pepper. Cook, covered, for 15 minutes. Uncover and continue cooking until the veal is very tender and the sauce thickens, 30 to 45 minutes longer.

6. Meanwhile, bring a large pot of lightly salted water to a boil over high heat. Add the pasta and cook until al dente, about 9 minutes. Drain, transfer to a serving bowl, and toss with the remaining 2 tablespoons of the lemon juice. Serve the veal, spooned over the pasta.

NOTE: Dried artichokes can be found in specialty food shops and some supermarkets. If you wish, substitute ½ cup dried porcini mushrooms or sun-dried tomatoes. Soak the mushrooms or tomatoes in the boiling water. Use the tomatoes and their water as they are, but you must strain the mushroom liquid. Lift the mushrooms out of the soaking liquid and set them aside. Pour the liquid through a cheesecloth, a coffee filter, or a paper towel–lined wire sieve placed over a small bowl. Rinse the soaked mushrooms to remove any clinging grit, and chop them coarsely.

Pheasant and Wild Rice Pie

You can substitute duck breasts or chicken breasts in this recipe. I just happened to be cooking lunch for a local shooting club and had yummy fresh pheasant available. You don't really need anything more with this dish than a green salad—perhaps spinach and endive would be tasty. If you find the mixture drying out as you cook, add a bit of chicken stock or white wine, just enough to keep it moist.

Makes 6 to 8

servings

12 ounces sweet Italian pork sausage, pricked with a fork

6 tablespoons (¾ stick) butter, plus additional for buttering the casserole

1 large onion, cut into quarters and thinly sliced

5 medium celery ribs, cut into ½-inch lengths

3 pounds skinless and boneless pheasant breast, duck breast, or chicken thighs, cut into bite-sized pieces

1 pound white mushrooms, thinly sliced

1 cup chopped fresh flat-leaf parsley

¼ cup red currant jelly

2 cups dry sherry

1½ tablespoons cornstarch dissolved in 2 tablespoons cold water

1 cup raw wild rice, cooked al dente according to package instructions

Freshly ground black pepper, to taste

1 sheet frozen puff pastry, thawed (about 8½ ounces)

1. Place the sausage in a large skillet and add enough water barely to cover. Bring to a simmer over medium heat. Simmer, partially covered, until cooked through, about 15 minutes. Drain, cool, and cut into 1-inch-thick lengths.

2. Preheat the oven to 400°F. Lightly butter a deep oval (or round) casserole large enough to hold all the filling.

3. In the casserole, melt the butter over medium heat. Add the onion and celery and cook until they've softened, about 5 minutes. Add the pheasant and cook, stirring often, until it loses its raw color, about 10 minutes. Add the mushrooms, parsley, and jelly. Cook, stirring often, until the mushrooms give off their liquid, about 5 minutes. Add the sherry, bring to a simmer, and cook for 5 minutes.

4. Ladle a tablespoon of juice from the casserole into a small bowl. Add the cornstarch and make a paste. Stir the cornstarch paste into the casserole until well blended, and let the mixture thicken, about 5 minutes. Stir in the wild rice, then the sliced sausage. Season with the pepper. Let simmer for 5 minutes and then turn off the heat to cool for 30 minutes.

5. Place the pastry over the filling, tucking the edges into the casserole like a sheet. (Or cut off any overhanging corners of pastry, and use them to fill in any gaps in the pastry lid.)

6. Bake until the pastry is golden brown and puffy and the filling is simmering, about 30 minutes. Serve immediately.

Shrimp and Asparagus Risotto

For a long time, I tried and tried to make risotto. My sister-in-law makes great risotto and mine never seemed to get soft and creamy without becoming a sticky mass. That was because I tried to avoid stirring all the time. Finally I paid attention to what others had told me: You must add the liquid only as it is absorbed and you must keep stirring. And you must.

This recipe can be altered to fit any mood. You could use scallops or lobster or chicken instead of the shrimp, and fresh artichoke hearts, green beans, or celery root instead of the asparagus. You could eliminate the bacon and sauté the onion in butter or olive oil. You can substitute vegetable broth for the chicken broth or use more wine. Just make sure you keep the liquid levels the same, and make sure that each addition of liquid is absorbed before adding the next cup.

Makes 6 to 8 servings

2 cups water

1 pound asparagus, trimmed, cut into 1-inch lengths

4 cups chicken broth, preferably homemade

6 slices of bacon, cut into 1-inch lengths

1 cup chopped onions

1 pound arborio rice

1 cup dry white wine

1 pound medium shrimp, peeled and deveined

1/4 cup fresh lemon juice

1/2 cup sour cream

1/4 cup chopped fresh chives

1/2 cup freshly grated Parmesan cheese, as needed, to taste

1. In a pot, bring the water, lightly salted, to a boil over high heat. Add the asparagus and cook until crisp-tender, about 2 minutes. Do not overcook. Drain, reserving the cooking liquid. Set the asparagus aside.

2. In a medium saucepan, combine the asparagus cooking liquid and chicken broth and bring to a simmer over medium heat. Reduce the heat to very low and keep at a bare simmer.

3. In a heavy-bottomed, medium saucepan, cook the bacon over medium heat, about 5 minutes. Using a slotted spoon, transfer the bacon to paper towels. Pour off all but 2 tablespoons of the bacon fat. Add the onions and cook until they're softened, about 3 minutes. Add the rice and stir until well coated, about 1 minute. Add the wine. Stir constantly until the rice has almost completely absorbed the wine, about 2 minutes.

4. Ladle about ³/₄ cup of the hot broth into the saucepan and reduce the heat to low. *Stirring almost constantly*, cook until the rice has absorbed the liquid, about 3 minutes, adjusting the heat as necessary so the mixture maintains a gentle boil. Ladle another ³/₄ cup of stock into the pan and stir until the rice has absorbed the liquid. Continue with this procedure until the rice is almost tender, 20 to 30 minutes.

5. Stir in the reserved asparagus along with the shrimp and the lemon juice. Stir for 1 minute. (There may be some broth leftover; if all of the stock is used before the rice is tender, add additional broth or hot water.) Stir in the sour cream and chives and keep stirring until the rice is barely tender and the shrimp are firm and pink, 2 to 4 minutes more. Remove from the heat. Stir in the Parmesan cheese. Serve immediately.

Venison Stew

On winter weekends, I have sometimes prepared lunches at a neighborhood shooting club. I served this venison stew on a freezing cold day with wide egg noodles tossed in a bit of butter, rosemary, and sour cream. If you can find lingonberry jam in the store, add a jar to the meat when you are browning it. It will add crispness as well as another flavor dimension.

Makes 6 to 8 servings

6 tablespoons (¾ stick) butter
4 tablespoons lard
8 garlic cloves, 4 chopped and 4 whole
5 pounds boneless venison stewing meat (shoulder or leg), cut into 1½-inch cubes
Salt and freshly ground black pepper, to taste
½ cup all-purpose flour
One 750 ml bottle hearty dry red wine
1 cup apple cider
½ cup plus 2 tablespoons sweet vermouth

1 pound venison, beef, or veal bones
2 medium onions, chopped
1 tablespoon chopped fresh rosemary
1 tablespoon chopped fresh thyme
1 tablespoon chopped fresh oregano
3 large leeks, white and pale green parts, well washed, dried, and cut crosswise into ½-inch-thick rounds
5 large carrots, cut into 1-inch chunks
3 large parsnips, cut into 1-inch chunks
1 large shallot, chopped
¼ cup applejack or Calvados liqueur

1. In a Dutch oven, melt 2 tablespoons of the butter and the lard over medium heat. Add the *chopped* garlic and cook until fragrant, about 1 minute. Push the garlic to the side of the pot.

2. Season the venison with salt and pepper. In batches without crowding, dredge the venison in ¼ cup of the flour, shaking off the excess. Brown the venison in the Dutch oven, turning it occasionally, until browned on all sides, about 8 minutes. Transfer the venison to a plate as it is browned and set aside.

3. Add the red wine, apple cider, ½ cup of the sweet vermouth, the venison bones, onions, *whole* garlic, rosemary, thyme, and oregano to the pot. Bring to a boil over high heat, skimming off any foam that rises to the surface. Boil, uncovered, until the liquid is reduced by about half, about 30 minutes. Remove and discard the bones.

4. Meanwhile, in a large skillet, melt the remaining 4 tablespoons of the butter over medium heat. Add the leeks and the remaining 2 tablespoons of the sweet vermouth. Cook, uncovered, stirring occasionally, until the leeks are softened, about 10 minutes. After the first 5 minutes, sprinkle with the remaining ¼ cup of flour and stir well. Turn off the heat when the leeks are cooked.

5. Return the venison with any juices that have collected on the plate to the Dutch oven. Stir in the leek mixture. Stir in the carrots, parsnips, and shallot. Bring to a simmer. Reduce the heat to very low and cover tightly. Simmer, stirring occasionally, just until the venison is tender, about 2 hours. Do not overcook, or the venison could dry out. During the last 10 minutes, stir in the applejack. Serve hot.

Early Summer Veal Stew

When the early days of summer have arrived, and corn and tomatoes are coming in—not yet perfect, but so desired—this stew is a wonderful way to get an early fix. If you have fava beans in your market and the energy to shell them, they are a tasty replacement for the corn.

Makes 4 to 6 servings

4 tablespoons (1/2 stick) butter
3 garlic cloves, coarsely chopped
2 pounds boneless stewing veal
Salt and freshly ground black pepper, to taste
2 tablespoons all-purpose flour
1 1/2 cups dry white wine or vermouth
1 1/2 cups veal or vegetable stock, preferably homemade, or water
6 medium carrots, cut into 1/2-inch dice
1 medium onion, chopped

4 medium tomatoes, seeded and cut into 3/4-inch dice
1 cup sour cream or crème fraîche
3 cups fresh corn kernels (cut from about 6 ears)
1/2 cup packed, *torn* sorrel or basil leaves (do not chop the sorrel)
1 teaspoon chopped fresh thyme
1 tablespoon fresh lemon juice
Chopped sorrel or chopped fresh basil for garnish

1. In a Dutch oven, melt the butter over medium heat. Add the garlic and cook until it's fragrant, about 1 minute. Using a slotted spoon, transfer the garlic to a plate and set it aside.

2. Season the veal with salt and pepper and toss it with the flour until coated. In batches without crowding, add the veal to the Dutch oven and cook, turning occasionally, until the veal is browned on all sides, about 10 minutes. Transfer it to the plate with the garlic.

3. Add the wine and bring to a boil, scraping up all of the browned bits on the bottom of the pot. Stir in the stock. Return the veal and garlic to the Dutch oven, and add the carrots, onion, and tomatoes. Bring to a simmer. Reduce the heat to low and cover tightly. Simmer until the veal is almost tender, about 1 1/2 hours. During the last 10 minutes, stir in the sour cream, corn, sorrel or basil. Just before removing the stew from the heat, stir in the lemon juice. Garnish with the chopped sorrel or basil and serve immediately.

10. Good Cheap Stuff

10. Good Cheap Stuff

There have been times (more than I care to admit) when I have probably spent as much money in the grocery store preparing for some grand experimental meal than it would have cost us to eat out at a five-star restaurant. But a shrewd cook does not have to spend a great deal of money to serve a meal that tastes like a million dollars. On the contrary, sometimes a lack of funds forces you to use a little imagination and to explore unfamiliar cuts of meat and fish—which can produce pleasantly surprising results.

That's what happened to me on a recent trip to the fish market, when I looked in my purse and saw that I had left my wallet at home. Happily, I discovered tilapia. I didn't have a lot of choice because I had so little money, and tilapia was by far the least expensive fish in the market. The fishmonger told me it was "a farm-raised fish, originally from Africa." I almost passed on it. I had always thought that "farm-raised" had to mean boring and tasteless. And the low price seemed to indicate that other people thought the same thing. I was wrong. Tilapia, it turns out, has a lovely flavor. It's a slightly sweet fish, white, with a nice texture, and I found that it is quick and easy to cook. No, you will not be eating sushi-quality tuna. But you will be eating something mighty tasty, and that's all that counts!

A lesson to be learned: Just because something is inexpensive or doesn't have "snob appeal," doesn't mean it isn't good. One of my guiding principles is that simple food is always the best food. So-called "peasant food," the simplest of all foods, is as delicious as gourmet food if properly and lovingly prepared. Rice, beans, and pasta—the peasant staples in many countries around the world—can be dressed up with seasonal vegetables and served beautifully. I personally and professionally owe a great deal to one particular peasant dish, the lowly lamb shank. Alison On Dominick Street won much of its initial fame thanks to a braised lamb shank that was truly soul soothing. When my chef Tom Valenti and I were planning our first menu, we tossed ideas back and forth on a daily basis for more than five months. We wanted wonderful, rich-textured food that would be "fine" in the fine dining sense, but also very approachable. One day Tommy said, "What about braised lamb shank?" I thought it was a great idea, embodying the personality I wanted the restaurant to have: rustic, robust, yet sexy. This was back in the late 1980s, and such inexpensive cuts of meat were not in vogue (or considered sexy). I wanted our food to be influenced by the "peasant food" of the southwest regions of France. Tommy's description of a lamb shank prepared with white bean puree sounded perfect.

Strangely enough, Tommy kept having second thoughts. He pointed out that both of us had always been associated with fine dining, and said he wasn't sure we should be doing lamb shank instead of a fancier and more traditional dish like a rack of lamb. But I knew we should be doing the braised lamb shank. The more Tommy questioned the dish, the more I was sure. Finally, I said that we had to have it. He could do anything else he wanted, but his lamb shank was so good, I didn't care that it wasn't "fine." It was homey and gutsy and wonderfully delicious. That was the kind of food I wanted, and that was that. And, thankfully, he finally agreed.

That braised lamb shank became Alison On Dominick Street's signature dish. Customers loved it so much and ordered it so frequently that we couldn't take it off the menu even in the heat of summer. After Tommy moved on to Cascabel, we would get calls asking, "Do you still have the lamb shank?" We did. A year later we replaced it with beef shin, which also received a wonderful reception. And like the lamb shank, it's an inexpensive cut of meat. We have since, on and off, brought back the lamb shank. Ten years later, customers still ask for it.

The less expensive cuts of meat such as lamb shanks, beef shin, or veal shoulder, that are cooked on the bone are very flavorful. But you have to remember that they require long, slow cooking times. They're well worth the wait. These "peasant foods" produce meals so rich you'll just want to keep on eating—and isn't that really what cooking is all about?

Tilapia with Shrimp and Tangerine Sauce

This dish is great served with wild rice and a little of the tangerine juice squeezed into the rice. Because there was no green in the dish, I found some fat California artichokes and we started with steamed artichokes.

Makes 4 servings

4 tablespoons (½ stick) butter
2 medium leeks, white and pale green parts, well washed, dried, and sliced into thin rounds
2 medium celery ribs, thinly sliced
1 garlic clove, minced
8 ounces small shrimp, peeled and deveined

¼ cup fresh tangerine juice (2 tangerines)
3 tablespoons chopped shallot
Salt and freshly ground black pepper, to taste
1½ pounds tilapia fillets, cut into 4 portions

1. In a large skillet, melt the butter over medium-low heat. Add the leeks, celery, and garlic. Cook, stirring often, until they're tender, about 10 minutes. Add the shrimp, tangerine juice, and shallot. Cook, stirring occasionally, until the shrimp are pink and firm, about 2 minutes. Season with salt and pepper. Using a slotted spoon, transfer the mixture to a platter and cover with aluminum foil to keep warm.

2. Add the tilapia to the skillet. Cook, turning once, until the fillets are opaque when flaked in the center, about 5 minutes total. Arrange the fillets on top of the shrimp mixture, and serve immediately.

Braised Lamb Shanks

Here is the recipe that put Alison On Dominick Street on the map. It has been printed in various periodicals through the years, but I'm including it for all of you who didn't clip it. All my thanks to Tom Valenti.

Makes 6 servings

10 lamb shanks (you'll have leftovers if you're lucky)

Salt and freshly ground black pepper, to taste

$\frac{1}{2}$ cup olive oil

5 cloves garlic, crushed

1 large onion, diced

$\frac{1}{2}$ bunch celery, cut in medium slices

2 carrots, cut in medium slices

3 cups red wine

2 bay leaves

6 anchovy fillets

2 cups veal stock

Two 32-ounce cans Italian plum tomatoes, strained and crushed

20 black or green peppercorns

5 cups White Bean Puree (recipe follows)

1. Preheat the oven to 325°F. Season the shanks with salt and pepper. In a large sauté pan or a heavy-bottomed casserole, heat the olive oil. Add the shanks in batches and brown them well on all sides, 15 to 20 minutes. Transfer the shanks to a roasting pan as they brown and set them aside.

2. Put the garlic, onion, celery, and carrots in the sauté pan, and cook for 30 seconds, being careful not to burn any particles that have stuck to the pan. Pour half the wine into the pan and scrape up any ground bits from the bottom. Add the contents of the pan and the remaining ingredients (except the bean puree) to the roasting pan with the shanks.

3. Put the roasting pan on a burner and bring the contents to a simmer. (The shanks should be almost covered with liquid. If necessary, add some water.) Cover the pan with aluminum foil, transfer it to the preheated oven, and cook them until the meat is very tender, about 2½ hours. Remove the shanks from the liquid and keep them warm. Strain the liquid, transfer it to a saucepan, bring to a boil, and reduce for 5 to 10 minutes, until it has the consistency of a good maple syrup.

4. Serve the shanks with the sauce on top of white bean puree.

White Bean Puree

2 pounds Great Northern beans

2 bay leaves

4 garlic cloves, 3 crushed and 1 finely minced

3 to 4 sprigs fresh thyme (or a pinch dried)

1 cup white wine

6 cups canned chicken stock

Salt and freshly ground black pepper, to taste

1 cup olive oil

1 to 2 tablespoons butter, as needed

1. In a pot, soak the beans for several hours, preferably overnight, changing the water 3 or 4 times. Drain.

2. Put all the ingredients except the minced garlic, olive oil, and butter in a large saucepan and bring to a simmer. Cook, uncovered, until the beans are very tender, about 1 hour and 40 minutes, adding a little more chicken stock or water if the liquid is absorbed before the beans are tender.

3. Puree the beans in a food processor, adding the olive oil slowly and the minced garlic to taste. If the puree seems too thick, fold in a tablespoon or two of butter.

Summery Rump Roast with Roasted Red Peppers and New Potatoes

Makes 6 to 8

servings

The last method of cooking most people think about in the summer is stewing or braising, but this recipe, served outdoors on a cool summer night with a loaf of peasant bread, will bring a smile to most faces.

One 3½-pound rump roast, or 3 pounds
    chuck or round steak
Salt and freshly ground black pepper, to
    taste
6 large ripe tomatoes, chopped
1 large onion, thinly sliced
1½ cups fresh corn kernels (cut from
    3 large ears of corn)
1 cup chopped fresh basil
3 garlic cloves, chopped
2 tablespoons chopped fresh thyme,
    plus more for garnish

⅔ cup fresh grapefruit juice
One 750 ml bottle dry white or red
    wine, or as needed
24 small red or white new potatoes,
    well scrubbed but unpeeled (about
    2 pounds)
3 medium red bell peppers, seeded
    and cut lengthwise into 1-inch-
    wide strips
¼ cup olive oil

    1. Using a sharp, thin-bladed knife, cut the roast crosswise into 6 to 8 thick "steaks." You can have the butcher do this for you, if you prefer. Season with salt and pepper and set aside.

    2. In a large bowl, combine the tomatoes, onion, corn, basil, and garlic. Spoon one third of the mixture into a Dutch oven. Top with half the beef. Sprinkle with 1 tablespoon of the thyme. Spoon half of the remaining tomato

mixture over the top, then layer in the remaining beef, and sprinkle with the remaining 1 tablespoon of thyme. Top with the remaining tomatoes. Pour in the grapefruit juice and enough wine barely to cover the meat. (If you run out of wine, use water or beef broth.)

3. Bring to a simmer over medium heat and cover tightly. Reduce the heat to very low. Cook, stirring occasionally, until the meat is very tender, 3 to 3½ hours.

4. About 1 hour before serving, preheat the oven to 450°F. Place the potatoes and red pepper strips in a roasting pan and toss with the oil. Season with salt and pepper. Roast, stirring occasionally, until the potatoes are tender, 35 to 45 minutes.

5. To serve, skim any fat from the surface of the braised meat sauce. In individual soup bowls, place a piece of meat, then a serving of potatoes and red peppers, then spoon the meat juices over all. Serve immediately.

Flank Steak with Mushrooms and Balsamic Vinegar

I have often served this on toast points. Another good accompaniment is Fried Pota-toes, page 189.

Makes 4 to 6 servings

One 2-pound flank steak
1 large garlic clove, peeled
1 tablespoon olive oil
Freshly ground black pepper, to taste
3 tablespoons butter
6 ounces mushrooms, thinly sliced

2 tablespoons high-quality balsamic
  vinegar
1 cup dry sherry
1 tablespoon Worcestershire sauce
4 scallions, trimmed and sliced
  crosswise into $\frac{1}{4}$-inch-thick pieces

1. Position a rack about 6 inches from the heat source and preheat the broiler. Rub the steak all over with the garlic clove. Finely chop the garlic and set it aside. Brush the steak with the olive oil and season it generously with pepper.

2. Broil the steak, turning it once, until medium-rare, about 10 minutes total. Let stand for 3 minutes before slicing.

3. Meanwhile, in a large skillet, melt the butter over medium heat. Add the chopped garlic and cook until it's softened, about 2 minutes. Add the mushrooms and stir well. Stir in the vinegar. Cook until the mushrooms give off their liquid, about 5 minutes. Add the sherry and Worcestershire sauce and bring to a simmer. Cook until the mushrooms are tender, about 2 minutes.

4. To serve, using a sharp, thin-bladed knife held at a 45° angle, cut the steak into thin slices. Serve the sliced steak with the mushroom sauce spooned over it. Garnish with the sliced scallions.

Fried Catfish in Cornmeal

For a quick dinner, serve this catfish with packaged red beans and rice or Spanish rice mix. You can find these at any supermarket.

2 large eggs
$1/4$ cup milk
$1/2$ cup yellow cornmeal
$1/4$ cup all-purpose flour
1 teaspoon ground red pepper
  (cayenne)

$1/4$ teaspoon kosher or sea salt
$1/2$ cup peanut or vegetable oil
2 pounds catfish fillets, cut into serving
  portions

Makes 4 to 6

servings

1. In a shallow dish, beat the eggs with the milk. In another shallow dish, combine the cornmeal, flour, red pepper, and salt.

2. In a large skillet, heat the oil over medium heat until very hot, but not smoking. Dip the fish in the egg mixture, then turn it in the cornmeal mixture to coat both sides. Cook in the oil until the underside is golden, about 2 minutes. Turn carefully and cook the other side, about 2 more minutes. Serve hot.

11. Saucettes and Sidekicks

11. Saucettes and Sidekicks

I used to hate making sauces and side dishes (gravies and dressings included) because they seemed too complicated. Sauces that professionals make require straining, and heating to certain temperatures for each layer upon layer. Side dishes just seemed like extra preparation. The hassle factor and the intimidation factor were so great, I never really tried to make my own sauces from scratch, and as for side dishes—well that's why I like to make everything in one pot!

I finally gave in to learning about sauces after serving enough meals where an element seemed to be missing. Ignoring my library of cookbooks, I started my own independent sauce-making experiments by thinking long and hard about what it was I was trying to create. I'd read that sauces were originally used to disguise foods that were going bad in the days before refrigerators were invented. Most of those thick, rich French sauces were the true highlight of a particular dish. But that was not what I wanted in a sauce. As far as I'm concerned, a sauce should complement the meal, not disguise or overwhelm it. The sauce should be the thread in the quilt of a particular dish, helping to meld the flavors and adding texture. There is no reason that a sauce has to be a hard thing to make, if you keep that in mind when you prepare it.

In the summer months, there is nothing better than what I call a "raw sauce." My inspiration for my first raw sauce came one very hot night when we were grilling a butterflied leg of lamb. You don't really need to have a sauce with a lamb that's been marinated and grilled, because its own juices are usually enough. But as the sun was setting and I was getting ready, I realized I had forgotten to grill the peppers that I'd planned to use as a garnish for the lamb. Not

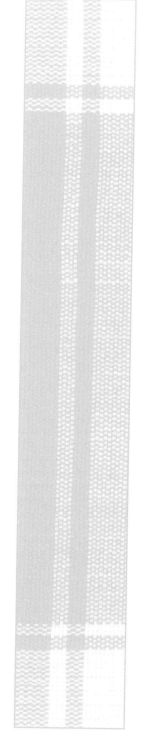

wanting to waste them, I threw the peppers in the Cuisinart. They pureed into a perfect chunky sauce. I decided to add a bit of onion, which I would never ordinarily chop in a food processor because the layers turn into a watery mush. The onion provided a perfect zing. Now I was truly inspired. I decided to go Mediterranean and threw in a few olives and a bit of garlic. Then I added a little salt and ground pepper and a squeeze of lemon, and, presto, I had a wonderful room-temperature sauce.

I have used pureed peppers as a base for my raw sauces many times since that breakthrough night. I've also added fruits and made sweeter versions for pork, and a hot pepper for beef. The point is, once I overcame my aversion to sauce-making, I discovered the fundamental ingredients for preparing a very simple sauce with almost unlimited possibilities and variations.

I take the same approach to salad dressings. While I was living in L.A., I was dating a man who made the most wonderful Dijon dressing. I remember the evening when he taught me to prepare it. First, you make a paste with the mustard and the vinegar. Then you add oil to get the consistency you want. Then you finish it off with some salt and pepper, and maybe some garlic, and you have dressing.

To this day I have followed the same basic Dijon dressing method. Of course, I'll change the seasonings, use different flavored mustards, and experiment with different vinegars. But the nice thing is, it always works, and it always tastes good with just a basic vinegar and a decent Dijon mustard. I have also used this Dijon dressing-base for warm sauces, replacing the oil with melted butter, using wine instead of vinegar, and/or substituting horseradish cream for the Dijon. Looking back on it, I am amazed that such a wealth of ideas could come from one very simple dressing. But then again, that's what creative cooking is really all about.

Gravy is another matter. I've watched in awe over the years as the chefs in my restaurants made silky-smooth brown sauces. Again, I hesitated to put in the work to learn how to make them. Then, one day, I was cooking a roast at my parents' house, and my father exclaimed, "What—no gravy?" Given that paternal reproof, I realized that I had to make gravy, or at least give it a darn good try. Although I had little or no experience making gravy, I knew that you had to add flour to the pan drippings to thicken it. I put the roasting pan on the stove top, turned up the heat, and added a couple of tablespoons of flour. I ended up with little clumps floating all over the place, so I took out the whisk and whisked hard. That just turned those little clumps into little lumps. Frustrated but determined—and not wanting to hear from my father throughout the meal that there was *no gravy*—I threw the whole mess, the drippings, the juices, and the little clumps, into the food processor. To my amazement and relief, it worked. I had a very nice and somewhat smooth gravy. I added a little sherry to make it smoother still, and I was done—and my father was well pleased. I have since learned to make a paste with the flour and a bit of the juices before adding it to the pan. But both ways work. No, it's not as smooth as the chef would make it, but it tastes great. And at the end of the day, who cares. If you wanted the kind of gravy a professional chef would make, you'd go to a restaurant.

I have also learned how to make a simple but tasty roux. That came about as a matter of necessity when I went through my gumbo and fish stew phase, because a true gumbo has to be made with roux and okra. When you get down to it, a roux is simply a combination of flour and butter, or another fat in the case of a darker roux. It needs attention so it doesn't burn. But basically, you are just slowly browning flour in fat until you have the color and intensity you want. When added to a stew, sauce, or soup, the roux will thicken it, and make a smooth consistency. I now make a roux almost any time I want to thicken a sauce or enrich its taste. And if the roux happens to burn, you can always throw it out and start over again, because it doesn't take a lot of time.

The hassle factor is really nonexistent if you follow a few basic principles. Most anything can be put in a food processor or blender. A cooked sauce can be strained if it's too thick, or you can add a roux if it's not thick enough. For raw sauces, adding in a bit of oil will make the sauce smoother. You do not have to be a restaurant chef to make very tasty sauces, gravies, and salad dressings.

As for side dishes, my question is, "How do you choose?" The answer is, "It depends." What is the main course—is it light? Do you have enough or do you need to supplement it with a heavier side dish. Think about what tastes good with what. Ultimately, it's all going to be on the same plate and should taste good if someone were to mush it all together.

You can always lightly steam vegetables and call it a day. I don't use a steamer, for no good reason except that I lent mine to someone and I never replaced it. I simply put an inch or two of water on the bottom of the pot, put the vegetables in, and let them steam with a cover on, turning them once so the bottom vegetables don't become boiled vegetables. I also look to the season. Again, summer is easy with so many fresh vegetables available. In the fall you have squash and root vegetables. In the depths of winter you can turn to pasta. As spring comes around you can find peas and artichokes. These days you can find many vegetables, such as asparagus, year round (sometimes for a price).

Be adventurous. Beyond steaming, you can sauté, roast, fry, make puddings and pilafs. I serve wilted greens a lot because they are so, so simple and so, so good. Experiment with small-sized pasta such as orzo.

I do believe that whatever one chooses, it should be simple. Your main course is your star. You are just complementing it. If the appetizer is the star's audience warmer, the side dishes and the sauces are his supporting actors.

Tropical Barbecue Sauce

A couple of mangoes, heading toward the other side of ripe, inspired this recipe. I have since made it with peaches and nectarines, and it is always good. Terrific as a marinade/baste for grilled pork ribs (use your favorite—baby backs, spareribs, or country-style ribs), it is also fantastic with pork chops, pork loin roast, or even chicken. But whatever you use it for, please be sure that any of the sauce that has come in contact with raw meat or poultry will be thoroughly cooked, as it can be contaminated by the raw meat. By the way, that doesn't go just for this sauce.

Makes about 4 cups of sauce, enough for 5 pounds of meat or chicken

8 small ripe beefsteak tomatoes

2 ripe mangoes, pitted, peeled, and chopped

1 medium green bell pepper, seeded and coarsely chopped

1 medium grapefruit, peeled, seeds removed

1 cup fresh orange juice

$^1\!/_2$ cup red wine vinegar

$^1\!/_3$ cup fresh lemon juice

$^1\!/_2$ cup chopped fresh flat-leaf parsley

1 tablespoon Dijon mustard

4 garlic cloves, chopped

1 cup olive oil

Salt and freshly ground black pepper, to taste

1. In a food processor fitted with the metal blade, process all of the ingredients except the salt and pepper until thoroughly pureed, about 1 minute. Season with salt and pepper.

2. Transfer to any non-aluminum bowl, cover, and refrigerate until ready to use.

Clementine Dressing

In the late fall, I am always tempted to purchase those little crates of Clementines that begin to appear, so I do. There are always so many in the crate that I have developed a recipe to use them up. This recipe works best on arugula with a bit of red onion. Toasted almond slivers thrown on top add a flavorful dimension and a bit of crunch.

Makes about 1½ cups

4 Clementines, peeled, with any white pith carefully removed (see Note)
¼ cup white wine vinegar
1 garlic clove, chopped

¾ cup extra-virgin olive oil
Salt and freshly ground black pepper, to taste

In a food processor fitted with the metal blade, pulse the Clementines, vinegar, and garlic until chopped. With the machine running, gradually add the oil through the feed tube. Season with the salt and pepper. Use immediately or on the day it is made.

NOTE: If desired, substitute 2 regular or blood oranges for the Clementines.

Fresh Mint Sauce

Coming from a family where lamb was never served without mint sauce, I learned to make my own. You can find mint sauce in most markets, but why spend your hard-earned dollars when this is so easy to make? Serve this sauce with any lamb dish. I also put it in the juice for Lamb Shepherd's Pie (page 148).

4 tablespoons chopped fresh mint,   2 teaspoons sugar
½ cup rice vinegar

Makes ½ cup

In a small bowl, combine all the ingredients well. Serve immediately or store in the refrigerator until ready to use.

Creamed Baby Spinach with Leeks

This is an easy match for any grilled steak or beef roast, and it's also great with salmon.

Makes 4 servings

½ cup (1 stick) unsalted butter

8 small leeks, white and pale green parts, well washed, dried, and cut into ½-inch-thick rounds

1 medium red onion, thinly sliced

8 cups packed baby spinach leaves; or 10 cups young spinach leaves, tough stems removed, well rinsed but not dried

1 cup half and half or light cream

¼ teaspoon freshly grated nutmeg

Salt and freshly ground black pepper, to taste

1. In a large, heavy-bottomed saucepan, melt the butter over medium-low heat. Add the leeks and onion. Cover and cook, stirring occasionally, until the vegetables are very soft, about 20 minutes.

2. Add the spinach and cover. Do not stir. Cook until the spinach is damp from the steam, 3 to 5 minutes.

3. Add the half and half. Increase the heat to medium-high and cook until the liquid reduces by about half, 3 to 5 minutes. Season with the nutmeg, salt, and pepper.

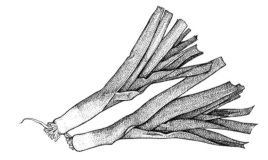

Sauerkraut with Horseradish and Lingonberry Jam

I created this recipe for the shooting club where I used to work. I was at a loss for something to serve with venison chops. The wonderful Willie Salm, the owner of the club, is German, so I started playing with sauerkraut—and this is the result. I have since served this dish with pork and beef, and it has always proved to be an unusual and surprisingly tasty treat.

Makes 8 servings

4 tablespoons (½ stick) butter

1 large onion, thinly sliced

3 medium leeks, white and light green parts only, well washed, dried, and sliced into ½-inch rounds

4 medium shallots, thinly sliced

1 pound sauerkraut, drained and rinsed

One 10-ounce jar lingonberry jam

2 tablespoons horseradish cream, or use

2 tablespoons heavy cream and 1 teaspoon freshly grated or prepared horseradish

1 cup (4 ounces) dried cherries (optional)

1 tablespoon chopped fresh rosemary (optional)

1 cup sour cream

1. In a large saucepan, heat the butter over medium heat until foamy. Add the onion, leeks, and shallots. Cook, stirring occasionally, until very tender, about 15 minutes.

2. Add the sauerkraut and mix well. Stir in the jam and horseradish cream, along with the dried cherries and rosemary, if using them. Bring the mixture to a simmer. Reduce the heat to low and simmer for 15 minutes. Just before serving, stir in the sour cream and heat through without boiling. Serve warm.

Orzo with Ricotta

You can do a lot with this recipe. Add 1 cup chopped ripe tomatoes, or ½ cup pitted chopped olives, or any herb that complements the main course.

2 cups orzo (rice-shaped) pasta
¼ cup olive oil
2 garlic cloves, chopped
2 tablespoons chopped fresh basil or
    rosemary (optional)

1 cup ricotta cheese, preferably fresh
Salt and freshly ground black pepper,
    to taste

Makes 4 to 6

servings

1. Bring a large pot of lightly salted water to a boil over high heat. Add the orzo and cook, stirring occasionally, until al dente, about 9 minutes. Drain well.

2. In a large skillet, heat the oil and garlic (and basil, if using it) over medium heat, stirring occasionally, until the garlic is tender but not browned, about 3 minutes.

3. Add the orzo and mix well. Stir in the ricotta, then season with the salt and pepper. Serve hot.

Fried Potatoes (Hash Browns)

Simple, simple, simple. Pan-fried potatoes go with so many dishes, it's good to have a recipe handy.

¹/₄ cup peanut oil
¹/₂ large onion, chopped
4 medium all-purpose potatoes, cut into
   ¹/₂-inch cubes

Kosher or sea salt and freshly ground
   black pepper, to taste

Makes 4 servings

1. In a large skillet, heat the oil over medium-high heat until very hot but not smoking. Add the onion, reduce the heat to medium, and cook until it's softened, about 1 minute.

2. Add the potatoes and mix well. Cook, turning occasionally, until the potatoes are browned on all sides and cooked through, 15 to 20 minutes. Season with salt and pepper. Serve immediately.

Creamy Eggplant with Rosemary

If you have any of this left over, puree it in the food processor for a great pasta sauce base. This dish sits proudly next to any roast lamb or beef.

Makes 6 to 8 servings

1 cup olive oil, approximately

3 garlic cloves, finely chopped

3 leeks, white and light green parts only, well washed, dried, and cut into $1/2$-inch-thick rounds; or 1 cup slivered onions

2 medium eggplant, cut into $3/4$-inch-thick rounds

2 medium ripe tomatoes, cut into $1/2$-inch-thick rounds

Salt and freshly ground black pepper, to taste

1 cup sour cream

1 teaspoon chopped fresh rosemary

1. In a large skillet or flameproof casserole, heat 1 tablespoon of the oil over medium heat. Add the garlic and cook until it's soft, about 2 minutes. Add 1 more tablespoon of the oil, and the leeks. Cook, stirring often, until the leeks are tender, about 5 minutes. Scrape the vegetables into a bowl and set aside.

2. In batches, using about 2 tablespoons of oil for each batch, cook the eggplant over medium-high heat, turning once, until it's browned on both sides, about 4 minutes per batch. (The eggplant absorbs quite a bit of oil.) As each batch is done, place it on paper towels to drain.

3. Place half the browned eggplant back in the pan (overlapping the slices to make one layer), then top with half the sliced tomatoes. Spoon the leeks over the tomatoes. Top with the remaining tomatoes, then the remaining eggplant. As you go, season each layer with a little salt and pepper. Spread the sour cream on top, then sprinkle with the rosemary.

4. Cover tightly and place over low heat. Cook, periodically using a turkey baster to baste with the olive oil at the bottom of the skillet that the eggplant releases, until the sour cream and oil "melt" into one, and all is soft and bubbly, about 30 minutes. Serve hot.

Corn Pudding

In the late summer when wonderful fresh corn is abundant, I try to use it as much as possible. Although I adore plain old corn on the cob, it's fun to do something different. Originally I served this with grilled split cornish game hens (which I roast the rest of the year). It is a great accompaniment to anything grilled or roasted—and should you yearn for a taste of summer in January, it can be made successfully with frozen corn.

3 cups fresh corn kernels (cut from
about 6 large ears)
2 cups yellow cornmeal
1 cup sour cream

1 cup low-fat milk
3 large eggs
1 tablespoon honey
1 teaspoon baking powder

Makes 6 to 8

servings

1. Position a rack in the center of the oven and preheat to 350°F.

2. In a medium bowl, mix all of the ingredients well. Spread the mixture into a 2-quart shallow baking dish.

3. Bake until the pudding is puffed and golden brown, about 40 minutes. Serve hot.

Swiss Chard Noodles

Big, fat egg noodles are pure comfort food. Made with a lot of butter, this may not be the healthiest dish, but it certainly tastes of home and hearth. You can serve it with any stew (that doesn't have potatoes in it) or a roast. The addition of Swiss chard adds a lovely flavor and a touch of green—and the truffle oil adds a bit of elegance.

Makes 6 to 8 servings

½ cup (1 stick) butter

1 pound Swiss chard leaves, well rinsed but not dried, thick ribs discarded, and leaves shredded

1 garlic clove, finely chopped

1 pound egg noodles

Salt and freshly ground black pepper, to taste

2 tablespoons truffle oil (optional)

1. In a large skillet, heat the butter over medium heat. Add the Swiss chard and garlic. Cook until the Swiss chard is tender, about 10 minutes. Keep warm.

2. Bring a large pot of lightly salted water to a boil over high heat. Add the egg noodles. Turn the heat down to medium so the water doesn't boil over. Cook until the noodles are tender, about 5 minutes. (Egg noodles don't take very long, so don't overcook them.) Drain.

3. In a serving bowl, toss the noodles with the Swiss chard mixture. Season with the salt and pepper. Drizzle with the truffle oil, if using it. Serve hot.

Wilted Greens in Lemon and Garlic

We grew up having to have something green at suppertime—a habit that has stayed with me as an adult. I find that any greens sautéed in lemon and garlic go with almost any main course. It's tasty, quick—and healthy.

4 tablespoons olive oil
4 garlic cloves, thinly sliced
$1/2$ medium red onion, thinly sliced
(optional)
2 pounds spinach leaves or dandelion
greens, tough stems removed, well
rinsed but not dried

$1/2$ cup fresh lemon juice
Salt and freshly ground black pepper,
to taste

Makes 4 to 6

servings

1. In a large, deep skillet, heat the oil over medium heat. Add the garlic, and the onion, if using it, and cook until the garlic is soft, about 2 minutes. Turn down the heat to medium-low. Stuff all the greens into the skillet, mixing well a couple of times to coat the leaves a bit with the oil. Pour the lemon juice over the greens.

2. Cover and cook until the greens are wilted, 4 to 6 minutes. Season with the salt and pepper. Serve immediately.

VARIATION: Broccoli Rabe in Lemon and Garlic: Substitute 2 pounds broccoli rabe, coarsely chopped, for the greens. Cook as directed until tender, about 15 minutes.

Wild Rice and Corn Pilaf

Serve this dish with any game or poultry and you're sure to be happy. As a variation, I cooled the pilaf down, tossed it with chopped tomatoes, oil, and vinegar, and served it on a bed of arugula for a first-course salad.

Makes 6 servings

3 tablespoons butter
1 medium onion, chopped
2 cups fresh or frozen and thawed
    corn kernels

1 cup raw wild rice, cooked according
    to package instructions
Salt and freshly ground black pepper,
    to taste

1. In a large skillet, melt the butter over medium heat. Add the onion and cook, stirring occasionally, until it's tender, about 5 minutes. Add the corn and cook until heated through, about 2 minutes. Add the cooked rice and sauté, stirring often, until it's hot, about 5 minutes.

2. Season with salt and pepper. Serve hot.

Celery Root and Ricotta Cheese Risotto

I made this risotto to go with Tuscan Stewed Chicken Thighs (page 110). It was pouring outside and going to the store was not an option I cared to entertain. I had a knob of celery root and some leeks and, of course, a tub of fresh ricotta cheese, which I keep on hand for such evenings. And I was very glad—the result made me very happy. It was pure comfort, a grown-up version of cream of celery soup.

1 quart chicken broth

4 tablespoons (½ stick) butter

1½ cups short-grained rice, such as arborio

3 medium leeks, white and pale green parts, well washed, dried, and chopped

1 cup peeled and chopped celery root (celeriac) or celery

1½ cups ricotta cheese

Salt and freshly ground black pepper, to taste

Makes 4 to 6 servings, or more as a side dish

1. In a medium saucepan, bring the broth to a simmer over medium heat. Reduce the heat to very low and keep the broth barely simmering.

2. In a heavy-bottomed, medium saucepan, melt the butter over medium heat. Add the rice and stir until well coated, about 1 minute. Add the leeks and celery root and stir until the leeks wilt, about 1 minute.

3. Ladle about ¾ cup of the hot broth into the saucepan and reduce the heat to low. Stirring almost constantly, cook until the rice has absorbed the liquid, about 3 minutes, adjusting the heat as necessary so the mixture maintains a gentle boil. Ladle another ¾ cup of hot broth into the pan and stir until the rice has absorbed the liquid. Continue with this procedure until the rice is al dente, with a slight "bite" in the center. The entire process will take 20 to 30 minutes; be flexible with your timing. (There may be some broth left over; if all of the broth is used before the rice is tender, add additional broth or hot water.)

4. Stir in the ricotta until heated through, about 1 minute. Season with salt and pepper and serve immediately.

Celery Root and Pecan Stuffing

Makes 12 to 16

servings

Most people think that stuffing is only for Thanksgiving, but it's not. Stuffing is easy to make and can dress up a chicken any night of the week. It's basically dry components mixed with wet components, and using flavors that taste good together. Look at those instant stuffing mixtures—you are just adding liquid. Well, if you take the same amount of dry, which can be bread, or a mixture of rices and bread, or nuts and dried fruits, and mix with liquid—you're going to have a stuffing. If the mixture is too wet and gloppy, add more dry, bit by bit. If it's too dry, add some juice, wine, or sherry. Just think about what you like to eat. If you don't like to eat and you are being forced into making this dinner, then just follow the recipe below.

4 tablespoons (½ stick) butter

6 medium leeks, white and pale green parts, well washed, dried, and cut into 1-inch-long pieces

1 medium celery root, peeled and grated

3 garlic cloves, minced

1 small apple, your favorite kind, peeled, cored, and chopped

½ cup fresh apple cider

5 cups ½-inch, slightly stale, crusty peasant-style bread cubes

1 cup finely chopped pecans

1 teaspoon chopped fresh rosemary

1 teaspoon chopped fresh thyme

¾ cup fresh Clementine or orange juice, approximately

Salt and freshly ground black pepper, to taste

1. In a large skillet, melt the butter over medium heat. Add the leeks, celery root, and garlic. Cook, stirring occasionally, until the leeks are tender, 10 to 15 minutes. Stir in the apple and the cider. Bring to a simmer and cook for 5 minutes.

2. In a large bowl, combine the bread cubes and pecans. Add the cooked vegetables, the rosemary, and the thyme. Add enough of the citrus juice to moisten the stuffing. Season with salt and pepper. Use immediately. Do not overstuff the bird; the stuffing will expand when cooked. Place any leftover stuffing in a buttered casserole and bake it as a side dish.

Chestnuts and Brussels Sprouts in Maple Syrup

Chestnuts and Brussels sprouts are a great autumn duet. Fresh chestnuts are best. If you have to use the vacuum-packed or canned ones, add them to the sprouts only during the last 10 minutes of roasting, or they will be overcooked. You'll probably want to prepare the fresh chestnuts the day before roasting them. And use pure maple syrup, which has a milder, less cloying taste than the artificially flavored, supermarket pancake syrup. You can substitute honey, but use ¼ cup instead of ½ cup and blend ¼ cup of orange or apple juice into the honey.

Makes 8 to 10 servings

1 pound chestnuts, peeled (see Note)
2 cups trimmed Brussels sprouts
½ cup olive oil

½ cup pure maple syrup
Salt and freshly ground black pepper,
    to taste

1. Preheat the oven to 450°F. In a medium bowl, toss the chestnuts and Brussels sprouts with the oil. Spread them in a large roasting pan.

2. Roast, stirring occasionally, for 20 minutes. Stir in the maple syrup. Reduce the oven temperature to 350° and continue to roast until the Brussels sprouts are just tender when pierced with the tip of a knife, about 20 minutes longer. Season with salt and pepper. Serve hot.

NOTE: To peel the chestnuts, preheat the oven to 400°F. Using a small, sharp knife, cut an X into the flat side of each one, cutting through the tough outer skin to the thin inner skin and the flesh beneath it. Spread the chestnuts on a baking sheet. Bake, stirring occasionally, until the skins are curled, about 30 minutes. Wrap the chestnuts in a kitchen towel to keep them warm. Remove the peel and thin inner skin from each chestnut. The chestnuts can be prepared, stored in a Ziploc plastic bag, and refrigerated for up to 2 days.

12. Welcome to

Auntie Pasti Night!

12. Welcome to
Auntie Pasti Night!

Do you ever wonder what to do with all the left-over food that accumulates in your refrigerator? It can be a real problem. If the food is only a day or two old, you feel guilty about throwing it away. But you feel just as guilty, not to mention pretty lazy, if you just toss a bunch of leftovers on a platter and serve them without any special preparation or creative presentation. Ironically, I learned how to solve the leftovers problem with some round-about inspiration and motivation from my husband.

When I first moved back to New York City after giving up my acting career in Los Angeles, I didn't cook very much. I worked in restaurants and they fed me. The hours were so long that on my days off I just slept and ordered Chinese food. This pattern continued while I was putting together Alison On Dominick Street. When I did cook, it was on weekends in the summer when I was visiting my parents, and that usually required cooking for a minimum of eight people. To this day, if I have to cook for two or thirty, it doesn't make a bit of difference—it's just more shopping and more food, and all the merrier. So I really started cooking seriously again when I met Harry and we started dating.

At the time, Harry was living in a one-bedroom bachelor pad in Sag Harbor that was so small I called it "The Mouse House." It had a kitchen with a nice counter, but Harry used the counter as his writing desk, so making dinner was a careful study in how not to mess anything up. After dinner, the leftovers were usually wiped up and thrown out. This wasn't my house, so it was hard for me to save anything; and if I did, it was usually tossed before I got back the next weekend.

As our relationship developed, I began cooking in The Mouse House more and more frequently, and it got a bit frustrating for me to have to wait until Harry put away the manuscript he was working on so I could start the evening meal. Eventually, I said we needed a bigger house, one where my remains weren't wiped clean each week. Although he bought me my very own dresser, put it together, and presented it with a long stemmed rose, as our relationship grew, so did our need for space—rather, *my* need. And it wasn't fair that he had to dismantle his desk every time I was inspired by the colorful produce at the farm stand, or that he had to live in fear that his computer might be rendered useless by a wayward flick of the hand during my cooking experiments in his kitchen/office.

Finally, we decided to start looking for a bigger house, and found the one we live in now. The first time we saw the place, I fell in love with the kitchen. It might not be fancy, but it's a warm country kitchen with a butcher block and room for a kitchen table. When we agreed to buy the house, Harry decided he should marry me. He figured that if we were going to buy a house, we might as well get married. He presented me with chocolate chip cookies and Champagne and a proposal.

When we first moved into our house, I was the happiest person on earth. I was about to get married, and I had a kitchen big enough to cook and eat in. I would cook us dinner most nights, but it was usually just the two of us, and the refrigerator began exploding with leftovers. I had forgotten how to cook for two. I think at least four others could have joined us on any given evening, and I still would have had something left for the next day.

For better or worse, however, Harry doesn't like what he calls "old food," and as far as he's concerned, leftover food is old if it's been in the refrigerator more than an hour or so. Countless times, I pulled the remains of the previous night's yummy meal out of the refrigerator and heard the same wary question coming from over my shoulder.

"Little," my husband would ask, sniffing the leftovers, "are you sure this food is still good?"

"Of course, it's still good, Bigger One," I would reply, adding that it might even be better than it was the previous night if he happened to be sniffing at a piece of braised meat or a pot of stew.

Having offered such reassurances again and again, I thought Harry might start going into the refrigerator to see what was there to make a lunch, but bachelor habits die hard. If it was Wednesday, he certainly wasn't going to miss out on his London broil sandwich from the local deli. And if it was Thursday, he still couldn't believe that the steak I had made on Tuesday would be good—it was *old!* Finally, I decided that I had to take action on the leftovers front once and for all. Too much good food was going to waste, and I was spending too much time and money at the grocery store.

My breakthrough came one sultry summer Sunday afternoon. On Saturday night, I had made a grilled butterflied leg of lamb with grilled vegetables. On Friday night, I had made corn, and I still had two ears in the refrigerator. There was also a foot-long link of my husband's favorite sausage in the freezer. I was determined not to ruin the day by making a trip to the market. Hoards of people enjoying the east end's summer offerings were milling about in town, and shopping wasn't a whole lot of fun under those conditions. I had also been to the store every day, and the vegetable stands were always picked-over on Sundays.

I went to the refrigerator, pulled everything out, and—bingo!—I envisioned a platter of antipasto. We had bread that was on the verge of being stale, which I could brush with olive oil and garlic. I sliced the lamb and sausage, and sautéed them in a pan with olive oil and garlic. I tossed the grilled vegetables with a bit of balsamic vinegar. The kernels of corn came off the cob, and I made a salad with a tomato and a leftover onion half. I found some bits and pieces of cheese, left from dinners the previous week; these I sliced thin. Then I spied a forgotten jar of artichoke hearts, and quickly roasted them. Because Harry likes pasta plain with olive oil, garlic, pepper, and Parmesan cheese, I made that, too. I lined a platter with radicchio and placed everything on it. After adding a sprinkle of olives, dinner was ready. It looked beautiful.

Harry called over from his office and asked what we were having for dinner. I knew better than to tell him we were going to eat leftovers, so I said we were having a sort of antipasti. I don't think he was really listening, because when we sat down to dinner a few minutes later, he looked at the platter and said, "Little, this is beautiful. Which of your Aunties did this recipe come from?"

"Auntie Pasti," I replied with a smile.

Henceforth, Sunday nights became our Auntie Pasti nights, and my husband has happily devoured all the "old food" I have put on his plate.

In the meantime, making wonderful meals out of leftovers has become a challenge I can't resist. When I am cooking more formal types of dinners, I often get more excited about the possibilities offered by the leftovers than I do about the dinner at hand. Chicken potpies with the dark meat left clinging to the carcass. Steak tidbits sautéed in steak sauce and served on toasted bread that has gone a bit dry. Risotto with almost anything stirred in at the end. Soups made from a puree of the previous night's vegetables and a can of stock, finished with a bit of cream. Rice tossed with vinaigrette and left-over duck. Rice pudding for dessert. And on and on.

As my husband has slowly begun to learn, "old food" that is wrapped properly and stored in the refrigerator can still be good food. Unless something smells bad or is covered with slimy green stuff, there is really no reason it can't be turned into something else. With the right presentation and a little imagination, you'll waste not and want not.

Welcome to Auntie Pasti night!

Auntie Pasta Salad

The day I made this salad I used the left-over asparagus from the night before. It was such a success, that I absolutely recommend making fresh asparagus if none is left over. You may want to add a few more capers, or some additional chopped tomatoes, depending on how many are left in the pasta. As a lunch, this salad stands alone. For dinner, I served it with grilled chicken and a white Beaujolais.

2 cups Gemelli with Salted Capers and
 Tomatoes (page 72), approximately
1 ripe large tomato, chopped
10 asparagus spears, cooked, and
 coarsely chopped
2 medium celery ribs, chopped
1/2 cup chopped onion

4 radishes, thinly sliced
2 tablespoons balsamic vinegar
2 tablespoon olive oil or mayonnaise
Salt and freshly ground black pepper,
 to taste
4 hard-cooked eggs, peeled and sliced
 into 1/4-inch-thick rounds

Makes 4 to 6

servings

1. Place the pasta salad in a shallow serving bowl and let it stand at room temperature for 30 minutes.

2. In a medium bowl, toss the vegetables with the vinegar and oil. Stir into the pasta. Season with salt and pepper to taste.

3. Arrange the sliced eggs over the top. Serve immediately.

Savory Bread Pudding

This recipe is as yummy as its ingredients. After you have looked over what's around to cook with, try to make the best flavor combinations possible.

The first time I had this idea, I had herbs and vegetables that weren't going to last, and we were going out of town. We had half a loaf of really good bread that was a little hard, and beets and goat cheese—it was phenomenal. That time I used some wilted dill I had on hand, and walnuts as well. Celery root and leeks are a mellow combination that goes well with almost anything. I have used cream cheese instead of the sour cream. Somehow, as long as I treat the eggs with respect, it always comes out just fine.

Makes 8 servings

Make sure your vegetables are almost cooked through before you add them to the pudding. If you don't want to sauté them, or you are using root vegetables that will take too long, just steam them instead.

I have added Canadian bacon or bits of sausage to this and made it almost a complete meal.

4 tablespoons (¹/₂ stick) butter

2 medium leeks, white parts only, well washed, dried, and thinly sliced (1 cup)

1 cup peeled celery root or celery ribs, cut into ¹/₂-inch dice

1 tablespoon chopped fresh herbs, such as thyme or oregano

1 cup packed chopped spinach, arugula, or basil leaves

Salt and freshly ground black pepper, to taste

1¹/₂ cups milk

1 cup heavy cream

¹/₄ cup dry vermouth or white wine

6 large egg yolks plus 2 large eggs

¹/₂ cup sour cream

6 cups slightly stale ¹/₂-inch bread cubes—walnut, olive, semolina, pumpernickel, or any bread that isn't sweet

3 ripe medium tomatoes, sliced into ¹/₂-inch-thick rounds, then cut in half

¹/₂ cup freshly shredded cheese, whatever you like

1. Preheat the oven to 325°F. Lightly butter a 2½-quart baking dish.

2. In a large skillet, melt the butter over medium heat. Add the leeks, celery, and thyme or oregano. Cook, stirring often, until the celery is tender, about 5 minutes. Add the spinach and cook until it's wilted, about 3 minutes. Season generously with the salt and pepper.

3. In a medium saucepan, heat the milk, cream, and vermouth over medium heat just until it comes to a boil. In a medium bowl, whisk the egg yolks, eggs, and sour cream until well combined. Gradually whisk in the hot milk mixture. Strain into another bowl.

4. Spread one third of the bread cubes in the prepared dish. Cover with half the leek mixture. Top with another third of the bread, then the remaining vegetables, and the remaining bread. Arrange overlapping tomato slices over the top, then sprinkle with the cheese. Pour the egg-and-milk mixture over all. Run a knife around the inside of the dish to help the egg mixture run under the bread.

5. Place the baking dish in a larger roasting pan. Place in the oven. Pour enough hot water into the larger pan to come halfway up the sides of the baking dish. Bake until a knife inserted in the center of the pudding comes out clean, about 1 hour. Let the pudding stand for 5 minutes before serving.

VARIATION: Beet and Chèvre Bread Pudding: Use walnut bread or sprinkle the bread cubes in the baking dish with ½ cup chopped walnuts. Eliminate the tomatoes. Stir 3 or 4 medium beets, cooked, peeled and cut into ¼-inch-thick rounds, into the cooked leek mixture. Substitute 1 cup crumbled goat cheese (chèvre) for the grated cheese.

My Macaroni and Cheese

I love macaroni and cheese. Nobody seems to be making it anymore. I rediscovered it when I was cleaning out the refrigerator and found several cheese ends including a couple of slices of mozzarella that my husband wasn't about to touch, and I didn't want to throw away. Sometimes I cook up some bacon or Canadian ham and throw it in too. I highly recommend it.

Makes 4 to 6

servings

12 ounces elbow macaroni (3 cups)

1 cup milk, at room temperature

½ cup fromage frais, fromage blanc, or sour cream; or 4 ounces cream cheese

¼ cup dry vermouth or white wine

2 large eggs

1½ cups shredded cheese (any cheese that is in the house—use up all those ends that no one is going to eat)

½ cup crushed cheese pastry sticks (my favorite for the topping) or cracker crumbs

2 tablespoons butter

1. Preheat the oven to 350°F. Lightly butter a 2-quart baking dish. I use an oval copper baking dish, which gives a stately presentation.

2. Over high heat, bring a large pot of lightly salted water to a boil. Add the macaroni and cook until barely tender, about 7 minutes. Do not overcook. Drain well. Return to the empty pot.

3. Meanwhile, heat the milk, fromage frais, and vermouth over low heat, stirring often, until very hot but not simmering, about 5 minutes. In a small bowl, whisk the eggs. Gradually whisk the hot milk mixture into the eggs. Return the milk mixture to the saucepan. Cook over low heat, stirring constantly, until lightly thickened, but do not boil. Stir in three quarters of the shredded cheese. Stir the milk and cheese mixture into the macaroni.

4. Transfer the macaroni to the prepared baking dish. Sprinkle with the remaining cheese and the crumbs. Dot with the butter. Bake until bubbling, about 35 minutes. Serve hot.

Veal Pasta Sauce

We were lucky enough to have some leftovers from our veal shank supper, as I had made enough for four and there were two of us. I was very happy to have the shanks in the freezer, but I found when I reheated them that the meat came off the bones. So I turned them into pasta sauce, and we had a magnificent meal. You can follow the same guidelines using any leftover meat stew.

1 cup leftover Lemon Veal Shanks
    with Dried Artichokes (page 156),
    or any beef, pork, lamb, or veal stew
4 ripe large tomatoes, seeded and
    chopped; or use 3 cups drained
    chopped canned tomatoes

2 cups dry white wine
$1/2$ cup sour cream
1 tablespoon chopped fresh rosemary
1 pound ziti or rigatoni

Makes 4 to 6

servings

1. In a large saucepan, bring the leftover veal stew, tomatoes, and wine to a simmer over medium heat. Reduce the heat to low. Simmer until the sauce is thickened, about 45 minutes.

2. Stir in the sour cream and rosemary and cook for 5 minutes more. Stir well to break up the meat into small chunks.

3. Meanwhile, in a large pot of lightly salted water over high heat, cook the pasta until al dente, about 9 minutes. Drain well and return to the pot. Add the veal sauce and mix well. Transfer to a warmed serving bowl and serve immediately.

Second Day Soup

A soup, a loaf of bread, a big green salad, and a hunk of cheese can make the perfect Sunday supper. Leftovers can be turned into a wonderful soup easily and quickly with the help of a blender or food processor. The instructions below should be considered more a guideline than a recipe. You can use any vegetables or beans, any stock, and add meat or not, depending on what is in the refrigerator. The addition of egg noodles or pasta or rice provide yet another texture. I like to use chicken stock most of the time, although I find with root vegetables such as beets, a beef stock makes a richer and more satisfying soup. On a hot summer day, use those left-over cucumbers or carrots with buttermilk and dill to make a refreshing cold soup. (If making chilled soup, refrigerate it for at least 1¹/₂ hours before serving.) Hot or cold—let your imagination run free, pick up your spoon, and enjoy!

Makes 6 to 8

servings

2 tablespoons butter

2 tablespoons all-purpose flour

1 medium onion, chopped

2 garlic cloves, chopped (optional)

2¹/₂ to 3 cups coarsely chopped cooked vegetables, such as asparagus, broccoli, or carrots

4 cups chicken broth, or 2 cups chicken broth and 2 cups milk or half and half

2 cups bite-sized cooked meat or chicken (optional)

2 tablespoons chopped fresh herbs— your favorite to match the vegetable

A pinch of freshly grated nutmeg (optional)

Salt and freshly ground black pepper, to taste

Sour cream or chopped pimentos, for garnish (optional)

1. In a large pot, melt the butter over medium-low heat. Add the flour and cook without browning for 2 minutes. Add the onion (and garlic, if using it) and cook until the onion softens, about 3 minutes.

2. Combine the onion mixture and the vegetables in a food processor or blender. (If using a blender, you may have to work in batches.) You may want to

save some vegetables for garnish. Process the vegetables, adding broth as needed to help you reach the desired consistency, from creamy smooth to chunky. If you want a very smooth soup, add the maximum amount of stock and pass the puree through a fine mesh sieve.

3. Return the soup to the pot and stir in any remaining broth (and the meat, if using). Stir in the herbs and optional nutmeg. Bring to a simmer over medium-low heat, stirring almost constantly. Reduce the heat to low and simmer, stirring often to avoid scorching, until very hot and lightly thickened, about 15 minutes. Season with salt and pepper.

4. Serve hot, topped with a dollop of sour cream, a sprinkling of pimento, or additional chopped herbs.

VARIATIONS: Bean Soup: Substitute $2\frac{1}{2}$ to 3 cups cooked beans (just about any kind—black, cannellini, garbanzo, or pinto) for the cooked vegetables. Garnish each serving with 1 tablespoon dry sherry.

Second Day Soup with Rice or Noodles: Stir 1 cup cooked rice or noodles into the soup during the last 5 minutes of simmering.

Warm Pork Loin Salad

I served this dish with a mushroom risotto made with a couple of mushrooms and leeks that were on their last legs. It made a perfect Sunday supper. If you have left-over beef, follow the same instructions, but add a little horseradish to the dressing. For a heartier salad, add some sliced boiled or roasted potatoes.

Serves 4 to 6

1 head Belgian endive, leaves separated

4 large tomatoes, thinly sliced

1 medium radicchio, cored and coarsely chopped

2 tablespoons olive oil

1 tablespoon coarsely cracked black pepper (crush whole peppercorns in a mortar or under a heavy skillet or keep coarse-ground pepper in your pantry)

1 to 1 1/2 pounds left-over sliced pork loin or any sliced roast meat

1/4 cup high-quality balsamic vinegar

1/2 cup fresh orange juice

2 tablespoons grainy mustard

1/2 cup sour cream

1. Divide the endive leaves among individual plates (or arrange them on a large platter). Top with equal amounts of the sliced tomatoes, then the radicchio.

2. In a large skillet, heat the oil and 1 1/2 teaspoons of the pepper over medium heat. In batches, add the sliced meat and cook just until heated through, about 1 minute on each side. Arrange over the salad(s).

3. Stir the balsamic vinegar into the skillet. Whisk in the orange juice, then the mustard. Whisk in the sour cream and the remaining 1 1/2 teaspoons of the pepper. Heat through, but do not boil.

4. Spoon the warm dressing over the salad(s) and serve immediately.

13. Sweet Everythings

13. Sweet Everythings

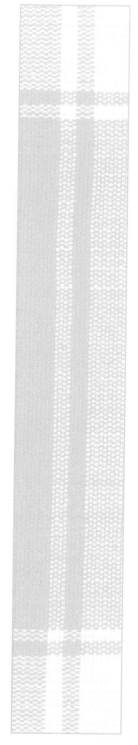

No one loves dessert more than I do. Cakes, cookies, pies, pastries, soufflés, tarts, trifles, parfaits, sorbets—next to my son and husband, these are a few of my most favorite things. The problem with dessert is making it, especially if you're trying to do it from scratch instead of merely breaking out a carton of store-bought ice cream, as I have done more times than I should admit. When you're baking, all kinds of things can go wrong—the weather, the altitude, the oven, anything can affect the delicate process.

Even so, you can lose your fear of making great desserts by following a few simple principles: First, pick a couple of desserts you really love to eat. My second principle: Stick with those selections at least until you can make them with your eyes closed. And third: If your choices are the kind that can be served in many different variations simply by switching certain toppings and fillings, all the better.

I overcame my own dessert-making phobias by discovering and developing variations on recipes for tarte Tatin. It happened almost by accident. One day, I found a small cast-iron skillet at the back of my kitchen closet. I had guests arriving for dinner and hadn't figured out what to make for dessert. I loved tarte Tatin, and I remembered that someone had once told me it should be made in a cast-iron pan. So tarte Tatin it was.

Tarte Tatin has all the characteristics of a dessert for great kitchen suppers: It's rustic, homey, tastes wonderful, is easily altered, hard to ruin, has great history, and everybody likes it. Tarte Tatin is said to have been developed by two sisters (Les Demoiselles Tatins) in the Loire valley. These two sisters served the tarte in their restaurant, and the recipe made its way to Paris and became, for better or sometimes worse, a staple of hearty bistro cooking. The original tarte was made with apples, and for many years I thought it could only be made with apples—a mistaken impression I would eventually correct to my relief and delight.

It happened to be fall when I attempted to make my first tarte Tatin, so there were plenty of wonderful apples available at the local farm stands. That made my choice of desserts seem all the more appropriate, but I couldn't help wondering if it was an omen that I was in for a fall. To put it bluntly, I had virtually no idea what I was doing. I did have a package of frozen puff pastry in my freezer, which I had purchased after discovering that one of the pastry chefs at my restaurant used frozen puff pastry in a pinch. Perhaps I'm not fussy enough, or my taste buds aren't refined enough, but I hadn't detected any great difference between the frozen puff and the fresh-made. And the frozen was certainly good enough for me to use at home, not to mention infinitely easier.

After retrieving the puff pastry package from the freezer, I sliced the apples, but didn't peel them. I know you're supposed to peel, but I feared they wouldn't hold their shape. Besides, I was too lazy and too frazzled to peel. I had about five cookbooks open, but all the recipes seemed too complicated. Finally, I decided just to forge ahead and trust my instincts. I cooked the apples in butter and sprinkled sugar on top. Everything got all melted and bubbly. The apples got soft but held their shape fairly well. I added a tablespoon of Calvados for no good reason other than I had some in the house and I thought it might add a bit of zing. It did. At this point, it occurred to me that with a little more liquid and cooking time, this would make a lovely sauce for vanilla ice cream. I thought maybe I should give up while I was ahead. I didn't.

Instead, I grappled with the all-important decision of what to do with my defrosted pastry. One recipe said to lay the pastry over the outside of the pan; another said to tuck it inside the pan. I chose the first option because it just looked right to me. Then I put the pan in the oven. The aroma of apples and sugar filled the kitchen. I kept the oven light on so I could peek through the window, having learned the lesson of opening the oven too soon: Too many times has my cake deflated or my popover failed to pop.

When the pastry looked all puffy and golden, I took it out. Now the hard part was literally at hand. Somehow I was supposed to turn this beautiful golden puff over onto a plate. As far as I understood it, this process had to occur while the pan was hot, otherwise the sugar would begin to harden and the apples would stick to the pan (which they do sometimes anyway). In the meantime, the melted sugar and butter mixture was bubbling out of the pastry in a couple of places, and the pan was hot, hot, hot.

It was time to get practical. I put the pan down on the butcher block and placed a large glass platter thick enough to withstand the heat over the tarte. I picked up the pan by the handle with the platter on top, slipped a pot holder underneath, placed my other hand under the glass platter, took a deep breath and awkwardly turned the tarte out onto the platter. The butter/sugar came rolling out and burned my wrist: I learned then and there that it was far better and far safer to place the pastry on the inside of the rim and tuck it in around the apples, rather than letting it hang over the outside of the pan.

Luckily, I managed not to drop the platter, so the tarte stayed intact. Only one piece of apple stuck to the bottom, and that was easy enough to scrape up with a spatula and replace. No one would know the difference. I have since tried several methods of turning the pan, and have even gone so far as to wrap the pan and platter with aluminum foil, which I cut off after I turn the tarte. That may have been a bit dramatic, but it worked—and it spared my wrist from another burn. I have also played with the amount of butter, juice, and liquor I might add to reduce the splash. The thing I discovered that is worth remembering is that all of it—or at least almost all of it—works. I have made neat tartes and messy ones, and they all taste good.

I truly get joy from making this tarte. It takes well to many different fruits, so the recipe can be altered with the season and my mood. It's fairly easy, and pretty much cooks on its own, so you can get other things done while it's baking. I am particularly fond of pears, apricots, peaches, and plums, in addition to the traditional apples, but I advise against using bananas because the cooking time is too long. Since making my first tarte Tatin, I have gotten a lecture from my pastry chef on peeling the fruit, which, mostly out of laziness, I still don't do very often. Besides, I find that the skin really does help the fruit keep its shape, and most importantly, I *like* the skin.

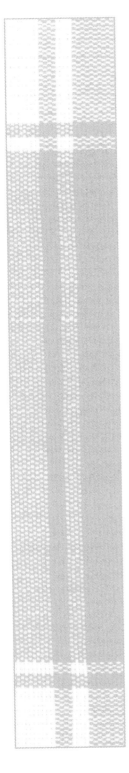

One word of caution if you try your own tarte Tatin: Cast-iron pans should not be washed. They rust, as I learned the hard way. Be sure to wipe the pan with a damp rag. Pour in a couple of tablespoons of coarse salt and scrub with the salt until the pan comes clean. Wipe the pan clean with another damp rag. You can also "season" the pan with a bit of oil to keep it from rusting. Just rub a teaspoon of oil, such as safflower or another light, fairly tasteless oil, in the bottom of the pan, then wipe thoroughly.

Tarte Tatin

What I love most about this recipe is that I can use almost any fruit except bananas (which were almost a disaster). For drier fruits, I add more butter, and for wetter fruits (like plums) I use less. Apples are always good, and may be the best. If you didn't read the introduction to this chapter, you may want to do so now as it tells the story of my first tarte Tatin.

12 tablespoons (1½ sticks) butter, cut into ¼-inch cubes

4 large apples, such as Rome or McIntosh, peeled, cored, and cut into ½-inch-thick wedges

½ cup sugar, as needed, depending on the tartness of the apples

2 tablespoons fresh lemon juice

1 tablespoon Calvados or applejack liqueur

1 sheet thawed frozen puff pastry (about 8½ ounces)

Makes 4 to 6

servings

1. Preheat the oven to 375°F.

2. In a heavy 9-inch skillet, preferably cast iron, heat 2 tablespoons of the butter over medium heat. Remove from the heat and arrange the apple slices in concentric circles in the pan, sprinkling the sugar and lemon juice over the apples and dotting them with the remaining butter as you go—you will have more than one layer. Remember that the bottom layer is what you will see when the tart is inverted, so keep it as neat as possible. Sprinkle with the liqueur.

3. Return the pan to medium heat. Cook, without stirring, until the juices are bubbling and golden brown, and the apples are tender but not mushy, about 10 minutes. Remove from the heat. Place the puff pastry over the apples, tucking the pastry in around the inside of the skillet like a bed sheet (be careful not to burn your fingers on the hot juices).

4. Bake in the preheated oven until the pastry is golden brown, about 30

(continued)

minutes. (You may want to place a piece of aluminum foil under the skillet to catch any juices that might bubble out.)

5. Immediately place a large, rimmed serving platter over the top of the skillet. Holding the platter and skillet together, carefully invert to unmold the tarte and fruit onto the platter. (If you're feeling nervous, place the skillet on a large sheet of aluminum foil, then cover the skillet with the platter. Wrap the whole thing up with the foil. When you invert the foil-wrapped skillet and platter, the foil will catch any hot sauce. Open up the foil to remove the platter.) If any apples stick to the skillet, remove them with the tip of a knife and put them back onto the tarte. Pour any sauce in the pan over the tarte. (The tarte can be prepared up to 2 hours ahead. If desired, reheat it in a preheated 350° oven for 10 minutes before serving.) Serve warm.

VARIATIONS: Pear Tarte Tatin: Substitute 6 Bosc pears, peeled, cored, and cut into $1/2$-inch-thick wedges for the apples and poire Williams liqueur for the Calvados.

Peach and Blueberry Tarte Tatin: Substitute 6 ripe peaches, peeled, pitted, and cut into $1/2$-inch-thick wedges for the apples and peach-flavored liqueur for the Calvados. Sprinkle $1/2$ cup blueberries over the cooked peaches before topping with the pastry.

Plum Tarte Tatin: Substitute 6 large ripe black plums, such as Black Friar, pitted and cut into $1/2$-inch-thick wedges for the apples and plum liqueur or crème de cassis for the Calvados.

Plum Tart

Here's a simple tart with the easiest piecrust ever: It's based on a cookie crust, thick and rustic, firm enough to keep all the liquid in the pie and great-tasting. You can prepare this recipe as a savory crust by omitting the sugar and adding a couple of tablespoons of herbs. As for the plums, I like the black ones—they are the juiciest and the sweetest.

FOR THE FILLING:

8 plums, preferably Black Friar, pitted and cut into quarters

1/3 cup sugar

1/4 cup fresh orange juice

2 tablespoons plum liqueur or crème de cassis

4 tablespoons (1/2 stick) butter, cut into small cubes, plus additional for the pan

FOR THE CRUST:

8 ounces cream cheese, at room temperature

1 cup (2 sticks) butter, at room temperature

1 3/4 cups all-purpose flour

1/2 cup sugar

2 tablespoons finely ground hazelnuts (almonds, pistachios, or walnuts are fine too)

Makes 6 to 8

servings

1. Preheat the oven to 350°F. Lightly butter the inside of a 9-inch springform pan.

2. To make the filling: In a medium bowl, toss together the plums, sugar, orange juice, and liqueur. Set aside.

3. To make the crust: With an electric mixer or in a food processor, blend the cream cheese with the butter, add the flour, sugar, and nuts and process until they form a soft ball of dough. Press the dough firmly and evenly into the bottom and up the sides of the prepared pan to make a 1/8- to 1/4-inch-thick layer. This should be a thick crust—it's a cookie! Pour the plum mixture into the crust and dot with the butter cubes.

4. Bake in the preheated oven until the juices are bubbling and the plums are tender, about 45 minutes. Let stand in the pan on a wire cake rack. Remove the sides of the pan and serve warm or cooled to room temperature.

Dark Chocolate Cake with Almonds and Orange

Serves 6 to 8

Bless this cake. I made it over 25 years ago in junior high school. It was probably the first cake I made that I fell in love with. Over the years I have played with the recipe, but I always come back to the original version. It is easy and so-o-o good.

If you wish, bake the cake in a springform pan. You won't have to invert it, but then you won't have a smooth top to give the cake a finished look.

You can use the icing over any cake. I have poured it over a store-bought pound cake, served ice cream on the side, and enjoyed a perfectly tasty dessert.

FOR THE CAKE:

2 oranges

4 ounces semisweet chocolate, finely chopped

1/2 cup (1 stick) butter, at room temperature, plus additional for the pan

2/3 cup sugar

3 large eggs, at room temperature

1 cup finely ground almonds, any kind (natural, blanched, slivered, sliced, or whole)

1/4 cup dry fine bread crumbs, all-purpose flour, or finely ground shortbread cookies

FOR THE ICING:

2 ounces unsweetened chocolate, finely chopped

2 ounces semisweet chocolate, finely chopped

4 tablespoons (1/2 stick) butter, at room temperature

2 tablespoons honey

2 teaspoons orange- or almond-flavored liqueur, such as Grand Marnier or Amaretto (optional)

Lightly sweetened whipped cream or crème fraîche, for serving (optional)

1. To make the cake: Preheat the oven to 375°F. Generously butter an 8-inch round cake pan. Line the bottom of the pan with waxed paper, and butter the paper.

2. Grate the zest from the oranges and set it aside. Squeeze the juice from the oranges and set it aside.

3. In the top of a double boiler over hot, not simmering water, heat the chocolate until it is almost completely melted. Add the orange juice. Heat, stirring often, until smooth. Remove the top of the double boiler from the heat and let the chocolate mixture stand for about 10 minutes, until tepid. (If you don't have a double boiler, put 1 tablespoon of water in the bottom of a heavy pot. Heat until very warm to the touch. Lower the heat and then add the chocolate. Melt over a very low heat, stirring to keep the chocolate from scorching on the bottom of the pot.)

4. In a medium bowl, using a hand-held electric mixer on high speed (if you have one, otherwise use a wooden spoon), beat the butter and sugar until light in color and texture, about 2 minutes. One at a time, beat in the eggs, beating well after each addition. Do not worry if the batter looks curdled. After the last egg has gone in, beat for 1 minute.

5. Beat in the cooled chocolate, ground almonds, bread crumbs, and orange zest until well combined. Spread evenly in the prepared pan.

6. Bake until a toothpick inserted in the center comes out with a moist crumb, about 30 minutes. Let the cake stand in the pan on a wire cake rack for 10 minutes. Invert onto the cake rack and peel off the waxed paper. Cool completely.

7. To make the icing: In the top of a double boiler (see step 3), combine all the icing ingredients. Place over hot, not simmering, water, and heat, stirring often, until the chocolate melts and the icing is smooth, about 8 to 10 minutes. Remove the top part of the double boiler from the heat. Stir until the icing is slightly cooled and begins to thicken, 3 to 5 minutes.

8. Place the cake on a serving platter. Tuck strips of waxed paper underneath the cake. Pour the icing over the top of the cake. Using a flexible metal spatula, spread the icing over the cake, letting the excess drip down the sides. Cool at room temperature (or if the kitchen is warm, refrigerate with a piece of waxed paper gently laid on top) until the icing is set.

9. Remove the waxed paper strips. Serve the cake at room temperature. For an extra indulgence, add a dollop of whipped cream or crème frâiche.

■ ■ ■ ■ ■ ■ ■ ■ ■ ■ ■ ■ ■ ■ ■

Chocolate Cheesecake

A real oldie, this recipe. I first learned to make this cheesecake when I was working for a now-defunct caterer to support my then-career—acting. My job was to make what seemed like hundreds of these cheesecakes, which we also sold retail. After I moved to Los Angeles, far from the catering kitchen (located in the basement of a rock 'n roll club!), I went for years without making another cheesecake. One day, while cleaning out files that had moved across the country many times, I came across my recipe written on the back of a paper towel. Cheesecake. It seemed so corny and so old-fashioned, and it is. It is also still so good.

Makes 8 servings

12 ounces semisweet chocolate, finely
    chopped
$^1/_3$ cup water
1 tablespoon orange-flavored liqueur,
    such as Grand Marnier

4 large eggs
$1^3/_4$ cups sugar
2 pounds cream cheese, at room
    temperature
2 teaspoons vanilla extract

1. Position a rack in the center of the oven and preheat to 350°F. Lightly butter an 8-inch round springform pan that is at least 2 inches deep.

2. In a heavy pot, melt the chocolate with the water and liqueur. When melted, remove from the heat and let stand until cool.

3. In a large mixing bowl, using a handheld electric mixer at medium speed, beat the eggs with the sugar until well combined, 3 to 5 minutes. Gradually beat in the cream cheese, $^1/_4$ pound at a time, until the mixture is very smooth, 5 minutes. Beat in the cooled chocolate and the vanilla. Spread the batter evenly in the prepared pan.

4. Bake in the preheated oven until the top edges of the cheesecake are puffed and golden brown, about 1 hour. Let the cake cool in the pan for 30 minutes. Run a sharp knife around the inside of the pan to release the cheesecake from the sides (if they haven't already pulled away during the cooling process).

Remove the sides of the springform, cover the cake with plastic wrap, and refrigerate for 30 minutes before serving. Bring to room temperature before serving, unless it is a very hot day, in which case, take it out of the fridge at the last minute and enjoy it cold.

VARIATIONS: Marble Cheesecake: Reduce the amount of chocolate to 6 ounces and the amount of water to 2 tablespoons. Melt the chocolate, water, and orange liqueur together. Make the cheesecake batter, but do not stir in the melted chocolate. Spread the cheesecake batter in the prepared pan. Drizzle the melted chocolate over the top of the batter. Draw a knife through the batter and the chocolate to create a marbleized look. Bake as directed.

Vanilla Cheesecake: Delete the chocolate, water, and orange liqueur. Stir $1/2$ cup sour cream or full-fat yogurt into the cheesecake batter instead of the melted chocolate mixture. Bake as directed.

Peach Bread Pudding with Crème Anglaise

This is a modified version of a recipe we served when we first opened Alison On Dominick Street. The variations are limited only by your imagination. It can easily be altered to accommodate the season and your taste buds. In fall or winter, substitute 2 or 3 peeled, cored, and thinly sliced apples or pears for the peaches; raisins, currants, or dried cranberries for the dried cherries; pecans or walnuts for the almonds; and Calvados or applejack for the amaretto.

Makes 6 to 8 servings

The first time I made bread pudding I was in one of my usual frenzies, having committed myself to cooking a lunch for 30 at my parents' house. I had planned to serve just-picked berries and peaches for dessert, but when I was rummaging through my parents' refrigerator, I found a massive quantity of bits and pieces of old bread. It made me crazy that no one was ever going to eat them. So I made peach bread pudding and served it with the berries on top. It was a big hit—even on a hot summer day!

You can make a lighter version of this recipe if it seems too rich by substituting half and half for the heavy cream. And you can eliminate the crème anglaise and use a fruit puree, sorbet, or ice cream instead.

FOR THE PUDDING:
1¹/₂ cups milk
1¹/₂ cups heavy cream
³/₄ cup sugar
2 large eggs plus 6 large egg yolks
1¹/₂ teaspoons vanilla extract
¹/₂ teaspoon almond extract
6 cups 1-inch slightly stale bread cubes, such as croissants, brioche, sandwich, or walnut bread, in any combination (see Note)

4 ripe peaches, peeled, pitted, and cut into ¹/₂-inch-thick wedges
³/₄ cup dried cherries
¹/₂ cup coarsely chopped almonds
1 teaspoon ground cinnamon

FOR THE CRÈME ANGLAISE:
1 cup milk
1 cup heavy cream
¹/₂ cup sugar
6 large egg yolks

<table>
<tr><td>⅓ cup amaretto or peach
   liqueur</td><td>1 pint fresh raspberries or blueberries,
   for serving</td></tr>
</table>

1. Preheat the oven to 325°F. Lightly butter a 2-quart shallow baking dish.

2. To make the pudding: In a medium saucepan, heat the milk, cream, and sugar over medium heat until simmering, 3 to 5 minutes, stirring often to dissolve the sugar. In a medium bowl, whisk together the eggs, egg yolks, vanilla, and almond extract. Gradually whisk in the hot milk mixture. Strain the custard into another bowl and set aside.

3. Spread about 2 cups of the bread cubes in the prepared pan. Top with half the peaches and half the cherries. Repeat the layering with half the remaining bread, the remaining peaches and cherries, and a topping of the remaining bread. Sprinkle the nuts over the top. Pour the custard over all. Sprinkle with the cinnamon.

4. Place the baking dish in a large roasting pan. Place the pan in the oven and pour enough hot water in the roasting pan to come halfway up the sides of the baking dish. Bake until a knife inserted in the center of the pudding comes out clean, about 1 hour.

5. Meanwhile, make the crème anglaise: In a medium, heavy-bottomed saucepan, heat the milk, cream, and sugar over medium heat until simmering, 3 to 5 minutes, stirring often to dissolve the sugar. In a medium bowl, whisk the egg yolks. Gradually whisk the milk mixture into the egg yolks. Pour the mixture back into the saucepan. Cook over medium-low heat, stirring constantly with a wooden spoon, until the sauce is thick enough to coat the spoon but not boiling (180° to 185°F. on an instant-read thermometer), about 3 minutes. Strain the sauce into a medium bowl and whisk in the amaretto.

6. To serve, spoon the pudding onto dessert plates. Spoon the sauce around the pudding, and sprinkle with the berries.

NOTE: If the bread is fresh, toast it lightly in a preheated 350° oven for about 15 minutes, and lightly butter the toasted bread.

Ginger and Caramelized Pear Cake

This incredibly spiced recipe comes from Michael Chamberlain, my business partner and cook extraordinaire. When Michael makes it, he leaves out the pear layer (that's my invention), and serves a wedge of cake with a Port-Poached Pear (page 230) and the ginger whipped cream on the side. Both ways are wonderful—it is simply a matter of time and how much work you want to do. Instead of the gingered whipped cream, I often serve this with a scoop of Häagen-Dazs Dulce de Leche ice cream. Any good quality vanilla ice cream will suffice.

Makes 6 to 8

servings

FOR THE PEARS:

4 medium Bosc pears, peeled, cored, and cut into ½-inch-thick slices; or 8 small Seckel or Forelle pears, peeled, halved lengthwise, and cored

2 tablespoons fresh lemon juice

½ cup (1 stick) butter

¼ cup packed *dark* brown sugar

½ cup poire Williams or pear eau-de-vie liqueur

2 teaspoons ground cinnamon

¾ teaspoon dry mustard

¼ teaspoon ground cloves

1 cup (2 sticks) butter, at room temperature

¾ cup packed *dark* brown sugar

⅓ cup unsulphured (light) molasses

⅓ cup cooled, brewed strong coffee

4 large eggs

1 cup buttermilk

FOR THE GINGER CAKE:

¼ cup peeled and finely chopped fresh ginger

2½ tablespoons granulated sugar

2⅔ cups all-purpose flour

1¼ teaspoons baking soda

1 tablespoon ground ginger

FOR THE GINGER WHIPPED CREAM:

1 cup heavy cream

2 tablespoons confectioners' sugar

½ teaspoon vanilla extract

¼ teaspoon ground ginger

1. Position a rack in the center of the oven and preheat to 350°F. Lightly butter the inside of a 10-inch springform pan, dust with flour, and shake out the excess.

2. To prepare the pears: In a medium bowl, toss the pears with the lemon juice. In a large skillet, stir the butter and sugar over medium heat until the sugar is dissolved and the syrup is boiling, about 6 to 8 minutes. Add the pears and mix gently. Pour in the liqueur. Bring to a simmer. Reduce the heat to low. Cook until the pears are tender but not falling apart, about 10 minutes. Remove from the heat and cool in the pan until easy to handle. Using a fork, overlap the pears in concentric circles in the bottom of the prepared pan. Discard the skillet juices.

3. To make the cake: In a small bowl, combine the chopped ginger and the granulated sugar. Let stand, stirring occasionally, until the sugar dissolves and forms a syrup, about 30 minutes. Sift the flour, baking soda, ground ginger, cinnamon, mustard, and cloves together and set aside.

4. In a large bowl, using a handheld electric mixer at high speed, beat the butter and brown sugar together until light in color and texture, about 2 minutes. Beat in the molasses, coffee, and the ginger/sugar mixture. Beat in the eggs one at a time, beating well after each addition. Do not worry if the mixture looks curdled.

5. Reduce the mixer speed to low. Alternating in thirds, add the dry ingredients and the buttermilk, mixing just until smooth and scraping down the bowl as needed with a rubber spatula. Do not overmix. Spread evenly over the pears in the pan.

6. Bake until a toothpick inserted in the center of the cake comes out clean, about 30 minutes.

7. Meanwhile, make the ginger whipped cream: In a chilled medium bowl, whip the cream, confectioners' sugar, vanilla, and ground ginger until it forms soft peaks. Chill until ready to serve.

8. Cool the cake in the pan on a wire cake rack for 10 minutes, then invert the cake onto a serving platter. If any pears stick to the pan, transfer them to the top of the cake with the tip of a knife. Serve warm, with a dollop of the whipped cream.

Michael's Port-Poached Pears

Here are the special poached pears that Michael likes to serve with Ginger Cake (see preceding recipe). I think you'll agree that they are special enough to be served on their own, perhaps with gingersnaps on the side.

Makes 8 servings

4 cups ruby port
2 ounces fresh ginger, peeled and cut into $\frac{1}{8}$-inch-thick rounds
2 cinnamon sticks
1 vanilla bean, split lengthwise

$\frac{1}{4}$ cup sugar (more if you want it very sweet)
$\frac{1}{4}$ cup fresh lemon juice
4 cups cold water
8 large Bosc or 16 small Seckel pears

1. In a saucepan large enough to hold the pears in one layer, bring the port, ginger, cinnamon, and vanilla bean to a boil over high heat, stirring to dissolve the sugar. Reduce the heat to medium and simmer for 10 minutes.

2. Meanwhile, in a medium bowl, stir the lemon juice into the cold water. One at a time, peel the pears, remove the core through the bottom of each pear with a small melon baller or the tip of a sharp paring knife, and place the pears as they are peeled in the lemon water to keep them from discoloring.

3. Drain the pears and add them to the simmering port syrup. Simmer, turning frequently, until the pears are tender and evenly colored, about 20 minutes. Using a slotted spoon, transfer the pears to a deep dish, standing them upright.

4. Increase the heat to high and boil the syrup until reduced to about $1\frac{3}{4}$ cups, 15 to 20 minutes. Pour the syrup evenly over the pears and cool. Cover and refrigerate until well chilled, at least 2 hours. (The pears can be prepared up to 2 days ahead.) Bring back to room temperature and serve the pears in shallow bowls, with the syrup.

14. Our Daily Bread

14. Our Daily Bread

Give me good bread and fresh butter, and I am a happy girl. Good bread is not that hard to bake, and it's even easier to buy. With the resurgence of artisan bakers and the availability of decent breads at most supermarkets, the only reasons to bake your own bread are that you long for the musty smell of yeast, and/or the sight of a golden glow of a crust fresh from the oven. Those are very good reasons, I'll admit. But let me remind you that unless you own a bread machine, baking bread is extremely time-consuming. Many cooks save it for a weekend project.

Since the birth of our son, Harrison, I don't seem to have any free weekends, so I don't bake much bread anymore. The exception is the stollen I bake at Christmastime. And as my husband can attest, baking the stollen loaves to fill the standing orders from members of our family alone is a three-day project that requires me to take over half the downstairs as well as the entire kitchen.

When I was growing up, we used to spend Christmas at my grandparents' house in St. Louis, where my father was raised. I remember being so excited when the plane took off from New York that I spilled hot chocolate all over myself. Everyone on board seemed to be staring at me as the stewardesses tried to mop up the mess I'd made. I remember how embarrassed I felt, not just because of the stares, but because I knew that I would arrive in St. Louis with a big brown stain on my little white dress with the red smock. I wanted so much to be a big girl.

My father has only one sister, but there was always a large extended family on hand for Christmas. I remember tall men in dark suits, women in long dresses, white tapers in silver candelabra, the tree twinkling with multicolored lights and ornaments. And I remember—who could forget?—my great Aunt Louise, our family's answer to Auntie Mame. At one of these Christmas dinners, Auntie Louise had her dress unzipped in the back. When I asked her why, she replied that it was hot and she needed an air hole. Auntie Louise lived to be 103, and spent much of her later years traveling on a Norwegian cruise line. It didn't matter where the boat was going, she always went on the same one, and she always sat at the captain's table and danced with the captain and her favorite crewmen.

Although I was too young to remember—much less get the recipes for—all the food we had at our Christmas dinners in St. Louis, I do have very vivid memories of my grandmother baking the Christmas stollen. It took two full days, during which my brother and I had to tip-toe around the house so that the dough wouldn't fall during one of its three risings. After chopping candied fruit rinds and almonds and pouring them into the mix, my grandmother would stir the batter with a wooden spoon that seemed to be as long as a broom handle. Then she would knead the dough again and again with her strong arms until it had just the right elasticity. Never would she even have dreamed of using an electric mixer as I do now.

I remember stealing into the kitchen with my brother to look at the bowls of stollen batter sitting tantalizingly on the counter under their dish towels. Our anticipation would become excruciating as we watched for the first bump in the cloth that let us know our tip-toeing around the house had served its purpose. If we were especially well behaved, my grandmother would reward our patience and satiate our hunger by treating us to a batch of fresh-baked oatmeal chocolate chip cookies. This is baking to me. And this is why I now buy a lot of bread. However, I've discovered some general principles that apply to both buying and baking. Let's discuss baking first.

Baking Bread

You have two basic choices for what kind of bread to bake—a quick bread or a yeast bread. Quick breads are baked with baking soda and baking powder, as opposed to yeast. Usually, quick breads are sweeter than yeast breads, and are served for breakfast or at tea. Classic quick breads are those biscuits that are so good for gravy-dipping; scones made with or without raisins, nuts, and other sweet treats; and my favorite as well as everyone else's, good old banana bread.

I have baked many quick breads, and I've found that the two things that usually go wrong are 1) the addition of too much liquid, which makes the bread gooey; or 2) the addition of too much baking soda, which gives the bread an odd flavor that can only be described as baking soda-ish. The best way to avoid these pitfalls is to use a little common sense, which, I concede, is sometimes hard to do if you're running late and the evil kitchen witch knows it. In following a quick bread recipe, as in following other types of recipes, it's best to go slowly, gradually adding small portions of liquid or baking soda until you achieve the proper balance. To avoid a gooey bread, take note of the consistency of your batter. It should be like a thick, pureed bean soup. The baking soda flavor is a harder one to fix before baking. You can taste your batter—if it tingles or slightly burns your tongue, you have probably added too much.

My experience with yeast breads has also given me a few pointers that are handy to have in mind even when buying bread. Bread made with water is chewier and crisper than bread made with milk. Sweeteners in breads make it more tender and moist. Salt will give it a firmer crust and crumb, creating a denser loaf because it slows down the growth of the yeast. Test your yeast before you start. if you don't get the bubbles initially, do not proceed—your yeast is dead.

The taste of bread will be determined by the quality and kind of flour and water that you use. We will never be able to truly copy a French bread because our water is different. White bread is made from white flour. Whole-wheat bread is made from whole-wheat flour, and wheat bread is made from a mix of the two. The most common stronger-tasting breads are pumpernickel, sourdough, and rye. Pumpernickel and rye breads are made from rye flour. They are denser than wheat breads, though they usually have some wheat flour added because rye flour doesn't have the same rising power. They are also more sour than white bread. Sourdough bread is made from any variety or combination of flours with a sourdough starter, which involves a special treatment of the yeast. It gives the bread a tangy flavor.

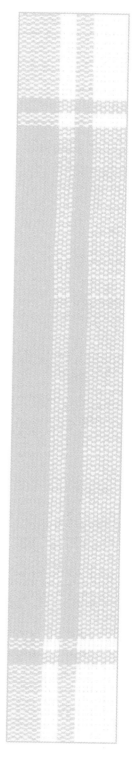

Your choices in buying bread will naturally be determined by what your local store carries. I have found that most supermarkets offer round boules and baguettes, which are always good bets. Sometimes you will find a dense potato bread as well. The trick to making bread an asset to your supper is to know what you are looking for to complement the meal. If you are serving stew, you want a peasant-type bread that will absorb the sauce. If the bread is too dense, the sauce will just roll off. If the bread is very airy, it will turn to mush.

I have two rules for buying bread. Rule number one relates to the flavors of the main course I'm planning to present. If I am serving a dish with a great deal of flavor, I serve a simple bread. If I am serving a simple dish, I pick a bread that is going to complement the flavors in the dish: a rosemary or olive bread with a leg of lamb, for example. Corn bread with pork loins. A raisin nut roll with a roast chicken. Rule number two relates to the thickness or thinness of my main course. The thicker the dish, the thicker the bread, and the thinner the dish, the thinner the bread. If I am serving a delicate fish fillet, I will serve a thinly sliced white or wheat bread. If I am serving short ribs, I want a thick, hearty slab of bread. I have made a mess of a simple grilled cheese because I used a bread that wasn't quite dense enough to hold the cheese (or maybe I used too much cheese).

In buying bread, you have three basic choices: artisan bread, machine bread, and what I call "in-between" bread. Most artisan breads are baked in brick ovens, which give them thicker, crispier crusts. But what makes artisan breads special is that the wheat has been grown specifically for making the bread. Just as a chef might have a farmer grow certain vegetables, a baker may select or choose a certain wheat or grain grown in a specific manner. And just as there are different types of apples, there are different types of wheat. Each loaf is made by hand and usually in small batches, which, I find, means that the bread will always be more interesting. Many artisan breads incorporate herbs, nuts, or seeds. Almost all of them are good, but I especially like walnut breads. You can also find interesting shapes in artisan breads, which make the presentation more dramatic.

Perhaps surprisingly, machine-made breads can be quite good, as well.

There's a semolina baguette at our local grocery store that my husband absolutely adores. When surveying a selection of machine-made breads, try to smell the bread. If it has a bit of fragrance, that's good. It should smell slightly yeasty. Most of the breads seem to have seeds, which is fine with me. Some people don't like seeds because they get stuck in teeth and make a mess on the dinner table, but I don't care. Often you will find bread that is labeled "baked in store." Assuming that the labeling is technically correct, you should be aware that many times the dough was *not* made in the store. The quality of these breads is okay, but stores often don't bake them properly, and you might have an unpleasant surprise in the middle of the loaf (I'll leave the nature of such surprises to nightmarish imaginations). In order to guard against purchases you'll later regret, lightly touch the loaves as you inspect them. The loaves should have some spring. If your finger sticks through the crust, you don't want it.

Loaf breads are made in pans. They should be easy to slice, and they are best served with smoked fish, for breakfast, in sandwiches, or with soup. You will usually find several basic offerings: white, oatmeal, whole wheat, or a variation containing several grains and seeds. I have found orange-flavored, honey-flavored, and maple syrup–sweetened breads. Loaf breads usually have a soft crust. Depending on the ingredients, they may have a fine or a coarse texture. Grain and seed breads will obviously be more textured than a smooth white. They will also break up a bit more. Recently, I have started buying white bread again. I know all about the supposed lack of health benefits, but I just like white bread for sandwiches and toast. You can now get a wonderful quality in the supermarket, and white bread is especially good when you don't want the bread to impart a lot of flavor.

Besides artisan breads and machine-made breads, there are what I call in-between breads made by several large companies such as Eli's. These breads are mass-produced, but their baking usually involves some sort of hand-made touch or special flavoring. Although not quite as special or as fresh as locally baked artisan breads, in-between breads are certainly a far superior alternative to packaged breads if you're looking for a loaf that will impart some flavor. Often there is quite a selection ranging from raisin nut, ciabatta, and pumpernickel to sourdough and country loaves.

If I had to pick one bread to eat for the rest of my life, I would choose a

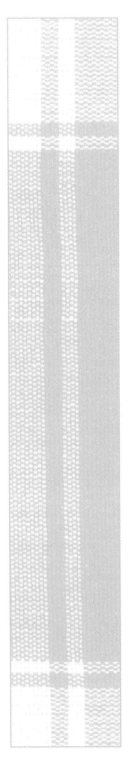

French baguette. I can't think of anything that couldn't be served with or on a baguette, regardless of whether the meal is breakfast, lunch, or dinner. Look for a firm crust that is not cracked and flaking. These days you can also find whole-wheat baguettes, if you like a grainy texture. I like my baguettes white, plain, and simple—now just pass me the French butter, please!

Christmas Stollen

Our family recipe—I pass it along to you with hopes that your kitchen will be filled with the love that ours had for many holidays. This recipe creates a very dense dry bread that is especially yummy served with warm (soft) butter. This is a large recipe, but you may cut it in half, though a whole loaf is a welcomed gift. If you do cut it in half, use a total of 1¹/₂ pounds of fruit in whatever combination you like.

Makes 8 loaves

TO PREPARE THE YEAST:
5 cups milk
¹/₂ cup sugar
3 envelopes active dry yeast
5 cups unbleached flour

FOR THE DOUGH:
1 teaspoon salt
1¹/₂ pounds (6 sticks) butter, melted
¹/₄ pound lard (usually found by the
    meat in the refrigerator section)
2 cups sugar

6 eggs
2 pounds blanched almonds, finely
    chopped
Grated rind of 2 lemons
³/₄ pound raisins
³/₄ pound dried citron, chopped into
    ¹/₄-inch pieces
³/₄ pound dried orange peel, chopped
    into ¹/₄-inch pieces
³/₄ pound dried lemon peel, chopped
    into ¹/₄-inch pieces
5 pounds unbleached flour, sifted

1. To prepare the yeast, in a saucepan, warm the milk with the sugar to lukewarm. Transfer it to a large non-aluminum—preferably non-metal—bowl.

2. Dissolve the yeast in the milk and sugar.

3. Stir in the 5 cups of flour, a cup at a time, beating until large bubbles form on the surface. Set the mixture aside, away from any drafts, and let it rise until doubled in bulk, about 2 hours.

4. In a large bowl, cream the salt, melted butter, lard, and sugar until smooth. Add this to the yeast mixture.

5. Add the eggs one at a time. Keep stirring until well incorporated.

(continued)

6. Add the almonds and the grated lemon rind. Stir again.

7. Add the dried fruits, mixing them in well.

8. Add the flour, a cup at a time, incorporating it well. You may need to divide the dough between 2 bowls if you don't have a very large bowl. When the dough is too stiff to stir with a spoon, knead it with your hands until it doesn't seem sticky and is smooth and has elasticity. Depending on where you live and the weather, you may need a little more or less flour. My grandmother used to knead for a good 20 to 30 minutes. I now use a KitchenAid mixer and accomplish the job in about 10 minutes.

9. Cover the bowl(s) lightly with a dish towel and set the dough aside to rise overnight (at least 8 hours) away from any draft and loud noise. The dough should rise to twice its bulk.

10. In the morning, butter and flour eight 9- or 10-inch bread pans.

11. Knead the dough down. First punch it in the middle and turn the edges to the center. Keep on doing this until the dried-out top has been fully incorporated back into the dough. You will knead for about 5 minutes. This kneading must be done by hand.

12. With a sharp knife, cut the dough into 8 pieces and shape it into loaves. Place each loaf in a bread pan, cover with a dish towel, and let rise again for an hour. Preheat the oven to 350°F.

13. Bake for 45 minutes to an hour. If the dough is rising too high and the tops are cracking, reduce the oven heat to 325°.

14. Remove the loaves from the oven and turn them out of the pans. You will know they are done if they are golden brown on top and sound hollow when tapped on the bottom. If they are still a bit soft, return them to the oven *out of the pans* for another 15 minutes.

15. Say Cheese, Please

15. Say Cheese, Please

My first trip to France thirty years ago introduced me to cheese. As a little girl, I didn't know that cheese had an existence beyond the presliced, ready-to-eat kind you find in supermarkets, or the precut cubes that grownups served on toothpicks at cocktail parties. On my first trip to France, I have to admit, I was more interested in the fresh croissants at the café around the corner from our hotel, but the cheese offerings in the restaurants intrigued me. Maybe it was because my parents would order cheeses for themselves but not for my older brother and me, presumably thinking that we wouldn't like the sophisticated tastes. I remember that some of the cheeses they ordered were incredibly stinky, or not pleasing to look at, but they glistened as they sat, proud and ready to be chosen for that night's dinner. On my next trip to France as an adult, I indulged in various cheeses at both lunch and dinner, and sometimes as an afternoon snack in a café. And that's when my love affair with cheese really bloomed.

When I began cooking dinners back in the States, I found that I could avoid making a first course by serving a cheese course after the entrée. But over the years, serving cheese has become much more than a convenience. I now serve cheese both as a refreshing change in the traditional American three-course routine, and as a delightful course in its own right. Instead of making a tart or baking a pie for dessert, I might serve cheese accompanied by a dessert wine or a port. On nights when gluttony reigns, I serve a five-course meal, and have cheeses along with everything else on the menu. And when I am dining all by myself, I often sit down with some creamy cheeses, a green salad, and a baguette, and come away from the table feeling perfectly sated.

Cheese is like wine in that it has its own vocabulary. How much of this vocabulary you need to know really depends on how much you want to know. You need very little knowledge to put together a mouthwatering cheese course. It might not be as sophisticated as a cheese monger would put together, but who cares? As long as you and your guests enjoy it, the cheese course has served its true purpose. And by gaining a working familiarity with the basics, you can increase your cheese course options and improve your presentations, even if you don't live in an area where there are wonderful cheese shops with nice knowledgeable people behind the counter and must fall back on the local supermarket or, if worse comes to worst, order by mail.

How to Design a Cheese Plate

Do not let the thought of designing a cheese plate throw you into a tizzy just because there are thousands of cheeses—it's just not that big a deal. If you were to design a crudités basket, would that worry you? Of course not. So just approach your cheese plate with that same worry-free attitude. Start by deciding how you are using the cheese. Is it to be served as an hors d'oeuvre or as an appetizer? Or are you going to serve cheese as a main course with a green salad and good bread? Perhaps you will choose, as I often do, to copy the French and serve it after the main meal and before, or instead of, dessert. It doesn't matter which option you select so long as you keep the overall purpose and a few key principles in mind.

First and foremost, you should try to serve a selection of cheeses that feature both different tastes and different textures, not only for the sake of variety but to expand your knowledge and tantalize your palate. The charts below provide a simplified map of your choices. The top chart is very basic. The bottom chart is nice information to know, but if it seems to complicate matters, don't worry about it. Just enjoy your cheese. The type of milk cheese you end up choosing will probably be determined by what is available in your area and where the cheese course fits in your menu. You may want to serve three cow's milk cheeses, or you may choose to serve one of each kind of milk. The type and the rind type may have no bearing on your choices if you are limited to the typically small range of selections available in a supermarket, but they can make some interesting conversation if you have a knowledgeable cheese monger in the neighborhood.

Texture	Taste	Milk Type
Soft	Mild	Cow
Semi-soft	Strong	Sheep
Hard	Sharp	Goat

Type	Rind type	
Veined	Bloomy rind (white mold)	
Cooked	Washed rind (with alcohol or brine to encourage bacteria growth)	
Uncooked	Natural rind (the bacteria grow without any helpers to create a rind)	
Fresh	None	

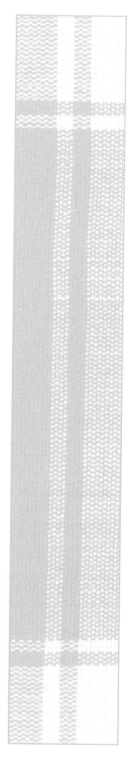

The more you explore different combinations of type, texture, and taste, the more fun you will have. There is no absolute rule about how many cheeses to serve on a cheese plate or board. Any offering from one to seven cheeses is acceptable and reasonable. If you are having a small dinner party, I think that one beautiful round of cheese, served with a good loaf of bread and some fruit, is just fine. If you are serving individual plates, three to five selections accompanied by some nuts or greens can be quite elegant. For a large dinner party, seven selections, well spaced on a cheese board should certainly be enough to please your guests.

How to Buy Cheese

Now that you've decided to serve cheese, you're off to the store. If your local cheese shop looks dirty, disorganized, and the cheeses are wrapped tightly in plastic, this is not a good sign. And if you whiff the scent of ammonia breaking through the funk, this is definitely not the place for you. No matter what the person behind the counter says, cheese should not smell like ammonia. If it does, that means the enzymes have gone to war with the amino acids and killed the cheese. So don't mistake "stinky" cheeses, which can be quite delicious, with ammonia-reeking cheese, which is no good at all.

If you have a choice of where to buy your cheese, scope out the shop with the friendliest cheese monger you can find behind the counter. You should be able to taste anything before you buy it, and you should be able to ask any question you want without feeling like an idiot. In any case, it's a good idea to look for a crowded shop, despite the headaches of dealing with the crush of fellow customers. The turnover of cheese will be high and the cheese mongers won't try to sell you something that has been sitting behind the counter too long. You might pay a bit more in this kind of shop, but until you really know your cheese, it's worth it. The little bit more you have spent might save you from spending even more money on a pound of cheese you're not going to enjoy eating. If you don't have a cheese shop nearby, go to the local supermarket, but keep it simple. In most deli departments, you can find a good aged Cheddar, a Roquefort, a reasonable Brie or a Camembert, and a decent goat cheese.

No matter where you buy your cheese, there are certain things you should look for. It's okay if the rind on a particular cheese looks ugly. But if the rind is cracked or swollen, reject it. The cheese is either bad, or hasn't been aged properly. If it is a cheese made by a small producer with specially fed animals (the "artisan" variety), it may be especially ugly to look at, but it may also be all the more tasty. Avoid any cheese wrapped in a wax rind (you have no way to determine how old it is), and any cheese with an unusual color, such as blue, other than blue cheese such as Roquefort, of course. Likewise, avoid cheeses that have a brownish or orange color near the rind because they are already well on their way to being spoiled. If there is any mold on the cheese itself (other than on blue cheeses), forget about it; that mold is not supposed to be there. If the cheese looks greasy, it's probably past its prime. If you're after Swiss cheese and you find that there are more holes in it than cheese, choose another one. No cheese should look shriveled or stick to the wrapper.

A soft cheese should feel supple, not runny. If the cheese is very runny, it could indicate that the manufacturer forced the process by exposing the cheese to too high a temperature. If you can, try to buy soft cheese on the day you are planning to serve it, because soft cheeses generally do not keep as well as hard cheeses. Hard cheese should not look dry or crumbly. If a cheese is spotted with white marks or looks like it has a mealy skin disease, do not buy it.

If you do get to taste before you buy, don't let anyone persuade you to buy something you don't like just because they insist it's a "great" cheese. If you don't like the taste of that particular cheese, it's not so great (at least for you)—and unless the person behind the counter is genuinely trustworthy, it may be bad. Cheese is not supposed to be bitter or sour. If it is supposed to be a "stinky" cheese, it may taste similar to the way it stinks, but even so, the flavor should be a bit milder than the stink. You should know that the cheese you get in France will always taste richer and smell stinkier than the cheese you can get elsewhere because it is made with unpasteurized milk. Cheese made with unpasteurized milk cannot be sold in the United States unless it has been aged for sixty days, and that aging process would kill a cream cheese. So don't be angry with your friendly cheese monger if his French cheese can't live up to what you were lucky enough to eat on your last trip to Paris.

Check the labels on cheese selections carefully. You want to know the place of origin. And you want to avoid copycat cheeses. Just as there is lots of fake balsamic vinegar on the store shelves, there are lots of fake cheeses. Check the small print on the wrapper, and make sure you're getting the real thing. For instance, the wrapper might say Cheddar—but is it a true aged Cheddar, or does the small print say cheese product? You may not always be able to obtain this kind of detailed information at a supermarket, but at a cheese shop, you can and must. If you find yourself at a cheese shop that can't or won't give it to you, don't spend your hard-earned dollars there.

Beware of shipping cheese home from a far-away place and/or buying by mail. Many cheeses (like many fine wines) do not travel well. If you must transport or mail cheeses, stick to hard and semi-hard varieties such as Cheddar and

Swiss, but remember—even those, if not carefully shipped, will be dry and mealy by the time they reach you. I learned this the hard way when carting home some cheese I had bought at a roadside stand in the Basque country. My husband and I enjoyed it thoroughly on the plane, but when we arrived home, after somehow getting it through Customs, the cheese started failing. It became dry and crumbly and just wasn't very good. We should have been gluttons and enjoyed the whole thing on the plane!

Buy only as much cheese as you are going to eat. Most cheeses, especially the softer ones, really don't keep more than a week. You might get a slightly longer life out of hard cheeses because they have a lower water content. To store a cheese for maximum life, wrap it tightly in plastic, but do not hermetically seal it. You can also use aluminum foil, but I don't recommend it because I have found that foil imparts an odd metallic flavor to the cheese. Goat's milk cheese fares very well when stored in a jar with a tight lid. Take out what you think you are going to use, and immediately rewrap the rest and put it back in the refrigerator. Cheese will keep longer the less it is handled, and the more stable the temperature it's in.

You want the cheese to keep as much moisture as possible. You can wrap hard cheeses in a damp cloth before wrapping them loosely in plastic. With all cheeses, you should use fresh wrapping each time. The old wrapping will have "stuff" on it that will keep it from sealing properly. If you can afford a twelve-dollar pound of cheese, using five cents worth of extra plastic wrap isn't going to break the bank. I always throw the original wrappings away, pulling off the labels and keeping them with the fresh wrapping.

Serving Cheese

There are certain classic foods to serve with cheese, such as apples, pears, and figs. For a more substantial cheese plate, you might choose to add saucisson or ham. Some baby greens make the plate look nice, but they don't serve a real purpose unless you have made a full-fledged salad. Nuts, dried fruits, and olives also complement cheese quite nicely. Or you can serve just cheese without any accompaniment. Bread and/or crackers of various types should be served alongside the cheese, but not on the same plate or board. (You don't want crumbs mixing into a delicate cheese even though it's all ending up in the same place, i.e., your mouth.) There are no hard and fast rules about which types of bread or crackers to serve with which types of cheese. The only thing I object to is salted breads and crackers. The idea is that the bread will complement the cheese. Generally, a mild cheese calls for a stronger bread, and a strong cheese calls for a blander offering. A dark raisin-nut bread, for example, makes a wonderful platform for a mild sheep's milk cheese. But when in doubt, remember that a fresh baguette will always do.

Virtually any wine you happen to be having with dinner will go with the cheese you decide to serve that night. Wine just goes with cheese. If you want to pick out something special for a cheese course, try to find wines that come from the same region as the cheese. The cows, sheep, or goats will have fed from the same terrain as the grapes have grown in, and therefore will usually be an excellent match. If you are serving cheese as a dessert course, consider port or a sweet wine.

The most important consideration when serving cheese is the temperature. Cheese should be at room temperature. Leave your cheese out for a good hour or hour and a half before serving. Remember to leave out only what you are going to serve. If you take the whole chunk out and serve only a third of it, the rest of it is only going to last a couple of days. Think about it—you don't leave out a carton of milk that you're not going to use, do you? The same goes for cheese, which is, of course, made from milk. But don't throw away those little end pieces when you're done. Blended with a little butter, they can be used to make a cheese spread or you can make a fancy macaroni and cheese (see page 208). Or you can make cheese soup. Or mixed grilled cheese. Or grate your cheese to liven up a salad.

I generally allow 1 to $2\frac{1}{2}$ ounces of each cheese on an individual cheese plate, and $2\frac{1}{2}$ to 4 ounces per person on a cheese board, with a little extra cheese added for good measure. The amount you will want to allot each person will depend on the rest of your menu and how well you know your guests' appetites. For large cheese boards, you should have a separate sharp knife for each cheese because you don't want the remnants of one cheese getting on another cheese with a different taste and texture. You might think you've created a taste treat,

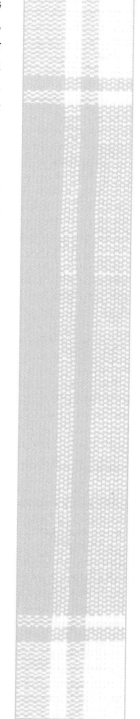

but your guests most likely will not. You do not need fancy cheese knives or a cheese board; a good paring knife or steak knife works just fine. For a cheese plate, I just give everyone an appetizer or a butter knife.

Cheese is so versatile, you've got to love it, even if the only cheese available to you is a large hunk of Cheddar. Just buy the best you can, add some interesting accompaniment, then take a sip of your wine and say cheese, please.

Rules to Follow So Your Cheese Will Always Please
1. If you don't like it, don't buy it.
2. If the outside looks funky and cracked, the inside will probably be worse.
3. Ammonia is what you clean with, not the way cheese should smell.
4. Take out only what you will need and leave the rest in the refrigerator.
5. Wrap cheese well, but don't smother it.

16. About Wine

16. About Wine

Wine is a subject I'm passionate about—but probably not in the way you might think. I am not an oenologist, which is a fancy name for a connoisseur of fine wines. Don't get me wrong. I do love fine wines. But I also love wines that some of the high and mighty wine tasters of the world might not consider to be so fine. Of course, just about everyone who is not a wine connoisseur, including myself, seems to get intimidated by those who are. I resent that because it makes people like us feel stupid when we are really anything but. Perhaps even worse, the intimidation factor prevents us from learning about and enjoying wines we really like. Remember these two things about wine even if you forget everything else in this chapter:

1. Wine is fermented grape juice (nothing more and nothing less).
2. Wine is meant to go with food, just as food is meant to go with wine.

When it comes to wine, I have a very simple and straightforward motto: "If it tastes good, drink it." If a particular wine doesn't taste good, the best things to do are to pour it out or to use it for cooking. Wine connoisseurs make far too much about showing off their expertise concerning the origins and nature of various wines, and the conventional wisdom about how to pair which wines with which foods. But picking a wine does not have to be a complicated or expensive proposition unless you want to make it so. Picking a wine, like picking the foods you want to eat, is supposed to be fun, a labor of love. When you make it a mind-numbing chore or an exercise in intellectual one-upmanship, you take both the fun and the love out of it.

Having said all that, I should point out that it can be useful to have some basic knowledge of wines, if only so that you end up drinking what you really like and avoiding what you don't like. It's not essential to know the names of every kind of grape there is, or to memorize the names and characteristics of every wine-growing region in the world. But you might want to familiarize yourself with and remember the names and regions of the wines you most enjoy and those you find disagreeable. My mother will drink almost anything—cheap wine, expensive wine, even wine that's been in an open bottle for a couple of days. My father, on the other hand, is very particular and very passionate. He absolutely loves a Beaujolais. And he absolutely despises French Rhone wines. You may find yourself becoming enamored of wines from a certain region, such as Burgundy (as opposed to Bordeaux), or wines from central California (as opposed to Napa or Sonoma). The important thing is to find out what grapes and regions are worth remembering and knowing about by tasting the wines and deciding whether or not you like them. It is not important—and in fact, it can be rather distasteful in every sense of the word—to force yourself to drink and learn about wines just because some condescending connoisseur tells you you should.

Quite some time ago, I had a client who liked to bring his own wines to my restaurant. He had a very impressive cellar of old wines, and on one occasion he brought in a very expensive Meursault. I don't remember the exact vintage, but as I recall, it was well over thirty years old. My client went on and on about how great his wine was before he finally invited me to taste it. As he poured a bit in our glasses, I noticed it was very dark for a white wine. He tasted first and seemed to be in bliss. Then I tasted it, and thought to myself that it didn't taste good. When my client asked my opinion of the wine, I blurted out, "It tastes . . . old." Needless to say, he wasn't thrilled with my reply, and his companion started laughing, which didn't help matters. My client wouldn't speak to me until after I had tasted his selection of red wine for the evening. I took a sip, and told him that his red wine was wonderful—and it truly was.

Later, as my client was paying the check, his companion pulled me aside and told me that after I had left the table, he had asked her if she thought the white Meursault tasted bad. She told me she had said yes, and added that after my client had taken a few more sips, he too had decided it didn't taste very good. Even so, the Meursault was very old and very valuable from a collector's point of view, and my client felt I should have recognized that. As a restaurant owner, I had made a mistake by unintentionally insulting a customer. But, be that as it may, the wine really didn't taste good. And my client's companion told me she appreciated my candor and the truth of my wine motto, "If it doesn't taste good, don't drink it."

Just as wine connoisseurs can be intimidating, so can the language and vocabulary of wines. I think of wine language as a bit like Latin for secondary school students: You only have to master it if you want to pass a wine course or impress other wine connoisseurs. If those goals are not part of your personal agenda, you are better off expressing your feelings, about wines and how they taste to you, in everyday language. I learned this through trial and error, and through a couple of experiences that initially made me wish I could disappear inside a bottle.

After Alison On Dominick Street opened and we were well reviewed and in the press, I began to be invited to some very important wine tastings. I was often the only woman at these events, which made me stand out. I knew something about wine—that is to say, what I liked and didn't like. The rest was like taking a course in pre-med-level chemistry. My eyes would begin to glaze over as educated wine enthusiasts spoke about the acid, the tannins, the percentages of different grape varietals, and how long which wines had fermented in what kind of barrels.

At the now memorable champagne tasting of a fine producer, I happened to arrive a bit late and had to walk across the room, making a very noticeable entrance I would have preferred to avoid. As I sat down and began to organize the information sheets, I noticed that some of the most prominent people in the wine industry were in the room, which only added to my sense of discomfort. After we had tasted the second champagne variety of the evening, they began comparing it to the first champagne, and engaged in a lively discussion about the mousse—what creates the mousse, how this mousse compares to the other mousse, and so on. But I just sat there wondering to myself, what is mousse? As you might imagine, I was praying that I wouldn't be called on for an opinion, but within a few moments, the moderator boomed, "Alison, what do you think?"

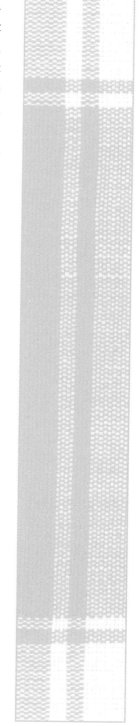

My face flushed because I felt that I did not have an intelligent answer to offer. But I took a deep breath, and said what I was thinking. "Well, I only know mousse to be something you eat or put in your hair, so I can't comment on that. But the bubble of this second champagne is nice, and it tastes good."

I felt like an idiot as the room suddenly fell silent. Then everyone around me burst into laughter, raising their eyebrows and twitching with a vicious know-it-all glee, while I wanted to disappear into a mountain of hair-styling-type mousse. After several painfully embarrassing moments that seemed like an eternity to me, someone had the grace to explain that the mousse is the bubble in the bubbly. I took another deep breath, and promptly replied, "Then why don't you just call it that?" The room fell silent again, but this time—*touché*—no one had a good answer. Finally, we all raised our glasses and made a toast to "the grand bubble" that is the essence of champagne Having gotten over the language barrier, I found myself enjoying the evening immensely, along with everyone else.

So how do ordinary people begin to choose a wine for their own meals? The easy answer is to find a friendly, knowledgeable wine shop with helpful sales-people who will not turn up their noses when you say you want to spend five to eight dollars. Form a relationship with one of these people, as you would any salesperson in any other type of shop you intend to frequent. Tell them what foods you are planning to eat, and let that be the starting point for the basic choice between red wine or white wine. It used to be conventional wisdom that you served white wine with fish and chicken, and red wine with meats and game. But I don't think there are any hard and fast rules anymore. I have served light reds with fish, and rich whites with meat. One of the best approaches is to think about the flavors of your food, and consider your choice of wine in much the same way you might choose a sauce or a gravy to complement that dish. Would you drown a light fish fillet like Dover sole in heavy brown gravy? If not, then your obvious choice is a light white wine. Would you gain anything by pouring a very light cream sauce over a piece of roast beef? If the answer is no, then you should pick a robust red wine to bring out the flavor of the meat.

What if you're located in a relatively remote area with no wine shops, or the one wine shop that is nearby happens to be run by a nasty curmudgeon who is more interested in making you feel like the village idiot than selling you something to drink? One option is to join a wine club by mail. Most wine clubs send out newsletters as well as catalogues of wine offerings that are often accompanied by descriptions and comments. Sometimes you will find ratings to help you through the maze of information. Some wine clubs offer mixed cases that include several different types of wine so you can sample a fairly broad selection and begin to know what you enjoy. You can also subscribe to the *Wine Spectator,* which comes out once a month and contains a wealth of useful information.

If you have a computer and are on the Internet, you can go to many different wine-related websites, including the *Wine Spectator* site and ask questions. Someone somewhere out there will e-mail you his or her ideas about the perfect wine to go with your dinner. If you are in an area that has a limited number of wine shops with a similarly limited array of choices, you are probably going to have to stick with the large producers such as Mondavi, Antinori, or Louis Jadot. But don't worry—there are still some very fine wines to be had.

General experimentation can be expensive, but trying different wines is really the only way to get to know what you like and which wine producers you prefer. I'm in the fortunate position of being able to taste wines all the time. When I'm working with my partner Michael Chamberlain on the wine lists for my restaurants, however, I do not always have the time or inclination to taste, so we also have several people in the wine industry we call upon for advice when we are trying to fill a spot on our restaurants' wine lists. In general, I like to look for wines that are not only well priced but also a bit out of the ordinary—for instance a red Meursault as opposed to a white, or a white Châteauneuf-du-Pape rather than a classic red. I also like good wines from unpopular or lesser-known regions. As a rule, it is wise to start at the low end of the price range and work your way up, rather than to start at the top and work your way down. The inevitable mistakes you'll make in the early going will be less costly, and as your knowledge of wine and of your own taste preferences increase, you'll be better at determining which of the higher priced wines are really valuable (to you) and which are merely higher priced.

If you don't want to follow any of this advice and simply want to rush into

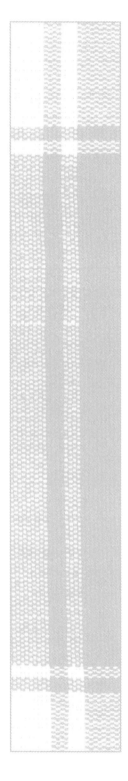

a store and get a bottle of wine, stay with the three most basic grape varieties—Chardonnay, Merlot, and Cabernet Sauvignon. Stick with the large producers, and do not buy anything that has a screw top. But most of all, do not let fear prevent you from trying something new. After all, what's the worst that can happen? The wine will get poured down the drain or it will end up in a sauce—and both you and the sauce will be the better for it.

17. You Can Be a Guest at Your Own Dinner Party

17. You Can Be a Guest at Your Own Dinner Party

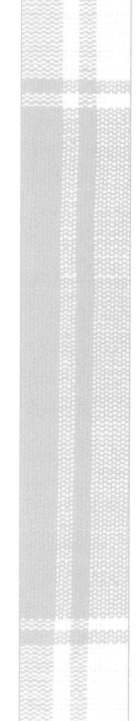

If home cooking were the same as restaurant cooking, you would never see your guests and they would never see you. Think about it. What if the chef at your favorite restaurant were in the dining room the entire time you were eating dinner? You couldn't help but wonder—and worry—about who was doing the cooking. When you're cooking at home, you have at least three roles to fill: you're the chef, you're the host, and you're also a guest at your own dinner party. I've been to many parties where I have never seen the host. Likewise, I have given parties where I have never seen my guests.

But why bother inviting people to dinner if you can't be with them long enough to enjoy their company? It would be much simpler just to dine out at a restaurant. On certain special occasions, you might find yourself tackling a menu that's so complicated you can't afford to sit down for more than a minute at a time. That should be the exception. And it's certainly not the rule when it comes to serving kitchen suppers. The point of kitchen suppers is to enjoy our friends and share our food. You'll find that entertaining can be a lot easier than you might think if you keep a few helpful hints in mind.

First and foremost, get yourself organized as far in advance as possible. If you plan even moderately well before you start cooking, you won't be making as much of a mad dash as dinnertime approaches. If you can set your table early in the day, for example, you'll at least *feel* organized. Should your guests arrive early, you'll appear to have been ready. And if worse comes to worst, you can look over at your pretty table and see that you have accomplished *something*, even if the rest of the kitchen looks like World War Three has just taken place, and you are ready to turn out the lights, lock your front door, and pretend that your guests have come on the wrong evening.

Second, think about your plates, glasses, and silverware before you decide on your menu and the number of courses you're going to serve. Do you have enough of everything on hand? Will the type and order of the courses you are considering require a lot of plate changes or washings in the middle of the meal? If you want to serve a green salad before dessert, for instance, will you need to reset plates and silverware, or will you feel comfortable having your guests use their entrée plates for the salad? The answer usually depends on what you served as the main course. I like nothing better than plopping a green salad on a plate that has the remnants of a yummy beef stew; it all seems to go together so deliciously. But if you have just served chicken or pork chops, it's not very appetizing to have the bones on the plate while you're munching away on the kind of delicate salad course my father calls "designer weeds." I can remember wonderful multicourse dinners during which the kitchen began to look like a yard sale with all the stacks of plates and bowls we had used, and I almost ran out of pretty dish towels to hide things under. This is okay, but plan for it.

You should also decide early on whether you want to serve all or part of the meal buffet style. There are a multitude of possible options and variations, each of which has its pros and cons. You can serve the first course at the table, and then serve the rest from a buffet, or you can buffet the first course and serve everything else at the table. You can have one big buffet, or you serve the whole thing. If there's going to be no more than four people, you are usually better off serving at the table. But if there are eight or more people on your guest list, I highly recommend a buffet unless you have a very large table, or serving help. Your tablecloth will stay neater. Your guests can pick and choose what they like, and help themselves to seconds. And it's easier to make the kind of presentations that elicit "oohs" and "aahs" if you use large serving platters and bowls rather than serving the courses on individual plates.

Regardless of which serving style you favor, be sure to make a schedule. You might not follow it exactly, but at least you will have some guidelines to fall back on if and when you find yourself teetering on the brink of catastrophe. When I cater large weddings, I always make a schedule. It is rarely followed to the tee. The bride may change her mind. The band may need a break, the wedding cake may start to topple over. But so long as we stick fairly close to the schedule, the show somehow goes on. As you are whirling around the kitchen, going off on tangents, and getting preoccupied by incidental tasks, it can be a lifesaver to have a piece of paper you can look at to remind you of the really important things that have to be accomplished when all is said and done.

Schedules have certainly saved my dinners—and my sanity—more times than I can count. As my husband can attest, it seems that just as I get home and start to cook dinner, one of my restaurants will call with a computer problem that requires a lengthy solution, and I lose track of what I'm supposed to be doing. My schedule puts me back on track. If I'm running very late, which all too often I am, I can also improvise better if I know in what order I need to do things. I try to plan for potential disasters, and have a contingency for every dish—bottled salad dressing for the one I didn't make, for example, or ice cream and cookies to replace the cake I just couldn't get around to baking. I'll also buy time by preparing some canapés that don't require cooking, such as smoked salmon or sausages or cheese, so my husband can keep our guests happy until I catch up.

If you are fortunate to have a kitchen large enough to entertain as well as cook in, you can be more adventurous. You can have your company in the kitchen for a glass of wine while you are putting what will hopefully be the finishing touches on the meal. Our kitchen is big enough for a table that accommodates six people, but my husband and our guests usually wind up in the living room, anyway. I hate the feeling of being left out (unless I'm in the middle of a disaster I don't want anyone to see), so I try to prepare menus that are ready to go, or stews and roasts that require only a few finishing touches. If you insist upon last-minute cooking, it's best to have no more than one dish to prepare. And you should still make sure to have all the necessary ingredients for that dish measured out and ready to go. Don't try to cook an entire meal as your guests are walking through the door or sitting down at the table. If you have to get up all the time to watch over the stove, what fun is the dinner?

Often, one of your guests will offer to help out in the kitchen. If you need his or her help, take it! If you don't need help, decline the offer politely. This is not a control thing. This is about having dinner on time, something I am still learning to do. If one of your guests happens to be a good cook, their help can be great because they will usually know what to do in the kitchen. On the other

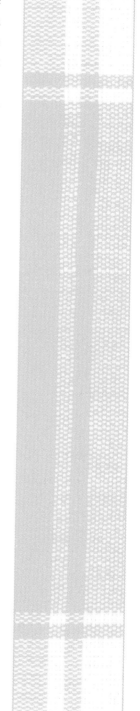

hand, they sometimes know a little too much, or think that they do. If you don't know your ever-so-helpful would-be helper very well, it's wise to start him or her out with simple tasks. But make sure you double-check whatever it is that he ends up doing. I once had a guest who insisted upon washing spinach leaves for the salad. It was a bit uncomfortable when we sat down to the first course and, crunch-crunch, found that bits of dirt were still embedded in the leaves. Had this been an old friend, I might have made a joke of it. Instead, we all had to pretend we didn't notice.

Many hosts are far too worried about what their guests will eat and not eat. I've found that most people are happy to be invited to someone else's home for dinner, and are more than willing to sample the dishes they are served. I might tailor a menu to some kind of dietary restriction, food allergy, or specific hate; I won't serve beets to one of my in-laws, for example, and I am forbidden to serve my husband anything that contains cilantro. And many times I do ask a guest if there is something he or she cannot eat. But by and large, I believe that a cook should get to cook whatever he or she wants to cook. When I meet with a future bride for the first time, I always find myself saying, "It's your wedding. Your guests are there to celebrate with you. You deserve to eat what you want to eat, and we will accommodate any restrictions on the basis of what you like or don't like, not on the basis of what your guests like or don't like." I feel the same way about serving dinner at home. If I'm the one doing all the work, I should enjoy what I'm eating. If I'm constantly worried about other people's tastes, I will never have fun.

One lesson I have learned from professional chefs is to keep the kitchen clean as I go. Most restaurant kitchens have limited workspaces, and they must be kept neat so there is room to prepare the massive amounts of food that need to be made for the customers. There are also gastronomic and sanitary considerations involved. Professional chefs don't want to mix foods that are not intended to go together, and they risk paying heavy fines to the health department if they fail to obey a long list of food-handling rules designed to prevent the spread of food-borne illnesses. You and I don't have to worry about being busted by the health department when we're cooking at home, but if you clean as you go, you will be a much happier and better-organized cook, and when you guests arrive, they will have no idea that you have used every pot in the house. One sure-fire trick I use to reduce muss and fuss is to line my kitchen floor with old newspaper. Then it doesn't matter what lands on the floor, and when I'm finished, I can roll up the messy newspapers and toss them in the garbage can.

If you have a dishwasher, empty it before you start cooking so it will be ready for use when the plates and platters start piling up at the end of the evening. As your preparations proceed, try to keep emptying your sink, as well. Unless it's absolutely necessary, I avoid washing in the middle of dinner; I merely straighten. I usually stack dirty plates and platters in the sink, and cover them with a pretty dish towel. If I run out of room in the sink, I place them on the counter and cover them with another pretty towel. This is not merely an act of procrastination or laziness; it's a matter of grace and graciousness. I'll never forget the time when my husband and I attended a dinner party at which the host kept Windexing the table, using stain remover on the tablecloth, and sweeping the floor between each and very course. We got the feeling that we were being wiped out as the evening dragged on. And that is not what kitchen suppers are about.

Just as it helps to clean the kitchen as you go, it's a good idea to build some time in your schedule for cleaning *yourself* up. Try to take your bath or shower early, and have your wardrobe for the evening laid out. Much to my husband's chagrin, this is an area where I admittedly don't always practice what I preach. When there's a break or time gap in the cooking process, I'll sit down and watch television or go outside for a breath of fresh air when I would be better off getting myself some clean clothes. Many of our guests have seen me flying upstairs to make a quick change, or heard the hair dryer blasting away as they have arrived. On other occasions, our guests have graciously accepted me as I was, dirty apron and all. That may be in keeping with the informal spirit of kitchen suppers, but I always feel better throughout the evening if I greet my guests in clean clothes.

As dinnertime approaches, be sure you recheck the list of dishes you're planning to serve before you call your guests to the table. On several semi-embarrassing occasions, I have made too many dishes and have simply forgotten to serve one of them. That means I didn't plan the menu properly; after all, if I forgot to serve something extra, we didn't need it anyway. But preparing too many dishes is wasteful, not to mention time-consuming. The opposite sce-

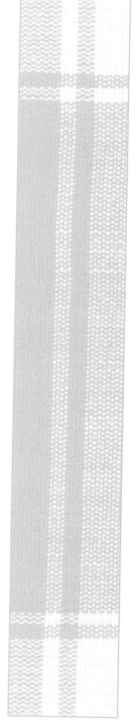

nario—forgetting something you cannot serve the meal without—though rare, can happen on a particularly stressful day. That's when having ready-to-serve contingencies in the cupboard or the refrigerator is crucial. When you forget to make a compote to go with the pork you're serving, a jar of store-bought applesauce seems like a godsend.

One of my dearest friends, a classic hostess with the mostest, always writes out her menus on fancy paper and shows them to her guests before dinner. I think this is a great idea. You can't forget anything, and if anyone has any aversions, they can silently determine how to escape the offending dish gracefully, or come and tell you they have a terrible migraine and won't be able to eat very much this evening. If this sounds too formal for you, just jot down your menu on a piece of scrap paper and pin it to the refrigerator for your own personal reference. That way you can remind yourself to take the bread out of the oven before the overwhelming aroma of burned flour fills your kitchen.

When dinner is finally ready and you get to sit down with your guests and raise a glass, keep a flexible plan for clearing and serving in the back of your mind, especially if you're offering more than one course. When I serve an appetizer course, for example, I prefer it to be something that I can pre-plate, such as soup, a salad, a tart, or a terrine. If you serve something that is going to be dished out at the table, in all likelihood the tablecloth will be destroyed, and I feel that this is an honor that belongs to the main course.

If you know the second course will be ready shortly after everyone is finished with the first course, rise and take your plate and the plate of the person next to you. If your second course is going to require a considerable amount of additional preparation time, leave your plate on the table and go back to clear when you are a few minutes away from its final presentation. Hopefully, one sweet guest or significant other will help you with this task, should you so desire. If not, finish clearing before you start to put the finishing touches on your next course or to make up individual plates. Have plenty of wine on the table so your guests can serve themselves while you are fussing with your masterpiece. If you have planned your menu with the right kind of foresight, this shouldn't take more than twenty minutes at most. Your dessert course should follow the same basic clearing and serving pattern.

Sounds easy enough, doesn't it? If you follow all these steps, and for some unknown reason, you find that nothing is working, don't worry. You've tried your best, and that's all you can ask of yourself. The kitchen gods just aren't with you, and unfortunately, no one has control over them. Your guests are your friends. They love you anyway. And if they don't love you, they came in the front door, so you know they also know the way out. In the meantime, here's an example of checklist items which you can copy or clip out and use as a ready-made planning guideline.

1. Compose your menu.
2. Make a schedule for when you are cooking what.
3. Make your plan for potential disasters.
4. Make a shopping list—and look to make sure—don't just assume—you have everything you need. If there is an item in the recipe you don't want to buy for whatever reason, make sure you have something you can substitute. Also, check your supply of flatware, plates, napkins, tablecloths, candles, etc. Remember, you want to make only one shopping trip if possible, not three or four.
5. When you go to the store, don't shop—buy. If there is time, you can explore the shelves a little, keeping your eye out for something that might inspire a delightful little twist. But usually, time is of the essence, and what you really need to focus on is getting exactly what you need for the menu you've planned.
6. Unpack and organize. Don't start cooking until you're sure you've brought home everything you're going to need.
7. Get out your recipes and recheck your cooking schedule so you can time your dishes appropriately. Make adjustments for any sudden inspirations that might have taken place during your shopping—I mean, buying—spree.
8. If there are no breaks in the cooking schedule, set your table before you start laboring over the stove.
9. Start your precooking preparations. Chop, slice, dice, and perform whatever tasks need to be done. But focus on one recipe at a time; don't flutter from dish to dish.
10. Cook.

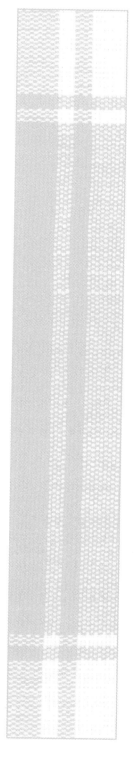

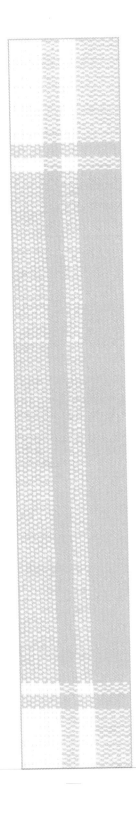

11. Clean as much as you can while you are cooking.
12. Check your table, check your kitchen, check your floor, check your cooking schedule, and check your menu for anything you might have forgotten.
13. If you missed something, go to your contingency plan.
14. Shower and dress or at least change your apron.
15. Put out some nibbles.
16. Greet your guests.
17. Put on the finishing touches.
18. Eat and enjoy!

18. What to Do When

All Else Fails

18. What to Do When All Else Fails

The act of cooking is an invitation to disaster. You should always remember that, but at the same time, you need not worry about it too much. Like life itself, cooking involves risk, especially when you are trying a new recipe or experimenting with variations on a familiar one. Sometimes that evil kitchen witch just shows up unannounced, and the good witch goes on vacation. The main difference between great cooks and mediocre ones is not the number of mistakes they make in the kitchen—in fact, a creative cook is likely to make more and much bigger messes than a less daring one—but the way they handle the disasters that befall them.

If necessity is the mother of invention, I used to feel like her unwanted stepdaughter. Like everyone else, I always wanted my dishes to be just as good as the recipes prescribed, if not even better. When disaster struck, my first impulse was to throw up my hands in dismay, and chuck the whole mess into the garbage for fear that my dinner guests would otherwise throw up their meals and chuck me in the trash instead. But, as I became a more experienced cook, I began to develop several methods for fixing seemingly unfixable kitchen disasters in fifteen minutes or less.

One quick fix was actually inspired by a disaster of someone else's making. When I was attending acting school in Boston, I shared an apartment with two male roommates. A very well-meaning friend had a huge crush on one of my roommates, and when my birthday rolled around, she offered to bake a surprise dessert. As fate would have it, I had somehow twisted my knee in my sleep, ripping the ligaments, and I was wearing a full leg cast and feeling supremely sorry

for myself. Her offer sounded like just what my good doctor would have ordered if he had been a good cook.

Unfortunately, my well-meaning friend was neither a good cook nor a good doctor. She arrived at our apartment bearing a fresh-baked pumpkin pie and a quart of Heath bar crunch ice cream. What she didn't know was that I hated pumpkin pie, and so did Bob, the male roommate she wanted so desperately to impress. I assume she did know that the ice cream needed to be stored in the freezer, but given her infatuation with my roommate, that must have slipped her mind, because she left it in a bag on the kitchen counter, where it naturally proceeded to melt while we ate.

When dessert time came, I had the dubious honor of getting the first bite of pumpkin pie, since I was the birthday girl. It was a bite I will never forget. My mouth burned like fire from an overwhelming onslaught of spices. I tried to disguise my reaction by turning toward my roommates, who were now in the process of taking their first bites of the pie. The cringing looks on their faces confirmed that they felt the same sensations I had suffered.

As it turned out, my well-meaning friend had misread her pumpkin pie recipe. She had put a cup of ginger in the batter instead of a teaspoon, and she had put in a teaspoon of sugar instead of a cup. If she had only tasted the batter as she went along, she might still have been able to salvage her pie by adding more cream and sugar to dilute the accidental ginger overload. Now it was too late. Or so I thought until I remembered the Heath bar crunch ice cream she had brought.

By this time, of course, the ice cream had completely melted, but it still contained the basic elements needed to fix the pumpkin pie, namely cream and sugar. I hobbled into the kitchen, and, mindful of just how badly my first bite of pie had burned, bolstered the melted ice cream by adding some more sugar and a generous dollop of vanilla extract. Then I returned to the dinner table with the container in hand, announcing with a mischievous wink that we had forgotten the sauce for the pie. My roommates were biting their lips in a hopeless effort to suppress their laughter, but my well-meaning friend proved to be a good sport. We poured the Heath bar crunch "sauce" all over the pie, and tried it again. Although I can't pretend that I suddenly gained a newfound love for pumpkin pie, my quick fix did extinguish the spice fire and make the ensuing bites at least palatable.

Years later, as I was starting a catering division to complement my restaurant business, that same sort of quick fix saved my life. I happened to be cooking lunch at a very exclusive shooting club for a very exclusive party of hunters. I was supposed to grill venison chops on the outside barbecue pit, but it was snowing, so that wasn't going to happen. Although the main lodge was elegantly spacious, the kitchen was rather cramped and the stove was tiny. My catering staff and I had all the burners going with pans of venison when the host of the hunting party informed us that ten extra people had arrived for lunch.

Things started to get a little frantic, and the evil kitchen witch tried to work her black magic on us. We were planning to serve ginger cake and ice cream for dessert, but somehow, we neglected to put the ice cream in the freezer while we were cooking the venison. The ice cream melted, and by the time we discovered our oversight, it was too late to refreeze it. But instead of panicking, I remembered the pumpkin pie disaster back in Boston. Fortunately, the situation I faced now was not nearly so dire, since the ginger cake, unlike the pumpkin pie, was quite tasty. I added a little vanilla extract to the melted ice cream, and poured it into a hand blown glass pitcher. The consistency was perfect. It made a great sauce for the ginger cake, and no one knew it was really just a quick fix—though I guess they will now!

As these anecdotes illustrate, the most important thing you can do when confronted with a disaster of your own making or someone else's is to keep your cool and your sense of humor. Be calm. And smile. More than once, I have turned a runny mousse into a yummy soup or chopped up accidentally overcooked meat and made it part of a mouthwatering bolognese sauce.

When catastrophes occur, the first thing I try to do is get rid of the evidence before anyone notices, which isn't always possible if there's ugly black smoke pouring out of my oven. That's where the smile comes in. If my well-trained husband has already escorted our guests out of the kitchen and into the living room for some drinks and hors d'oeuvre prior to the disaster, I'll take a quick break, and emerge from the kitchen to say sweetly, "Not to worry. Dinner will be delayed fifteen minutes or so." As my husband offers everyone another round of refreshments, I'll laugh lightheartedly, then turn around and march back to the kitchen before they see the tears streaming down my cheeks.

Needless to say, it's much easier to maintain your composure in the face of kitchen disasters if you have made contingency plans. You may want to go back and reread the "Pantry Pride" chapter with that in mind, because your range of disaster-solving choices always depends on how well you have stocked your pantry. Likewise, remember that most disasters are not all-or-nothing situations that leave no choice but to throw everything out and start all over again. In her brilliant book *The Making of a Cook*, Madeleine Kamman notes that the best approach is the most reasoned one. "Think it out first," she advises. "Can you salvage it?"

Oftentimes, one part of a dish survives the disaster. If you've ruined the meat but not the vegetables while cooking a stew, for example, you can switch from stew to pasta or risotto, both of which are quick to prepare. Just puree the veggies into a pasta sauce or stir them into the risotto. If it's the vegetables you've ruined and there are no other fresh ones in the house, look in the pantry. If you've made the proper contingency plans, you'll probably find some canned tomatoes on the shelf. They may not compare to fresh tomatoes, but if you roast them in the oven and serve them with chopped oregano, they can be quite tasty.

If nothing can be recovered and you're feeling completely cowed, there's always eggs and toast (unless the bread came to an untimely death, as well). The International House of Pancakes based an entire advertising campaign on having breakfast for dinner. A frittata (which is a baked omelet pancake) with chopped sausage and onion can be a wonderfully homey main dish. If you used up all the eggs in the hollandaise for the appetizer, you'll have to think of something. I recently stumbled across a recipe for a pasta made with potatoes and cream. Okay, so it may not be the healthiest of dishes, but it certainly tasted great, and when you're in a fix, you have to go with what you've got.

If you're feeling adventurous and your fear hasn't crippled you, just make something up. Call the dish whatever you want. The more the name you dream up sounds like a variation on a more conventional dish, the better. Is a guest going to really challenge you when you serve your "creamed fish risotto" by saying it's really overcooked fish and rice. I don't think so.

I must say that I treasure the quick-fix methods described below. They are my secret weapons in the never-ending war against the evil kitchen witch. Because of them, I usually manage to come out of disasters looking like a much better cook than I really am. I would be less than truthful if I claimed that I am more than happy to expose my weaknesses by sharing my secret weapons with you. But then again, I wouldn't be a good kitchen witch—or a good kitchen friend—if I didn't.

Disasters and the Sure-Fire Quick Fixes That Take Fifteen Minutes or Less

TOO MUCH SALT

Your stew, soup, or poaching broth is simmering away, looking all happy. Then you spoon a little out to taste the flavors that have melded together so perfectly, and bang—you realize that you must have added a handful of salt rather than a pinch. My first suggestion is to peel a large potato and stick it in the stew. It will absorb some of the liquid; then you can add a bit more fresh broth. My second suggestion is to add something sweet, but make sure you do it a little at a time so you don't go from oversalty to oversweet. Start with just a tablespoon of brown sugar, tomato paste, or honey to salvage meats and vegetables. If the problem involves fish, a squeeze of lemon will help. Even though it's not sweet, it works. Sugar and fish, other than sweet-and-sour concoctions, generally don't mix.

OVERSEASONING

For stews and soup, follow the same routine that I suggest for salt. If you have overseasoned, you can make a very plain sauce, then stir it into the stew or pour it over the meat. A cream sauce can also be a savior if your diet allows you to have cream. If not, a vegetable sauce made in the food processor from peppers and celery is quite good. For an especially quick fix, cook some onions in butter and balsamic vinegar or brown sugar to make a sweet onion sauce.

BURNED THINGS

If you're going up in flames: TURN THE BURNERS OFF. DO NOT THROW WATER. If you have one close by, grab a large pot cover to smother the flame. If it's a grease fire, throw baking soda or salt on it. Now that we have that covered, what do you do about salvaging dinner?

If you stayed on the phone too long and burned your garlic or onions, try putting them in a cheesecloth pouch and simmering them in boiling water with a squeeze of lemon for a few minutes. Or you can start with a fresh batch. But keep the burned ones. They can taste great if you crumble them on top of a stew, a salad, or fish.

If you burn the bottom of the pot, remove all but the last inch or two of what you're cooking, then put it in a fresh pot and continue cooking. The longer the food stays in the burned pot, the more burned it will taste. If you haven't rescued enough to serve for a main course, serve it over pasta, or stir it into risotto.

If you burn rice, take what you can out of the pot and sauté it with butter and onions—you will have just made toasted rice! You can also make burned or browned rice into rice cakes. Mix an egg into the rice, form it into patties, and sauté. You can also turn this into a dessert by sautéing it in butter and adding a tablespoon of sugar for each cup of rice.

If you burned the butter, just start all over again. If you don't have any more, try substituting oil.

OVERCOOKED THINGS

Vegetables lend themselves to purees. You can add a bit of cream to create a beautifully smooth and sumptuous dish. But if baby food consistency doesn't enchant you, chop up the vegetables and make a creamed dish, sauté them with some rice, or stir them into risotto.

Or serve soup: Puree or chop the vegetables fine and add chicken stock or vegetable stock a bit at a time until you have the consistency you want. Add a bit of cream, or maybe a bit of sour cream, and you have soup. Or if you have time, you can make a timbale or a soufflé—although after having one disaster, you are probably not in the mood to invite another one by attempting a soufflé.

If your pasta is a coagulated mess, try putting it into a colander and pouring boiling water with a tablespoon of oil over it. Gently pull it apart and return it to the pot with more oil or butter. If the pasta has so thoroughly overcooked that it's turned mushy, drain it carefully, then sauté it in butter or oil, and crisp the outside a bit. If you add some Parmesan cheese while you are sautéing it, it will coat the outside and get a toasty cheese flavor. You can try the same thing with bread crumbs or nuts instead of the cheese. The pasta will certainly be edible—and it may be quite tasty, depending on how mushy it was to begin with.

If you've unintentionally made sticky rice, you have a couple of choices. The first is to pretend that you intended to serve sticky rice, and toss it with a bit of warmed rice vinegar and a touch of lemon juice. Or you can sauté the rice with onion and a bit of oil or butter, and toss in any vegetable that will cook quickly.

Overcooked fish can be flaked and stirred into risotto. (Yes, I know that I keep coming back to risotto, but it's really an exceptionally good quick-fixer.) Fish can also be turned into a gourmet tuna casserole. But you probably won't have time for this on the night of the dinner. Instead, sauté some tomatoes, and add the fish at the last minute for a quick-fix pasta sauce. If your roasted fish dries out, poach it for a couple of minutes and serve it with a little of the poaching broth.

Overcooked meat is a very untasty problem. Always make sure to check your roast prior to putting it on the table, so that you don't make a beautiful presentation only to discover a gray monster hidden inside. If you do have a gray monster, whisk it away immediately. Then slice the meat very thin with a sharp knife. Place it on individual plates and pour gravy or the pan juices over the top. Steak sauce or mint sauce, thinned with a little preheated balsamic vinegar, will also work. Even ketchup thinned with vinegar and a dab of horseradish can do similar wonders.

Dried-out chicken or turkey is depressing. But you can still salvage either one by pulling the meat from the bones and sautéing it with vermouth or white wine and a little sour cream, then serving it over pasta. Or you can make a kind of hacked chicken or hacked turkey by shredding the meat, and mixing up a sauce of peanut butter thinned with rice vinegar, a little oil, and some hot pepper. You can also slice and simmer the meat in some stock with the pan juices (if there were any), then simply put it on a platter and serve.

UNDERCOOKED THINGS

This is usually a time problem. The best fix is just to keep cooking. But what if you've already kept your guests waiting an hour? In that case, you can slice and sauté undercooked meat or poultry. Or you can braise the slices in a little stock.

The thinner you slice, the quicker it will cook. Then, just make a beautiful presentation on a platter, and your guests won't know the difference. In fact, when they see the beautiful presentation, they will think they know why you have taken so long.

If you forget to put the potatoes in the oven on time, slice them very thin and sauté them in oil or quickly switch to pasta. If you have small potatoes, you can boil them quickly and serve them with parsley and butter. Or take a good look at your menu and reevaluate. If you are serving great bread, do you really need the potatoes?

THINGS THAT DON'T DO WHAT THEY SHOULD

If your popover doesn't pop, split it open and serve it with a stew or creamed/pureed vegetables on top.

If your soufflé falls, don't hide it—show it with pride. The fact that you even tried to make a soufflé should be good enough for your guests. A fallen soufflé can be served with a sauce or whipped cream if you feel you have to hide the damage, and it will still taste the same. If the soufflé cooked but didn't rise at all, hey, it's a new dish. You never told anyone you were making soufflé, did you? And if you did, just tell them you changed your mind. Slice it like a pie and serve.

When your meat doesn't brown and gives off too much juice, take it out of the oven, pour off the juice and save it for later. Then dry the meat with paper towels, add some fat to the pan, and brown the meat in the fat.

If your stew is seriously soupy, it may be that you added too much liquid. If so, pour a half cup to a full cup of rice into a loose cheesecloth pouch and put it in the stew; the rice will absorb some of the liquid. You can also save the rice for a subsequent lunch or dinner. Or you can add a thickener such as roux, cornstarch, or arrowroot. The quickest fix is flour paste, which is not as yummy as roux but a lot easier to use. Add one part flour to two parts water to make a paste, and whisk that into a boiling stock or the bottom of a pan. I do this one tablespoon at a time so as not to destroy the flavor of the stew and create another disaster I would have to fix by adding more wine or more stock.

If your stew meat is tough, try braising it in some wine or adding more acid to the stew. This will help tenderize the meat. Sometimes, you just have to let the meat cook more. You can't expect a tough piece of stew meat to cook quickly. You can also add a mild vinegar or lemon juice. But make sure to keep tasting! Otherwise, you will have to add something sweet to counter the acid needed to tenderize the meat.

If your sauces are lumpy, put them through a sieve or whirl them in the food processor, or both! I prefer the food processor method. You can add a bit of cream or an egg yolk to smooth things out. I have also added cream cheese, which tasted great with veal stew.

THE FINISHED RECIPE DOESN'T TASTE RIGHT

If a recipe does not come out tasting quite right, it is not necessarily your fault. Your taste buds are different from the taste buds of the person who wrote the recipe. Perhaps you feel like adding a little more of something than the recipe calls for, or perhaps you used some brand that was different from the one used when the recipe was tested. It's your food, so feel free to play with it. After all, you are the one eating it!

On those occasions when a recipe does not come out right because of a mistake you made, you can improve the taste in several ways. If you have used an oil that is too strong for the sauce or dressing, make a second batch with safflower oil or another mild oil and combine the two. I have done this when I used too much nut oil.

If a dish is too spicy, add something sweet or add some salt.

If your food has a case of the blahs, a spoonful of mustard, hot sauce, or horseradish will certainly wake it up. So will a tablespoon of balsamic vinegar. In stews and tomato dishes, a tablespoon of brown sugar brings out a nice flavor, as does a bottle of ale or strong beer. As with every quick fix, add a little bit at a time and keep tasting. If you have problems with delicate foods, such as fruits and vegetables, add a squeeze of lemon, lime, or orange to bring out flavor.

THERE IS NOT ENOUGH TO SERVE

On more than one occasion, I've discovered to my dismay that the beautiful huge bunch of rich green spinach that looked so big at the farm stand is barely enough for two people, never mind the party of eight we've invited to dinner.

When that happens, I slice an onion or some leeks, sauté them with butter, and add the spinach at the last minute. The result is a dish plentiful enough for everyone at the table.

If extra guests arrive when I am planning to serve individual portions of meat, such as lamb chops or veal chops, I slice the meat from the bones, make a bowl of pasta, and serve the meat on the side or over the pasta. I take whatever juices are available, mix in a bit of oil and garlic, and create a sauce. You can do the same thing with risotto, chopping up the meat and stirring it in.

Sauces can usually be stretched by adding stock and/or wine. But you might find that you simply have to rethink a dish. One night I was making a simple supper of chicken breast with ricotta, and two extra people arrived. I quickly added a little more ricotta, some chicken stock, and some Canadian bacon. The addition of wide egg noodles made plenty of food to go around. It was terrific.

DESSERT IS A DISASTER

I always keep ice cream in the freezer when I am having friends to dinner. I also stock up on chocolate to melt into chocolate sauce or grab a jar of store-bought chocolate sauce when I go shopping. Sometimes the time just flies by when I'm cooking the other courses, and I can't make dessert as planned. And there is nothing wrong with ice cream, with sauce or without. Fresh fruit, or even warmed up fruit jams, also make fine ice cream sauces. When I opened Alison By The Beach, the only dessert I *insisted* on having on the menu was an espresso coupe, which is chocolate and espresso ice creams with thick chocolate sauce, candied nut crunch, and a cookie. The espresso coupe is our best-selling dessert by far.

Ice cream can also come in handy when you have a pie-baking disaster. You've managed to make a piecrust with a perfect buttery, sugary, fruity filling, and it's in the oven bubbling away when all of a sudden that all-too-familiar black aroma creeps into the air. Or you take your masterpiece out of the oven, and the crust is mushy. Maybe the oven was on too high. Maybe you used too much liquid. Maybe the heat was uneven. Does it matter? Next time, yes, but not right now because dessert is not going to be what it was supposed to be anyway, and you need to salvage something.

Get your pie or tart out of the oven. Check the damage. If you've made a covered pie and it's only the top crust that is burned, just take the top off. If it breaks up, take off the pieces. Crush some nuts with brown sugar and butter and you've got a crumb topping. If the damage is worse, scoop out the innards and serve them over ice cream or with whipped cream. If you have time and there is a puff pastry in the freezer, you can make turnovers. Or, if the pastry is in shell form, just scoop the filling into the shells and serve it with ice cream or sauce. And yes, here again you can stir the mixture into a risotto. Just put some brown sugar and butter on top, bake it till the top gets crusty, and serve it as rice pudding.

Let's say you've made a cake and all seems okay until it's time to remove the cake from the oven. There's a big hole in the middle where there is supposed to be a mound, and it is mushy. Scoop or cut out the undone middle, and fill the hole with whipped cream or ice cream. If the center hasn't fallen too much, you can simply repair it with icing or whipped cream.

But maybe you've just turned the cake out of the pan, and, as you eagerly peek while lifting the pan, a strange looking hunk drops out while the rest is sticking happily in the bottom of the pan. If you can get the other piece out intact, you can repair it with icing, melted sugar, or cream whipped almost to the consistency of butter. You will have a strange line running through the cake, but if you cut the slices before serving, who's to know.

If the cake has fallen apart in chunks like a jigsaw puzzle, it's probably dried out. Cut it into smaller chunks and top it with a sauce and some ice cream. You'll have an ice cream and cake sundae! If there is enough cake to cut into squares for individual servings, no one will know the difference. You can also dry out some of those chunks even further and make a pudding, then put the chunks into a baking pan with the pudding and have bread pudding. If it's summer, cut the cake up, douse it with liqueur, make a quick custard sauce, and serve it as a trifle.

If you've turned your whipped cream into butter, you're either going to have to start all over again, or melt it down and serve it as a sauce instead of as whipped cream. If you didn't really need the whipped cream anyway, put it into the refrigerator until you have time to blend in some spices, herbs, smoked fish, or horseradish, which will turn it into an hors d'oeuvre spread for a later date.

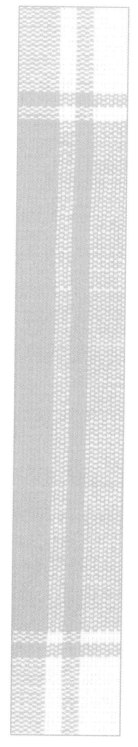

You can also add honey or brown sugar to the butter and serve it on toast. Or whip maple syrup, into it and use it for pancakes or waffles.

Whatever you do, when disaster strikes, it's good to have the following five rules in the forefront of your mind or taped to the door of your refrigerator:

1. Anything mushy can be stirred into risotto.
2. Anything dry and overcooked can be chopped into a pasta sauce.
3. Anything undercooked can be sautéed.
4. Anything sweet can be replaced with ice cream.
5. When disaster strikes, anything goes.

Appendices

Appendix A

Substitutions

Baking Products

BAKING POWDER:

1 teaspoon = $\frac{1}{4}$ teaspoon baking soda and $\frac{1}{2}$ teaspoon cream of tartar

= $\frac{1}{4}$ teaspoon baking soda and $\frac{1}{2}$ cup butter milk (reduce liquid in recipe by $\frac{1}{2}$ cup)

= $\frac{1}{4}$ teaspoon baking soda and 1 tablespoon vinegar or lemon juice

YEAST:

1 tablespoon active dry yeast (1 package) = 1 standard cake

BREAD CRUMBS

1 cup = $\frac{3}{4}$ cup of cracker crumbs

FLOUR (ALL-PURPOSE):

1 tablespoon flour = $\frac{1}{2}$ tablespoon cornstarch = $\frac{1}{3}$ tablespoon arrowroot (for thickening)

1 cup flour = 1 cup + 2 tablespoons sifted = 1 cup + 3 tablespoons sifted cake flour

   Sifting adds about 2 tablespoons flour to each cup.

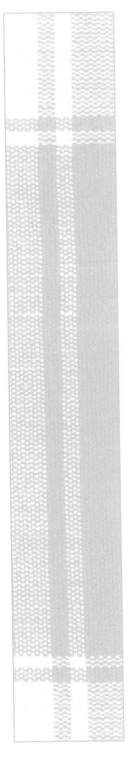

1 cup (¹/₂ pound granulated) = ³/₄ cup honey (reduce liquid in recipe by ¹/₄ cup)

= ³/₄ cup maple syrup (reduce liquid in recipe by ¹/₄ cup)

= 1¹/₄ cups molasses (reduce liquid in recipe by ¹/₄ cup)

= 2 cups corn syrup (reduce liquid in recipe by ¹/₄ cup—this is the least desirable substitution)

= 1³/₄ to 2 cups confectioners' sugar

= 1 cup light brown sugar

Light Brown Sugar:

1 cup = ¹/₂ cup dark brown sugar + ¹/₂ cup granulated sugar

Dark brown sugar:

1 cup = ³/₄ cup granulated sugar + ¹/₂ cup molasses

DAIRY

Butter:

1 cup = ³/₄ cup chicken fat

= ⁷/₈ cup vegetable oil

= ⁷/₈ cup lard

Egg:

1 egg = 2 yolks + 1 tablespoon water

Milk:

1 cup whole = 1 cup nonfat + 2 tablespoons butter

= 1 cup buttermilk + ¹/₂ teaspoon baking soda

To replace milk with buttermilk when baking, do not use any baking powder. It will curdle. Just use ¹/₂ teaspoon baking soda for 2 teaspoons baking powder. The buttermilk will introduce extra acid into the recipe, replacing the need for the acid in baking powder. Otherwise your cake will be flat.

1 cup half and half = $\frac{1}{2}$ cup light cream + $\frac{1}{2}$ cup whole milk

= $1\frac{1}{2}$ teaspoons melted butter + $\frac{7}{8}$ cup whole milk

1 cup whipping cream = $\frac{3}{4}$ cup whole milk + $\frac{1}{3}$ cup butter

1 cup sour cream = $\frac{3}{4}$ cup buttermilk + $\frac{1}{3}$ cup yogurt or butter

1 cup buttermilk = 1 cup yogurt = 1 cup milk + 1 tablespoon lemon juice or vinegar

Flavoring

1 teaspoon dried herbs = 1 tablespoon fresh

1 teaspoon ground allspice = $\frac{1}{2}$ teaspoon ground cinnamon + $\frac{1}{2}$ teaspoon ground cloves

1 ounce semi-sweet chocolate = $\frac{1}{2}$ ounce unsweetened + 1 tablespoon granulated sugar

1 ounce unsweetened chocolate = 3 tablespoons cocoa + 1 tablespoon butter

= 3 tablespoons carob powder + 2 tablespoons water

Lemon juice = equal parts water and vinegar = white wine

1 tablespoon mustard = 1 teaspoon powdered mustard

1 tablespoon shallot = 2 teaspoons onion = 1 teaspoon garlic

1 garlic clove = $\frac{1}{8}$ teaspoon powdered garlic = $\frac{1}{2}$ teaspoon dried garlic

1 tablespoon fresh ginger = $\frac{1}{8}$ teaspoon powdered = 1 tablespoon candied

2 cups tomato sauce = $\frac{3}{4}$ cup tomato paste + 1 cup water or wine

= 2 cups ketchup + 2 tablespoons lemon juice

1 cup ketchup = $\frac{3}{4}$ cup tomato paste + $\frac{1}{2}$ cup sugar + 1 tablespoon vinegar

Appendix B
Food Equivalents and
Serving Sizes

All the amounts below are approximate. When food cooks, it loses water and the cooked-down quantities will vary depending on the quality and the water content of the food you are cooking. It is helpful to know these things before you go shopping, so that you aren't disappointed when your spinach turns out to be only enough to serve one, or you discover that you have cooked enough rice for an army.

DAIRY

1 pound butter = 2 cups = 32 tablespoons = 4 sticks
1 pound cheese = 4 to 5 cups shredded
8 ounces cream cheese = 1 cup = 16 tablespoons
1 pound soft cheese (such as cottage) = 2 cups
1 cup heavy cream = 2 cups whipped

EGGS

3 to 4 large or extra-large = 1 cup
1 hard-boiled = $\frac{1}{4}$ cup chopped
6 to 7 egg whites = 1 cup
12 to 14 yolks = 1 cup
1 yolk = 2 tablespoons

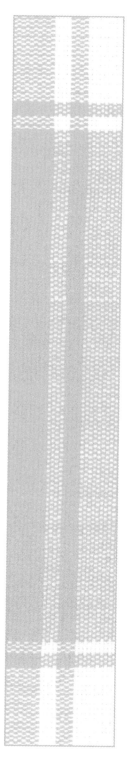

6 ounces chocolate chips = 1 cup

1 ounce unsweetened chocolate = 1 square = 2 tablespoons melted

1 pound cocoa = 4 cups

1 pound cornmeal = 3 cups = 12 cups cooked

1 pound all-purpose flour = 4 cups sifted = $3\frac{1}{4}$ cups unsifted

1 pound honey, molasses, or syrup = $1\frac{1}{3}$ cups

1 pound brown sugar packed = $2\frac{1}{4}$ cups firmly packed

1 pound confectioners' sugar = $3\frac{1}{2}$ cups

1 pound granulated sugar = 2 cups

FRUIT AND NUTS

As a general rule, 1 pound = $2\frac{1}{2}$ to 3 cups chopped or sliced

1 apple = 1 cup sliced or chopped

1 pound apples/pears = 3 medium = 3 cups sliced or chopped

1 pound bananas = 3 to 4 = $1\frac{3}{4}$ cups mashed

1 pound blueberries/strawberries/raspberries = 1 pint = 2 cups

1 pound cherries = $2\frac{1}{2}$ cups pitted

1 pound cranberries = 2 cups

1 pound dried fruit = $2\frac{1}{2}$ to 3 cups = $5\frac{1}{2}$ cups cooked

1 pound grapefruit = 1 medium = $1\frac{1}{2}$ cups chopped = $\frac{2}{3}$ cup juice

1 pound grapes = $2\frac{1}{2}$ cups

1 lemon = 2 to 3 tablespoons juice = 2 teaspoons grated rind

1 pound lemons/limes = 4 to 6 = 1 cup juice = 8 to 12 teaspoons
  grated rind

1 pound nuts = 3 cups whole = $3\frac{1}{2}$ to 4 cups chopped

1 orange = $\frac{1}{2}$ cup juice = 2 tablespoons grated rind

1 pound oranges = 3 medium = 1 cup juice = 6 tablespoons grated rind

1 pound peaches/plums/apricots = 8 to 12 = $2\frac{1}{2}$ cups sliced or chopped

1 pound raisins = $2\frac{1}{2}$ cups

GRAINS AND PASTA

1 pound dried beans = 2½ cups = 5½ cups cooked

1 pound bread = 12 to 16 slices

1 slice bread = ½ cup cubes = ¼ cup dry bread crumbs

1 pound bulghur = 2¾ cups = 3¾ cups cooked

1 pound noodles = 6 to 8 cups = 8 cups cooked

1 pound pasta/rice = 2½ to 3 cups = 7 to 9 cups cooked (depending on type and shape)

1 cup white rice = 6 ounces = 3 cups cooked

1 cup brown rice = 6 ounces = 3½ to 4 cups cooked

1 cup instant rice = 6 ounces = 2 cups cooked

1 cup Uncle Ben's rice = 6 ounces = 3½ to 4 cups cooked

1 cup wild rice = 6 ounces = 2 to 3 cups cooked

MEAT AND POULTRY

1 pound ground/diced meat = 5 cups cooked

One 3½-pound chicken = 3 cups cooked meat

VEGETABLES

1 pound asparagus = 16 to 20 medium spears

1 pound avocado = 2½ cups sliced

1 pound beets (tops removed)/parsnips/turnips = 2 cups cooked

1 pound broccoli/cauliflower = 2 cups chopped

1 pound Brussels sprouts = 4 cups = 32 sprouts

1 pound cabbage = 4 cups shredded = 2½ cups cooked

1 pound carrots = 3 cups chopped = 2½ cups shredded = 2 cups cooked

1 medium head celery = 4½ cups chopped

35 to 40 chestnuts = 2½ cups chopped

2 ears corn = 1 cup kernels

1 pound eggplant = 3 to 4 cups chopped

1 pound green beans = 3 cups chopped = $2\frac{1}{2}$ cups cooked

1 pound lettuce = 6 cups shredded

1 pound mushrooms = $1\frac{1}{4}$ cups chopped or sliced = $\frac{1}{3}$ cup cooked

1 medium yellow onion = $\frac{1}{2}$ cup chopped

1 pound pea pods = $2\frac{1}{2}$ cups peas

1 large bell pepper = 1 cup chopped

1 pound potatoes = 3 medium = 3 cups sliced or chopped = 2 cups mashed

1 pound spinach = 10 cups = 1 cup cooked

1 pound tomatoes = 3 medium = $1\frac{1}{2}$ cups cooked

One $14\frac{1}{2}$-ounce can tomatoes = $1\frac{3}{4}$ cups

SERVING SIZES PER PERSON

These amounts should be adjusted depending on how ravenous you and your guests are feeling.

Fish:

1 pound whole fish with bones

$\frac{1}{2}$ pound steaks

$\frac{1}{3}$ pound fillets

$\frac{1}{4}$ pound stuffed

Meat:

1 pound meat on the bone

$\frac{1}{2}$ pound steak

6 ounces cutlets

$\frac{3}{4}$ pound stuffed

Grains and Pasta:

$\frac{1}{4}$ cup uncooked long grain rice = $\frac{3}{4}$ cup cooked

$\frac{1}{4}$ cup wild rice = $\frac{1}{2}$ cup cooked

Pasta main dish: 4 ounces uncooked = 2 cups (I usually double this)

Vegetables and Fruit:

$\frac{1}{4}$ pound ($\frac{1}{2}$ to $\frac{2}{3}$ cup)

Salad:

$\frac{1}{6}$ pound greens (1 cup)

1 teaspoon dressing

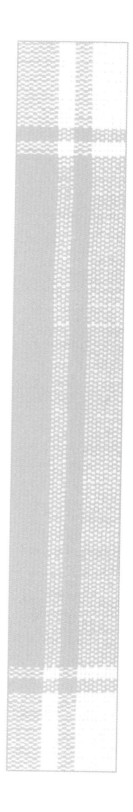

Appendix C
Food Storage Times

	Refrigerator	Freezer	Defrost in Fridge	Defrost Outside Fridge
Fresh meat	3–5 days	5–6 months	Allow 12 hours	Allow 8 hours
Ground meat	2 days	3 months	for the first	for the first 4
Sausage	7 days	6 months	4 pounds, after	pounds, after
Ham/bacon	3–5 days	2 months	1 pound per hour.	3 pounds per hour.
Cooked leftovers	2 days	2–3 months	Example: 16	Example: 16
			pounds = 24	pounds = 12
		hours	hours	
Chicken	2 days	6 months	1 day	
Game	2 days	2–4 months	1–2 days	
Cooked leftovers	2 days	5 months	6 hours	
Fish	2 days	3 months	6–12 hours (depends on the thickness)	2–6 hours

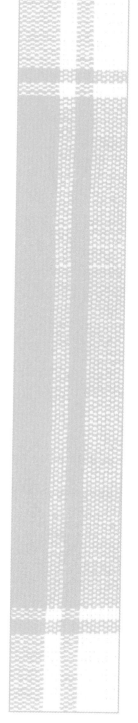

Bibliography

Bibliography

The New Food Lover's Companion, Sharon Tyler Herbst. Barrons Educational Series, 1995.

The Cook's Advisor, Camille Stagg. Stephen Greene Press, 1982.

The Lobel Brothers' Meat, Leon and Stanley Lobel. Running Press, 1990.

Kitchen Science, Howard Hillman. Houghton Mifflin, 1981.

On Food and Cooking, Harold Mcgee. Charles Scribner & Sons, 1984.

The Making of a Cook, Madeleine Kamman. Atheneum, 1971.

The New Making of a Cook, Madeleine Kamman. Morrow, 1998.

Completely Cheese, Anita May Pearl, Constance Cuttle, Barbara B. Deskins. Jonathan David Publishers, 1978.

Cheese Primer, Steve Jenkins. Workman Press, 1996.

Tastings: The Best from Ketchup to Caviar, Jenifer Lang. Random House, 1986.

The Best of Kitchen Basics, Jenifer Lang. Wings Books, Random House, 1996.

Beard on Bread, James Beard. Alfred K. Knopf, 1973.

The New York Public Library Desk Reference (Third Edition), Macmillan General Reference, 1998.

Index

Index

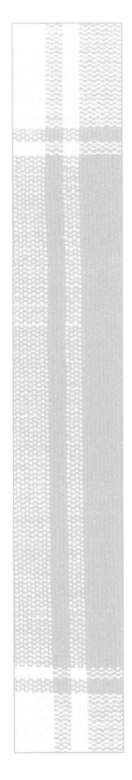